# NetSlaves
## True Tales of Working the Web

BILL LESSARD
STEVE BALDWIN

McGraw-Hill
New York  San Francisco  Washington, D.C.  Auckland  Bogotá
Caracas  Lisbon  London  Madrid  Mexico City  Milan
Montreal  New Delhi  San Juan  Singapore
Sydney  Tokyo  Toronto

## McGraw-Hill

A Division of The **McGraw·Hill** Companies

Copyright © 2000 by Bill Lessard and Steve Baldwin. All rights reserved. Printed in the United States of America. Except as permitted under the United States Copyright Act of 1976, no part of this publication may be reproduced or distributed in any form or by any means, or stored in a database or retrieval system, without the prior written permission of the publisher.

1 2 3 4 5 6 7 8 9 0   AGM/AGM   9 0 9 8 7 6 5 4 3 2 1 0 9

ISBN 0-07-135243-0

*This book was set in Concorde BE by North Market Street Graphics. Printed and bound by Quebecor Martinsburg.*

McGraw-Hill books are available at special quantity discounts to use as premiums and sales promotions, or for use in corporate training programs. For more information, please write to the Director of Special Sales, McGraw-Hill, 11 West 19 Street, New York, NY 10011. Or contact your local bookstore.

 This book is printed on recycled, acid-free paper containing a minimum of 50% recycled, de-inked fiber.

# Contents

|           | Acknowledgments | vii |
|---|---|---|
| **Level .90** | **Introduction** | 1 |
| Level .91 | The Purpose Behind This Book | 3 |
| Level .92 | Are You a NetSlave? Take the Quiz! | 7 |
| Level .93 | Virus Scan: A User's Guide to the New Media Caste System | 10 |
| **Level 1.0** | **Garbagemen: The Y2K Bug Is Eating My Pizza!** | 13 |
| Level 1.1 | Who Are They? | 15 |
| Level 1.2 | General Characteristics | 16 |
| Level 1.3 | The Story of Matt | 18 |
| **Level 2.0** | **Cops and Streetwalkers: Is That a Cellular Modem in Your Pocket or Are You Just Happy to See Me?** | 39 |
| Level 2.1 | Who Are They? | 41 |
| Level 2.2 | General Characteristics | 42 |
| Level 2.3 | The Story of Kilmartin | 43 |
| **Level 3.0** | **Social Workers: Click Here for a Clean, Well-Lighted Place** | 59 |
| Level 3.1 | Who Are They? | 61 |
| Level 3.2 | General Characteristics | 62 |
| Level 3.3 | The Story of Cindy | 64 |

| | | |
|---|---|---|
| **Level 4.0** | **Cab Drivers: Another Day, Another Startup** | 79 |
| Level 4.1 | Who Are They? | 81 |
| Level 4.2 | General Characteristics | 82 |
| Level 4.3 | The Story of Jane | 84 |
| **Level 5.0** | **Cowboys and Card Sharks: Turnkey Solutions Traced in Blood** | 99 |
| Level 5.1 | Who Are They? | 101 |
| Level 5.2 | General Characteristics | 102 |
| Level 5.3 | The Story of Zorn | 104 |
| **Level 6.0** | **Fry Cooks: Confessions of Real-Life "Dilberts"** | 119 |
| Level 6.1 | Who Are They? | 121 |
| Level 6.2 | General Characteristics | 122 |
| Level 6.3 | The Story of Boyd | 124 |
| **Level 7.0** | **Gold Diggers and Gigolos: Sex, Lies, and Hypertext** | 141 |
| Level 7.1 | Who Are They? | 143 |
| Level 7.2 | General Characteristics | 144 |
| Level 7.3 | The Story of Kellner | 146 |
| **Level 8.0** | **Priests and Madmen: Infinity in a Grain of Sand** | 163 |
| Level 8.1 | Who Are They? | 165 |
| Level 8.2 | General Characteristics | 166 |
| Level 8.3 | The Story of Barstow | 168 |
| **Level 9.0** | **Robots: Kill, Crush, Deploy!** | 177 |
| Level 9.1 | Who/What Are They? | 178 |
| Level 9.2 | General Characteristics | 180 |
| Level 9.3 | The Story of Hussein | 182 |
| **Level 10.0** | **Robber Barons: Who Needs Dynamite When We've Got IPOs?** | 199 |
| Level 10.1 | Who (We Think) They Are | 201 |
| Level 10.2 | General Characteristics | 202 |
| Level 10.3 | The Story of Welch | 204 |

**Sublevel −1.0 Mole People: Living Large in the Net's
               Hoovervilles**    225

(Bug Report: Virus Scan Has Detected Mole People on
             Your Hard Drive    227
Sublevel −1.1 Who/What Are They?    228
Sublevel −1.2 General Characteristics    229
Sublevel −1.3 The Story of Outis    230

**Afterword    Not Ready for Beta**    243

# Acknowledgments

This book would never have been possible without the help and support of the following individuals:

- Lisa Swayne—our agent, who worked tirelessly on our behalf and was always a source of inspiration.

- Susan Barry—our editor, who rescued our proposal from the gutter of Net obscurity and brought a bright wit and a skillful hand to our otherwise mad ravings.

- Kevin Hemenway, aka "Morbus"—our system administrator, Webmaster, and avatar of the Digital Underground, who provided a home for the NetSlaves Web site when no one else believed in it.

- Cheolan Kim of Pine Tree Design—who gave us a mascot and created many of the graphics which found their way into the final project.

Our family and friends provided enormous emotional sustenance during the year it took to research and write this book. Bill Lessard would like to thank his mother, his girlfriend Joanne, and his virtual brothers J.P., Freddie, Al, Rob, Matt, and Kyle. Steve Baldwin would like to thank his parents, Carl and Mary Ellen Baldwin; his daughter, Tess; Teri Baldwin; Kathy, Julio, and Luis Granda; Feargal O'Sullivan; Kaye Bettiga; and Juliet Hanlon.

We'd also like to thank our informal group of professional "perps" for their invaluable feedback. They include: Robin Miller, Steve Gilliard, Noah Robischon, Lev Grossman, Bryan Parola, Monique Elwell, Scott Samios, Nathaniel Wice, Josh Quittner, Chris Stamper, Gian Trotta, Andrew Susman, David Flores, Michele Masterson, Sal Cataldi, and others who regularly hang on the NetSlaves mailing list. And we owe a profound debt to Clifford Stoll, David Hudson, David Shenk, and Douglas Rushkoff, whose early encouragement provided us with the impetus to pursue this project.

We gratefully acknowledge the following journalists for writing about NetSlaves. They include Austin Bunn, Mary Huhn,

Judith Messina, Clive Thompson, Lisa Napoli, John Whalen, Thomas Hoffman, David Becker, Joanna Glasner, Laura Rich, Courtney Pulitzer, Adam Fisher, Ron Bel Bruno, Karl Taro Greenfeld, Adam L. Penenberg, Katharine Mieszkowski, Mel Duvall, and Ty Burr.

Our greatest debt belongs to those anonymous NetSlaves who were brave enough to step forward and tell us their stories. We wish we could tell you the names of these people, but because most still work in the technology business, they have asked to remain nameless.

Do you know where you are? You're in the jungle, baby!
—Guns N' Roses

# Introduction

## .91 The Purpose Behind This Book

"Did you receive my résumé?"

"One second. Let me check the pile." The sound of papers being shuffled, then a prolonged silence.

"Did you find it?"

"Yes, I'm reading it now."

More silence, then finally the sound of the recruiter on the other end of the phone clearing his throat. "Mr. Lessard, in going over your résumé, I see that you've had, on the average, one job per year for the past seven years."

"That's correct."

The man let out a tiny, mocking laugh. "Mr. Lessard, if this were California, I'm sure that potential employers would think you're a pretty stable guy. But this is New York. I'm afraid the clients I deal with would think there's really something wrong with you. Is there any reason why you've jumped around so much?"

"You don't understand," I stammered. "I'm in the Internet business. Everything's very unstable. The last place I worked merged and laid everybody off; the place before that went out of business and the place before that..."

"Mr. Lessard!" he interrupted, the mockery in his voice hardened into a curt directness. "You can say whatever you want, but facts are facts. No reasonable company would hire you with such a spotty résumé. I'm sorry, but I can't help you."

The phone clicked. I slumped on the edge of my perpetually unmade bed, listening to the dial tone. A rage welled up inside me, and for a moment I entertained the thought of calling the recruiter back and cursing him out. But the thought passed soon enough when it dawned on me that this guy really wasn't to blame.

Like most people, this headhunter had simply bought into the hype that goes something like this: if you work in the Internet business, you're a 25-year-old with a $30 million initial public offering (IPO). Anything less means you're an abject loser–after all, how could anyone "fail" in a business that's grown more explosively and created more wealth than we've seen since the Oklahoma oil boom, if not for some deep personal flaw?

The more I thought about the Net's Universal Success Myth–the idea that winners predominate in this business and losers are the exception–the more it grated on my own experience and the experiences of almost everyone I know in the technology business. I'm a living testament to the fact that most Internet careers are nasty, brutish, and short, and I'm not alone. My coauthor Steve, for one, is an impoverished Internet freelancer, who's been living a hand-to-mouth existence, without health benefits, for the past several years.

The rest of our colleagues are only slightly better off. Joe, we'll call him, is a talented programmer who's now licking his wounds from a bloody purge that took out 1,000 employees (his second dismissal this year alone) in an act of managerial desperation that reduced the size of the company by 50 percent. Suzie (another pseudonym) is a Web designer who left one place where she was pulling 14-hour shifts only to end up in another where she's working even harder—16 hours being the average day. And lest I forget, my friend John—his real name—has been in the technology business since 1987 and is currently winding up his 25th job—a fact that might well be entered into the *Guinness Book of Employment Instability*.

But hey, what's a little sweat? At least they're *all* eventually going to be rich, right?

Wrong.

For every barely postadolescent CEO who hits the jackpot with the company he started in his dorm room, there are thousands more who fail miserably. Even if the startup they work for doesn't go up in flames after six months and actually shows enough spark to slip an S1 past the Fed, few will ever see a big payday, unless they're lucky enough to be employee number 6 or under, with options to buy 300 gazillion shares at 25 cents a pop. The unlucky ones—and by that I mean the 4 million or so workers who labor every day in the tech business—work away in high-pressure, low-security positions where a pink slip is a far likelier thing to see in their inboxes than a Vegas-style payout.

There's a very good reason why people don't like to talk about how rough it is to really work in the Internet business. American culture and the mainstream media that claim to represent it are obsessed with success (when was the last time you saw a noncelebrity on the cover of *People* magazine?). Many journalists who write about the Net really don't know very much about the people in this medium—who they really are and what they really do. Let's face it, it's a lot sexier to talk about the American-Dream-come-true of some kid who made a pile of money selling a digital geegaw to a big conglomerate than to talk about armies of Silicon Schmoes putting in 90-hour weeks in two-bit electronic sweatshops. In the words of the innumerable publishers and agents who rejected this book before the good folks at McGraw-Hill rescued it from the gutter, "Who cares? Who wants to read about techies pissed off at their jobs?"

Steve and I are not so foolish as to believe that everyone working in the technology business is unhappy, but believe us, there's enough misery among the workers who are building tomorrow's "digital economy" to warrant a closer look. The Net is still a new medium and its history thus far has largely been written by the winners (if you don't know who the winners are, just skim through a copy of *Wired*, *Upside*, or any other sacred text of New Media hagiography).

And so, determined to set the record straight, we armed ourselves with a suction-cup microphone and 500 supersized coffees (light, three sugars), and journeyed forth—like two amateur anthropologists—to talk to everyone we could find in the Net industry who would talk to us in a personal way about their work lives. Many of the people we encountered were quite friendly and readily spilled the beans; others, fearing the retribution of the Volcano God in the Corner Office, drove us away with threats of flaying our skin into mousepads.

Our investigative journey lasted exactly one year—from the spring of 1998 to the spring of 1999. Even though both Steve and I considered ourselves fairly experienced Net veterans who thought we knew it all and had seen it all, our subjects quickly brought us down to size, teaching us much more than a thing or two about what working the Web is all about.

All the accounts you are about to read in the following pages are from real people who work at real Internet companies. To protect their identities, we've changed their names and the names of the companies for whom they work, and in a few instances, we've created character composites.

The result, in a lot of ways, is an homage to Studs Terkel's classic, *Working*, that's updated for the plugged-in '90s. Instead of covering a wide range of professions, we've focused on just one—the Net—and the many subspecies of real-life "Dilberts" (which we prefer to call "Net-Slaves") performing a wide range of jobs within it. However, as a definite leftover from *Working*, we've substituted everyday job titles for Net job descriptions, whose techno-speak frequently obscures what the worker actually does. For instance, itinerant Web freelancers have been labeled "Cab Drivers" and overworked, abused desktop support techs have been labeled "Garbagemen."

Why the switch? Well, two reasons:

1. To demystify the jargon-laced professional nomenclature which serves to compound confusion about the most widely misunderstood business phenomenon of our time
2. To take advantage of the discovery we made, in going over our dozens of interview tapes, that despite its claims to have broken all the rules, the Internet business is pervaded with an unspoken, but very real, pecking order

This hierarchical pecking order—or "caste system," as we've called it—forms the structure of this book (see Section .93 for more details). We start at the bottom and take you through its 11 levels, with each rung of the employment ladder depicted through an introduction, a profile, and a story exploring the character and behavior of each caste member we talked to.

For the record, we want you to know that while we believe that the conditions affecting technology workers constitute serious social issues which in turn merit serious sociological study (and perhaps even a political remedy), we've tried to avoid being preachy or pedantic. Our hope is that you have as much fun reading this thing as we did writing it. We want you to laugh—laugh out loud—at these bitterly funny accounts, and be drawn in by the voices of some very interesting people, most of whom you'll probably never read about in *Wired*.

Before sending you into the warped parallel universe that is "Internet Time," we'd like to leave you with one final pseudo-anthropological observation: people are nuts, no matter what profession they're in, but people forced to work like dogs with the carrot of stock options and untold wealth dangling under their noses are especially nuts.

If you don't believe us, turn the page.

## .92 Are You a NetSlave? Take the Quiz!

Before entering the New Media Caste System, we recommend that you take our short self-assessment test to orient yourself to what may at first seem a strange, alien environment, and to find out if you too suffer from the ills of indentured digital servitude. Please be candid–the results will not be tabulated and sent to some marketing organization (this is a book, not a sleazy Web site), and don't cheat–there's enough of that in the stories that follow.

**PART I: YOUR WORK LIFE**

1. At your last New Media job interview, you exhibited:
   - ☐ A. Optimism
   - ☐ B. Mild wariness
   - ☐ C. Controlled hostility
   - ☐ D. Hysteria

2. Describe your workplace:
   - ☐ A. An enterprising, dynamic group of individuals laying the groundwork for tomorrow's economy
   - ☐ B. A bunch of geeks with questionable social skills
   - ☐ C. An anxiety-ridden, backbiting bunch of finger-pointers
   - ☐ D. The final scene in *The Wild Bunch*

3. Describe your home:
   - ☐ A. Small, but efficient
   - ☐ B. Shared and dormlike
   - ☐ C. Rubble-strewn and fetid
   - ☐ D. Don't remember (but can describe the office)

**PART II: YOUR RELATIONSHIP WITH TECHNOLOGY**

4. My personal computer:
   - ☐ A. Maximizes my productivity
   - ☐ B. Is my best friend
   - ☐ C. Lets me work all kinds of crazy hours at home
   - ☐ D. Provides the only heat in my apartment

5. My alphanumeric pager:
   - ☐ A. Is a convenient way to stay in touch with my office
   - ☐ B. Goes off at 3:00 a.m. when someone in Hong Kong has a problem changing fonts in Word

☐ C. Has been temporarily disabled
☐ D. Has been permanently destroyed

**PART III: YOUR INTERNET KNOWLEDGE**

6. What does the "I" in "IPO" stand for?
    ☐ A. Initial
    ☐ B. Imaginary
    ☐ C. Impossible
    ☐ D. Insolvent

7. What does the "e" in "e-commerce" stand for?
    ☐ A. Electronic
    ☐ B. Enigmatic
    ☐ C. Error-prone
    ☐ D. Exploitation

8. What are the Three C's of the Internet?
    ☐ A. Content, community, and commerce
    ☐ B. Cults, chats, and clutter
    ☐ C. Chee-tos, chinese food, and Coke
    ☐ D. Cost, confusion, and chaos

9. What is the "Windows environment"?
    ☐ A. A graphical operating system
    ☐ B. A ploy for world domination
    ☐ C. A bug-ridden, proprietary disaster
    ☐ D. The corner office where your manager schemes against you

10. Who is the real Father of the Internet?
    ☐ A. Vinton Cerf
    ☐ B. Jerry Yang
    ☐ C. Barry Diller
    ☐ D. George Orwell

11. Why was the Internet created?
    ☐ A. To survive an atomic attack
    ☐ B. To boost the Dow over 10,000
    ☐ C. To give you another reason to drop out of school
    ☐ D. To give your employer a nifty way to bid out your job to a grade-school student in Pakistan

**PART IV: YOUR HOPES AND FEARS FOR THE FUTURE**

12. Why are you working in the Internet business?
    - ☐ A. To get rich
    - ☐ B. To get by
    - ☐ C. Because it's more fun than high school
    - ☐ D. Nobody else will take me

13. Describe yourself politically:
    - ☐ A. Libertarian capitalist
    - ☐ B. Luddite
    - ☐ C. Grassroots populist
    - ☐ D. Wired terrorist

14. Describe your religion:
    - ☐ A. Monotheist
    - ☐ B. Futurist
    - ☐ C. Satanist
    - ☐ D. Linux

15. What will happen on January 1, 2000?
    - ☐ A. Many older computer systems will simply stop working.
    - ☐ B. Your girlfriend will leave you for a venture capitalist.
    - ☐ C. Your health insurance will run out.
    - ☐ D. You'll be outsourced with no equity.

## *How to Score Your Results*

If you answered "A" to any of the preceding questions, your IEQ (Internet exploitation quotient) is zero–you're not a NetSlave, and you can probably put this book down without proceeding further. If you selected "B," you've probably just started working in the technology business or lead some sort of charmed (mythical?) existence the rest of us only dream about. For those answering either "C" or "D," your IEQ is off the charts and you should contact a mental health professional immediately, but not before getting a true diagnosis of your disorder in the next section.

## .93 Virus Scan: A User's Guide to the New Media Caste System

Not all NetSlaves are created equal. Knowing this and knowing where you fall within the tech biz's unspoken, but very real, pecking order is crucial to your survival in this industry. To help you out and to give people who are lucky enough not to be NetSlaves a hand at understanding the book they're holding, we have put together the following set of rhetorical questions. (Warning: Side effects may include dizziness, the sudden urge to kill your boss, and an unquenchable thirst for Mountain Dew.)

### Level 1.0: Are You a Garbageman?

Do you wear a cell phone, a beeper, or other electronic tethers? Do you spend more than 10 percent of your week compiling, solving technical complaints, or plugging components in and out of machines? Do you rage against a particular operating system (OS) kernel at completely inappropriate times (viz., the middle of the night)?

### Level 2.0: Are You a Cop or a Streetwalker?

Are your prurient interests so aroused or outraged by what you find on the Net that you've become a professional purveyor or repressor of all digital manifestations of the love urge? Are you paid to chase stalkers and other electronic undesirables?

### Level 3.0: Are You a Social Worker?

Have you distanced yourself enough from the unfiltered info-sewer flowing through the digital underground to consider yourself above it? Do you manage conversations for a living, or believe earnestly in "the power of communities" to change your life? Do you regard chat as a legitimate form of literature? Are you a sysop or a "guide," or are you otherwise involved in the digibabble industry?

### Level 4.0: Are You a Cab Driver?

Are you one of the itinerant, faceless drones who codes Web sites for a living? Do you think health insurance is for wimps? Have you ever been stiffed for a check, forced to wear a degrading "temp" name tag, or had to choose between feeding your cat and feeding yourself?

## Level 5.0: Are You a Cowboy or a Card Shark?

Do you mention the word "upside" or "bandwidth" more than once a day? Do you battle against "legacy applications," "scope creep," and other nightmares of the consultancy racket? Have you ever skipped town to avoid a crashed ERP? Do you take twice as long to complete projects just for a few more bucks in your pocket?

## Level 6.0: Are You a Fry Cook?

Do you sweat over six projects that are all due at once? Do you alternate between ass kicking and ass kissing? Are you haunted by legions of salespeople who have promised the client everything under the sun? Are you universally hated by your staff of developers who blame you for not properly "managing expectations"? Do you dream of a world without flowcharts?

## Level 7.0: Are You a Gold Digger or a Gigolo?

Do you know the difference between a vermicelli noodle and a line of C++? Do you care? Have you been able to parlay your complete technical ignorance into a plush spot in sales or business development? Is "schmoozing" an accurate description of your job responsibilities?

## Level 8.0: Are You a Priest or a Madman?

Do you earning your living making wild, unfounded claims about the future of the Internet? (By 2005, household pet-generated e-commerce will top 3 trillion.) Do you track the shoe telephony market? Does the term "insider trading" ring a bell with you? Have you taken to the lecture circuit to promote your new book, *Getting in on This Internet Thing: Digital Marketing Strategies for the Clueless and Psychotic*?

## Level 9.0: Are You a Robot?

Are you a technological genius whose lingua franca is 1's and 0's? Do you get your kicks spying on everyone's e-mail? Do you hire and fire with the same coolness as changing upstream providers? Has the "Humanity" file been deleted from your root directory? Are you the proud owner of six pagers, three Palm Pilots, and a dozen cell phones?

### Level 10.0: Are You a Robber Baron?

Have you rocketed to fame and fortune on hype alone? Have you recently led your company to a gangbusters IPO, despite the fact that you have absolutely no revenue or business model? Do you think that being rich will make up for your dorky, sex-deprived adolescence?

### Sublevel −1.0: Are You a Mole Person?

Do you think that updating your Web site is actually a fun thing? Do you enjoy spending hours chatting and trading files? Have you ever built a home page on GeoCities, or toyed with the idea of running your own magazine, radio station, or smut shack?

### How to Score Your Results

As with all therapy sessions, you are now in a safe, no-judgment zone. But a word of caution: If you fall into the upper register of the New Media Caste System, try to avoid running into Steve and me in a dark alley. In the meantime, you can pick up some helpful self-defense techniques from the Garbagemen, the first group of NetSlaves we encountered in our journey.

LEVEL 1.0

# Garbagemen

## The Y2K Bug Is Eating My Pizza!

## 1.1 Who Are They?

Steve and I began our journey trying to locate the most oppressed and widely despised group within the New Media Caste System. We searched high and low (mostly low) and found this group buried under the mass of tangled cables and pizza boxes that is the Great American Back Office.

Although they referred to themselves with such charming epithets as "desktop monkeys," "code janitors," and "pager scum," we decided that "Garbagemen" was perhaps the term most descriptive of what these people have to put up with on a day-to-day basis. Garbagemen do everything from getting up in the middle of the night to restart the server, to enduring the screams of clueless users who don't know how to open a Web browser, to debugging spaghetti software. In short, Garbagemen are the Net's sleepless, abused, and overworked sanitation engineers, damned with the task of cleaning up everyone else's technological messes.

With many of you out there still waiting for your e-mail to get fixed or the laptop to return from the shop ("You don't have it *yet?* It's been three weeks!"), Steve and I won't even attempt to rouse your sympathies. We too have had more than a few run-ins with these people, but after speaking to them under the strictest of confidence, we feel that we now understand their plight enough to declare that their so-called inefficiency isn't totally their fault.

Between the number of complaints they receive during normal business hours and the problems they have to fix while the rest of you are home in bed, Garbagemen lead a Sisyphean existence–they push the boulder to the top of the hill only to have it roll right back down and flatten them. Many of you probably have or have had jobs with comparable thanklessness quotients, but Steve and I suspect that you were paid a lot more money than Garbagemen are to put up with such abuse.

In any event, we offer you the following as a way of passing on our understanding of Garbagemen and the role they play in your professional life and, by extension, the New Media Caste System. We're not asking you to weep uncontrollably into your hankies once you've reached the end, but on behalf of our brother and sister NetSlaves who perform this despised function, we hope that we are able to raise your consciousness to the point that you at least scream at a lower decibel level the next time you can't get the printer to work.

## 1.2 General Characteristics

***Where they can be found:*** Wherever the immediate problem is—be it at the bottom of a mass of cables, in the charred remains of a fried hard drive, or at the other end of a sweaty receiver in overlit, overheated, and downright hectic triage wards, better known as Tech Support.

***Hours worked per week:*** 60 to ?? (including nights, weekends, and whatever odd hour the system chooses to blow up).

***Average age:*** 23 to 25. Being a Garbageman is a definitely a young person's game. Old people (that is, anyone over 25) wouldn't survive a week, between the hours and the stress.

***Education:*** Many Garbagemen are self-taught, or else they hold such bogus, but required (for employment), credentials as "Certified Spreadsheet Engineer" and "Licensed E-mail Technician."

***Mating habits:*** Garbagemen are not exactly the most outgoing of NetSlaves and therefore do not have much of a social life, especially when it comes to wooing and cooing. Although the final statistics are not in as of publication, it is safe to say, with a fair degree of accuracy, that Garbagemen are the least-sexed caste—their romantic activities being limited to checking out the voluptuous hindquarters of the new marketing chick in Building G and drooling over running scenes on *Xena* (frame-by-frame, slo-mo advancing through a videotaped copy of the latest episode being the preferred method).

***Percentage of the NetSlave population:*** 40 percent

***Average income:*** $20 to $25 per hour. (Admittedly, Garbagemen do earn more than higher-caste NetSlaves such as Cyber-Cops and Social Workers, yet we feel that they are indeed the lowest of the low because their quality of life is nonexistent.)

***Enemies:*** The administrative assistant with a voice like a chipmunk who calls 20 times a day screaming that "that screensaver message is back again!" The executive who won't stop downloading half-baked shareware that crashes his system.

***Last book read:*** Once tried to read *On the Road*, but gave up on it due to lack of technical references. Now only reads trade magazines. (*Router Weekly* is a common favorite.)

***Current technical fetishes:*** Advances in shoe telephony, Linux-based search engines, the growing acceptance of the IOU D-COM 2.06 protocol.

***Chance of upward mobility:*** High. NetSlaves at such a low and demeaning level in the New Media Caste System can only go up from here. Typical Garbagemen achieve advancement through additional certification programs ("Java in a Day," "Networking w/Fries–the Fast Food Method") or else get so burned out and disgusted with technology that they apply their hands-on skills to bricklaying.

*Career aspirations:* To telecommute from home in their underwear or as far away from operational problems as possible. (Can you say, "Tahiti"?)

## 1.3 The Story of Matt

*Matt could have been a big shot at Aggro Software, but he chose to become a Garbageman at an educational software company to pursue a "higher" purpose. What Matt didn't know was that there was no escaping Royster G. Pfeiffer, Aggro's billionaire CEO—you were either his loyal subject or his bitterest foe. For Matt, it would be the fight of his life.*

Matt Swift's cell phone was ringing. And ringing. And ringing. But he couldn't hear it. He was dead to the world and had a pillow thrown over his head for good measure. It had been yet another grueling 14-hour day of debugging. He'd arrived home at 11 p.m. in such a state of exhaustion that he'd left his clothes in a heap on the floor and climbed right into bed.

In other, less frenetic professions, Matt's long Saturday shift might have been enough to earn him a night's rest—but not so in the 24/7 world of the Internet, where sleep, at least for a NetSlave in Matt's position, was viewed as a retreat from the relentless needs of the work group. Matt was a QA (quality assurance) engineer for IntelliComp, a beleaguered educational software company in San Jose, California. Although Matt's title suggested that he held a high-and-mighty job, all it really meant was that he was the drudge who had to make sure that:

1. The developers were writing "clean" code.
2. They were working from the latest version (or "build") of the software.
3. They were keeping to spec—many a project at IntelliComp had been sabotaged by developers who, instead of producing the compiled equivalent of a gas-efficient economy car, insisted on delivering a stretch limousine, complete with hot tub, wet bar, and steam room.

Because he was easygoing by nature, Matt didn't enjoy wielding such dictatorial powers. But his job required him to play the bad guy role of nagger, nudger, and nitpicker of programming snafus committed by IntelliComp's prickly crew of code crunchers. Some of these highly paid geeks were egotistical prima donnas, others were outright flaky, but all bitterly resented being overseen by Master Matt. All Matt wanted was for his team to stick to the program (literally), but the coders didn't see it this way. They'd accuse him of cracking the whip or leading them on a death march, and they'd react as POWs often do:

with evil looks, resigned, sullen stares, and raised middle fingers when Matt had passed safely out of sight.

Adding to Matt's psychological stress was the fact that, day and night, he was electronically tethered to higher-level IntelliComp developers in several time zones, from California to London to Hong Kong–a small detail that disrupted his life with a never ending series of Priority 1 emergencies. If Matt got more than three hours of shut-eye in a given night it was truly a miracle.

It also didn't help Matt's nerves that his team was facing a completely unrealistic deadline–SmartSpell, IntelliComp's banner product and the project he supervised, was scheduled to ship the Gold Code of its 3.0 version in three weeks. If they failed, the company's archrival, Aggro Software, would beat it to market and crush IntelliComp like a bug. With IntelliComp's stock in the toilet and growing talk of layoffs, failure was not an option. To make matters worse, Aggro was doing everything in its power to run IntelliComp out of business. Its stealthy agents spread fear, doubt, and uncertainty in the trade press; concocted a fake acquisition rumor; and used the information gathered in private meetings with IntelliComp to launch its own product, SpellRight. In the final twist of the knife, Aggro planned to give away this product on the Web, cutting off IntelliComp's air supply for good.

Who knew that educational software could be so brutal?

Certainly not Matt. When he started at IntelliComp eight months ago, he brimmed with fresh-out-of-college dreams of creating a better world where clean code would consign misspellings and grammatical errors to the dustbin of history. Matt knew that achieving his dream wouldn't be easy, but he hadn't bargained for the dismal, enervating world he now found himself in–the endless trench battle involving boorish menu-bar gurus, political pissing matches, turf warfare, and cell phones that buzzed like enraged hornets throughout the night.

## *Taking the Call*

The last ring of the phone cut off, and Matt's voice mail kicked in. The caller left a screaming, incoherent message before calling again five minutes later. This time Matt woke up–or at least was conscious enough to fling off the pillows, roll over, and grab the phone from the cluttered nightstand.

"H-hello?" he groaned tentatively.

"Where the willed? You promise the willed!"

"I willed? I willed what?"

"MATT! WAKE UP! This is Steve Leung in Hong Kong. I need willed RIGHT NOW!"

Matt sprang up in bed, as if he'd received an electric shock.

"I uploaded the build before I left tonight," he said with panic in his voice. "Did you check the 'Development' folder on the network?"

"It not there! Do you think I call if there?"

"OK, OK—I'm on my way. You'll have it in 20 minutes."

Matt put down the receiver to scramble for his clothes. Instead of wasting precious seconds looking for something fresh to wear, he threw on the same rumpled, smelly rags he'd pulled off his exhausted body a few hours earlier, and ran out the door. He was halfway down the stairs when he realized he'd forgotten his glasses. He rushed back into the apartment to snatch them from the nightstand and grabbed his cell phone from its base station.

Taking the phone was a big mistake—like taping a giant "kick me" sign to his back, it was an invitation for abuse. Sure enough, not 10 minutes later, the evil gizmo started buzzing again. He knew it was Steve, but answered it anyway.

"Good morning!, IntelliComp," Matt said mockingly. "How may I direct your call?"

"Where the willed?"

"Look, I'm just pulling into the parking lot. Five more minutes, all right?"

Five minutes was indeed all it took. Matt dashed out of the elevator, sprinted across the cluster of cubes to his workspace, and was just moving the latest version of the software over to the "Development" folder when the phone on his desk started ringing. Matt picked it up immediately and screamed, "IT'S THERE! PRAISE HOLY JESUS! IT'S THERE!"

There was a moment of silence at the other end of the line, and then a click. Steve was gone, thank goodness.

Matt let out a long sigh and glanced at the clock in the lower-right-hand corner of his monitor. It read 2:51 a.m. He was too wired and mad to go back to bed, so he tried doing some work—a few e-mails had drifted in from London that needed answering, but Matt's mind was confused and his body felt compressed. Violent fantasies flashed through his mind. His mouth twisted into a demented smile as he thought about getting on a plane and shooting Steve, and then returning for his boss and the obnoxious C++ cretins who hated his guts. But he banished these evil thoughts from his mind. A gun, a light saber, even a hydrogen bomb couldn't undo the mess he'd gotten himself into—all by himself.

## Coming to a Boil

Few who knew Matt would suspect him of harboring such homicidal inclinations. On the outside he was the picture of Silicon Valley normalcy–bespectacled, well-groomed (by technology standards, at least), and about 15 pounds overweight. To a more perceptive eye, however, Matt, in the last few weeks, was moving toward the point of cracking up. The 80-hour weeks he'd been putting in, combined with the abuse that was the essence of his job function and the flat-out craziness of his boss, were morphing Matt into what is clinically termed "a basket case."

If forced to choose whom he hated the most, Matt would have picked his boss hands-down. Marty, as he insisted everyone call him, was a 40-something ex-hippie from U.C. Santa Cruz who had no business in the business world. Like many people in the Internet industry, he'd have been better off if he'd stayed where he belonged–tracking quarks in some supercomputing lab. Matt had no serious prejudices against '60s people, but it rankled him that this aging hipster's communications and managerial skills were nil, along with the fact that he'd explode at the first sign of trouble. Marty also had unorthodox ideas about what Matt considered proper workplace decorum. He smoked pot in his office, which didn't bother Matt much. But the fact that Marty brought his dog Floppy in each day and forced Matt to walk the canine with pooper-scooper in hand infuriated him.

A month before, Matt had sought the help of Dr. Link, a therapist who specialized in treating people in the technology business. Dr. Link was a man in his fifties who looked like an older version of Marty, but he played the role of caring mental health professional very well. He leaned back in his padded chair, listening intently to everything Matt said. He'd nod at all the right moments and even let out an "Oh, gosh," to demonstrate empathy for this young man's suffering. But when Matt had finished spilling his guts, the only thing the therapist could offer him was a tiny vial from the top drawer of his desk.

"What's this?"

"Planax–it's a very mild antidepressant I prescribe to all my patients when they're in major crunch mode."

"Is it addictive?"

"Like I said, it's very mild. The only side effect you should experience is slight drowsiness."

"OK, I'll try it out. But I think what I really need is a better job. And . . . aren't you going to ask me about my childhood?"

"We can talk about those things the next time you come," the doctor laughed heartily. "In the meantime, let's just see how you handle the beta."

As Matt half-expected, Dr. Link's pills were completely ineffective, aside from making his mouth dry and causing his eyes to water. They certainly didn't help him sleep. Matt never went back to Dr. Link. He was done with the so-called professionals—if he needed dope, he could get it from the guy on the corner. His best course of action, or so he concluded, was to face his problems head on.

And Matt had done so, by driving his team hard and crashing the time. The pace was killing, but Matt reasoned that if he could endure it for just another few weeks, he might be in the clear. But as Matt's sleep-deprived mind directed its attention to the clock again and saw that it was only 2:54, time started to behave in the weirdest way. It stretched and stretched, until Matt's numbed mind could no longer conceive of there being a tomorrow, or a day after that. Time became abstract and unreal—like some cryptic piece of code that might never execute.

"I've got to do something," he said wearily, "or it will never end."

Matt's eyes had a wild, glazed look to them, and he rocked back and forth in his chair. He saw for the first time that his mind was just like a server: if it was hit with too many packets, or its power supply dropped too low, its motherboard would blow up and heavy smoke would billow from the corners of its casing.

"I'VE GOT TO DO SOMETHING!" he shouted to the empty room.

A security guard making his rounds stopped dead in his tracks and shouted to Matt from across the wide-open production area. "You there, are you all right?"

Matt paid no attention to him, other than lowering his voice, as he repeated his mantra. "I've got to do something. I've got to do something."

The guard walked away quietly. Having worked in this building since the mid-'80s, he knew a meltdown when he saw one and had learned long ago that it was best to stay away—far away—from these technical types when they lost their marbles.

The clock read 2:55, and Matt, suspended in his state of waking sleep, gazed around at the few momentos he'd gathered on his desk. There was an old photo of an ex-girlfriend he hadn't spoken to in months; a snapshot of his parents, who he dimly remembered were still alive; and a picture of what looked like a high school graduation class.

In the front row, blurry and indistinct, was Matt–looking years younger, happier, and better rested. In the foreground, beaming a proud, patrician smile, was Royster G. Pfeiffer, the richest man in the world, standing with Aggro Software's 1997 crop of programming interns.

Matt, in his REM-deprived stupor, stared at Royster's smiling face and realized something that he'd never considered before. It was something so devastatingly clear and so obvious that it became, for a single moment, the only fact in the world: Royster G. Pfeiffer was behind it all. He was the man responsible for millions of hours of lost sleep, blasted nerves, and cell phone oppression, all across the world. He was the great Darth Vader, the destroyer of worlds, and his singular competitive megalomania had driven Matt, IntelliComp, and all of humanity to this deadly killing pace.

"GODDAMNED BASTARD, who do you think you are?" Matt screamed. "WHO DO YOU THINK YOU ARE?"

Matt was enraged, and it felt good. He swiveled his chair and cracked his knuckles, and started to type. Unsure of where his words would lead him, Matt began to type a long, scathing e-mail message to Pfeiffer that began with a passionate appeal to reason:

> If Aggro's products are so great, and you're so big and bad, then why must you create a noncompetitive marketplace? Why can't you play fair? Don't you see you're destroying everyone in the office productivity market, by driving us–our development cycles–to levels of insanity that are tearing us apart?

But Matt's opening sentences seemed weak, so he beefed it up with stronger stuff:

> You come to us offering the open hand of friendship, but then you curl it into a fist. You say you serve the customer, but your feral, pathological "win at any cost" mind-set doesn't even serve yourself–it serves only the forces of evil. We who were once your friends and loyal associates–who believed in you and everything that Aggro stood for–we condemn your scorched-earth, imperial stampede across the office productivity software space. Tell me who will stand by you when everyone else is dead, Royster–when you stand alone, your deeds revealed, your soul exposed to the all-seeing eye of Judgment?

He proofread the message once, corrected some misspellings, and signed it "Matt Swift, IntelliComp." It was a marvelous piece of ranting. Matt smiled at his work and bathed in the final prelaunch moments before firing his electronic missile into the ether. It thrilled every fiber of his being to vent his frustrations this way—he felt alive in a way he hadn't in months.

But Matt couldn't quite bring himself to hit the "send" button yet. For a long, long time, he sat very silent, staring at the incendiary rant smoldering in his outbox, thinking about everything that had brought him to this moment of truth.

## *Intern-to-Be*

In truth, Matt was neither a friend nor a loyal associate of Royster G. Pfeiffer. But two years ago, back when he was still in college, he'd spent a long, memorable summer at Aggro Software, up north in Bellevue, Washington. Aggro Software wasn't just some two-bit startup—it was the largest computer software company in the world, and the guiding, benign presence of Roy, as he preferred everyone to call him, pervaded every nook, cranny, and subdirectory of the vast campus. How the company and the brains behind it had conquered the world was a mystery, but one thing was clear: Aggro had worked very hard to get where it was and would hire only the most intelligent young minds—those at the rightmost reaches of the IQ bell curve—to keep it on top.

Competition for internships at Aggro was fierce, and Matt had gone up against candidates from the very best schools and had come out on top. But even Matt's stellar grades and glowing enthusiasm for next-gen applications development tools couldn't spare him from enduring Aggro's bizarre recruitment/mating process.

In midspring of his junior year, Matt saw an Aggro flier on the bulletin board of the computer lab, and he e-mailed his résumé to the address at the bottom. Weeks passed. He had nearly forgotten about the whole thing when, late one evening, he got the strangest of phone calls.

"Matthew Swift?" the no-nonsense, monotone male voice inquired, without so much as a hello.

"Yes, it is. Who's calling?"

"This is Aggro Software's Human Resources Department. We're calling to schedule a screening session. How does next Thursday at 7 p.m. PST look for you?"

"Oh!" Matt replied enthusiastically. "You liked my résumé! You're contacting me about the internship, right?"

"Sir, I am unable to confirm that information," the voice answered dryly. "Now, about next Thursday, is 7 p.m. PST acceptable?"

"Yes, it is."

"Thank you very much for your time."

"Wait!" Matt interrupted, as the voice was about to hang up. "Do you have any idea who will be interviewing me?"

"Sir, I am unable to provide that information."

"What is your name—for future reference?"

"I am unable to provide that information either."

"OK, well, uh . . . I'll be here next Thursday to take the call."

"Excellent," the voice responded, now showing the slightest trace of humanity. "Have a good evening."

The phone went dead. The mechanical voice had hung up, leaving Matt standing in the middle of his dorm room feeling quite puzzled, as if he were applying for a black ops mission for a secret branch of the CIA, instead of an internship with a software company. Matt asked several of his classmates about the phone call and they all confirmed that it was standard practice for Aggro. His friend Rick, who'd been an Aggro intern the prior summer and was now studying for his master's, was particularly illuminating on the matter.

"You mean, the way that person treated me was, like, de rigueur?" Matt asked him.

"You got it, dude."

"But it was like a scene from a Chuck Norris movie."

"That's because to them it is."

When Thursday came around, Matt was again thrown off guard. The screener called 20 minutes late, and when he did, he was the complete opposite of the robotic voice without a name.

"Hey, man," said the voice. "This is Tad! Is Matt in?"

"Yes, this is Matt."

"Matt, this is Tad Stone of Aggro Software. How are you doing tonight, buddy?"

"I'm fine. Yourself?"

"I'm great. GREAT! So glad to be talkin' to a fellow Cal Tech guy."

Tad then launched into an ecstatic monologue describing all the fun he had in school and how much fun he was now having working for Aggro. "The parties rock, man. The parties totally rock!"

Matt had no idea what to make of it, but he played along as best he could. After Tad calmed down a notch, he asked Matt some standard questions about his educational background and his feelings about technology. Matt gave it his thoughtful best, but was jarred when Tad's universal response to each of his answers was a vociferous "RIGHT ON!"

The "screening" lasted no more than 10 minutes before Tad, ending it abruptly, said, "Listen, dude. I gotta go."

"That's kewl," Matt said, some of Tad's surfer demeanor rubbing off on him (even though Matt hailed from Massachusetts and had only seen the ocean on television). "What happens next?"

"OK, well, you'll hear from someone next week. I'd like to get you up here to talk to some more people."

"Do you have any idea when?"

"Somebody will call you next week. Don't sweat it, OK? . . . I gotta go."

And with that, Tad got on his board and paddled back into the ocean to catch the next wave, or so it seemed to Matt, who walked down the hall to ask Rick about the latest call from Aggro. Rick's response was somewhat ominous.

"It's the second part of the game."

"What do you mean?"

"You'll see."

Rick would say no more and returned to reading a dense tract on artificial intelligence. Matt walked out of the room in a complete fog, but stayed optimistic. It seemed to him that he'd made a favorable impression on Tad and was very much on his way to scoring the coveted internship with Aggro after all.

The following week, Matt stayed home at night awaiting the follow-up, but the phone didn't ring. Perhaps Tad had smoked up a big bowl after their call and had completely forgotten their conversation. Another week passed. And then like some wacked-out clockwork, just as he had completely given up hope, Matt received notice from Aggro in the mail: he was to report to their campus in Bellevue the very next day (Saturday) for a series of interviews. The names and locations of the people he was to meet with were enclosed, along with the plane tickets.

Matt stood frozen in front of his mailbox, staring down at the envelope. "It's a big mind game," he mumbled to himself, finally realizing what Rick had meant.

## *Invitation to Bellevue*

Matt's realization that Aggro was messing with his mind was an important conceptual milestone, which eased his passage through the in-person stage of Aggro's recruitment process. After being met at the SEA-TAC International Airport by the official Aggro Software shuttle and whisked off to the sprawling campus in the woods, Matt's first interview began promptly at 9 a.m., and was followed in quick succession by six more.

The people he talked to were nice enough, but to Matt it seemed that there was something ersatz about them. Matt didn't believe that his interviewers had all been hatched out of pods or stamped out of the same DNA template in some laboratory, but their shared characteristics were hard to miss. All were white, highly educated, and extremely verbal, and all wore the same uniform: sky-blue oxford shirt, tan chinos, hiking shoes with thick, treaded soles, and cell phones or pagers strapped to their belts. They showed emotion only if they liked something Matt said, and would often signify their approval with a quick, chirpy "Super!" But most of the time, they just listened, avoided eye contact, and tapped at the keyboard in front of them.

As Matt approached the end of his long day, having been shuttled to various parts of the campus in the Aggro van, he began to suspect that while he was sitting in the van, invisible e-mails appraising him were darting around the campus among the people he'd seen. His suspicion was based on the fact that the subject matter of each interview began where the preceding one had left off, as if every person he saw had intimate, exact knowledge of what had transpired. It was an eerie feeling—almost as if Matt were a document that was being worked on and revised by a ghostly work group that existed in some parallel universe just behind the tall pines.

When his final interview ended at 7 p.m., Matt was at liberty. He hadn't even had a break for lunch—but the grumbling in his belly didn't matter. The hard part was over, and there was nothing to do now except wait in the perpetually falling drizzle for the shuttle to take him back to the airport. He was tired, but unfazed—he had run the gauntlet, he could handle the people, and the work seemed challenging, at least the way everyone described it.

The only thing that did give him the creeps, though, was the place itself. By day, the campus looked like, well, a campus. By night, it took on a wholly sinister character: the towering A-shaped buildings were straight out of Fritz Lang's *Metropolis,* and the fact that the parking lots were full and everyone was still working at such an hour on a Saturday night only added to the futuristically hellish effect.

## *Where's the Pisser?*

About three weeks later, Matt received a letter informing him that he'd been accepted into Aggro Software's internship program. He would be paid $10 an hour, would be entitled to subsidized housing, and would enjoy medical benefits, along with health club membership. Overcoming his past reservations about the place, he immediately called to accept it.

At the end of June, Matt lugged his one and only suitcase into the townhouse that would be his home for the next several months. Closing the door behind him, he was greeted by his roommate, a big burly football player–type guy stretched out on the couch, beer in hand, watching cable TV in the dark. He had trouble hearing the guy at first, because the TV was at full volume, with the sound of exploding bombs reverberating throughout the living room.

"My name's Matt!"

"WHAT?"

"I SAID, 'MY NAME'S MATT?'"

"RHETT?"

"NO . . . MATT! . . . WHY DON'T YOU TURN DOWN THE TV?"

"I CAN'T. I BROKE THE REMOTE."

The fellow then rose from his spot, turned off the TV, and made a more proper introduction.

"I'm Frank. What did you say your name was again?"

"Matt."

"Where do you go to school?"

"Cal Tech."

"That's cool."

"What about you?"

"University of Montana."

"That's cool. When did you arrive?"

"Last night. I wanted to make sure I was here in time for the party."

"What party?"

"Roy, the big cheese CEO, is having a party up at his house. Everybody told me not to miss it. His parties are supposed to be kick-ass. If you're gonna make it, you'd better start getting ready now."

Matt threw his bag in the bedroom and jumped in the shower. Even though Frank hadn't been there more than 24 hours, the place was already a mess—hair on the walls, hair clogging the drain, the toilet looking like something you'd see at a bus station. Being accustomed to dorm life, however, Matt ignored the mess and was ready to go when the shuttle came to pick them up at 7:30.

Frank entertained Matt and the other passengers with an endless supply of dirty jokes. He spoke in a booming voice that was hard to ignore. He was one of those people you either loved or hated, and most people in the van didn't seem to love him much. To his credit, Frank couldn't care less what anyone thought of him and kept the jokes coming as the shuttle whisked the Aggro interns through the exterior gates of Roy's mansion and began to climb a steep hill.

Matt expected to see something truly grand at the top of the hill—a modern-day Xanadu—but was surprised to see a large, generic split-level structure that looked like it had been airlifted out of a suburb. Roy's house was drab, but the view it commanded was beautiful: a panoramic view of hills, lakes, and forests. As the van parked, Matt could see small armies of khaki-shirted security guards checking the ID cards of people filing into the entrance.

"OK, MR. MONEYBAGS, WE'RE HERE!" Frank shouted. "LET THE PARTY BEGIN!"

Despite Frank's expectation of a Roman orgy, the party soon turned out to be quite boring. There were tables set out on the back lawn, manned by chefs in white uniforms who served everything from smoked salmon to pasta. The "entertainment" was no better, in Frank's estimation. A single forlorn DJ, set up in a small tent emblazoned with the "A" logo, was playing middle-of-the-road '80s pop tunes from the likes of Huey Lewis and Culture Club.

"What the hell kind of party is this?" Frank asked Matt.

"Relax. There's free beer."

Matt slapped a bottle in Frank's hand and that was sufficient to shut him up long enough for Matt to begin studying the scene. The party was crowded with a sea of young faces, interspersed with the occasional Aggro employee, who looked like everyone else Matt had met during his interviews: white, well-dressed, generic appearance, median age of 30.5 years, and so on. Matt could tell there was a lot of ass kissing going on. Each of the Aggro employees was mobbed by four or five interns who smiled and nodded a lot and seemed to be hanging on their every word. Matt scanned the crowd some more for the man himself, Royster G. Pfeiffer. A few minutes later, he spotted him at the farthest corner of the lawn, surrounded by a larger-than-average crowd of interns and various janizaries.

"There he is," Matt said to Frank, pointing toward Pfeiffer.

Frank looked, blinked, and responded in a completely obnoxious fashion. "What a nerd. I bet I could kick his ass with both hands tied behind my back."

Matt laughed. Roy did look like a nerd—he was tall, lanky, in his late thirties, with slightly stooped shoulders and thick glasses whose frames were older than the music that was playing. But what was most notable about him was his hairstyle, or lack thereof. It was the standard geek-issue, bowl-shaped cut, which, even from afar, looked especially greasy.

"You think with all the money he's got he could afford some shampoo," Frank quipped, and then suddenly asked Matt, "Hey, how much would you give me if I went up and asked Roy where's the pisser?"

"The what?"

"The men's room."

"You wouldn't dare," Matt said.

"Try me."

"All I've got is 20 bucks," Matt responded incredulously, handing him the money.

Frank jammed the bill in his shirt pocket, and went over to another group of Aggro interns and made the same offer.

"If you touch him, I'll give you $50," said one.

"I'll give you $100, but you have to actually piss on his leg," said another.

"I'll touch him for $50. C'mon, ante up, you guys."

Beer in hand, $150 of venture capital in his pocket, Frank strolled to the other side of the lawn, took a deep breath, and strode up to Roy, who was lecturing a small crowd of Aggro marketing people on the future of interactive CD-ROMs.

He came up behind Pfeiffer and flicked him on one of his bony biceps, flat out interrupting him.

"Hey man, where's the pisser?"

Pfeiffer half turned around, stunned. Frank stayed the course. "C'mon, dude, I gotta go bad. Where's the pisser?"

Roy remained speechless. It took him several seconds to recover.

"The pisser," said Frank. "You got one or do I have to use the lake?"

Frank did a pee-pee dance for effect, and Roy and the rest of the crowd stared in shock at his rudeness. To everyone's amazement, Roy cracked a slight smile as he gave Frank the directions.

"Through the house. Second door on the left."

"Thanks, dude," Frank responded, dancing away.

A wave of repressed laughter surged through the crowd. Those who weren't appalled by Frank's actions were impressed to no end. The consensus was that he was some sort of idiot savant—a genius when it came to computers, a maniacal boor when it came to everything else. By the time Frank had returned from "the pisser," he had become a genuine legend—no one in the history of Aggro Software had ever had the guts to talk to Roy that way before, much less get away with it.

"Just tryin' to have some fun, y'all."

"You're lucky you didn't get shot," said Matt.

## *Aggro's Untouchables*

Matt was slightly hungover when he reported to Building 8G for his first day. He was greeted by a plainclothes security guard, who escorted him up to his cube and gave him an ID and a password for his computer. When Matt had booted up and logged onto the machine, he found a tall stack of e-mails waiting for him. The first was from Roy himself, greeting all the interns; the rest were from someone named Ruth Thomas, who turned out to be his boss. Matt read through the e-mail carefully: it briefed him on the history of the project he'd be working on and listed a series of completion deadlines for his portion of it. He would be a beta tester for Know-X, a CD-ROM encyclopedia that was being relaunched in conjunction with a Web site. Matt took copious notes and was ready to hit the ground running, but nobody from the development team seemed to be around. In fact, Matt was the only one on the entire floor—the cubes surrounding him, as well as the offices that lined the walls, were completely empty.

It wasn't until 11 a.m. that people started filing in. The cubes filled up quickly, and most were occupied by an odd type of worker that Matt hadn't seen before. Unlike the preppy robots that seemed to make up much of Aggro's workforce, these people were a ragtag, grungy bunch of 20-somethings. Dressed in jeans and sneakers, they seemed to belong behind the counter of one of the local coffee bars, instead of hacking code in the antiseptic world of Aggro's Building 8G. But what was most shocking and refreshing about them was the definite "up yours" attitude they projected. Curious to learn more about this strange subspecies, Matt leaned over his cube and introduced himself to a thin blonde woman with pink streaks in her hair. Her response was not what he expected.

"You're one of them, aren't you?" she grunted.

"Them? What do you mean, 'them'?"

"C'mon, you're smart, you're from an Ivy League school, don't tell me you can't figure it out."

Matt sank down into his cube, stunned. He had no idea what this woman was talking about, but the situation did become clearer once he introduced himself to the lead developer.

"Hi, I'm Matt Swift," he said, offering his hand.

The developer's eyes trailed down immediately to his security badge and he smiled sardonically. "Purple, huh? Well, I'm blue. I don't like you, but I guess we're stuck with each other. . . . My name's Rich."

Matt put his extended hand away. He thought it best not to push the familiarity issue—there was some type of class warfare going on here that could get him in trouble. Instead, he listened intently as the developer explained the work flow.

"As you've probably read in your e-mail, the Know-X project's due August 20. That leaves us 11 weeks before they freeze the code. The good news, for you at least, is that we're way ahead of schedule on the toolbar piece that you're responsible for. In fact, if you bust your ass, you could finish debugging it in a month and spend the rest of your time here enjoying the perks afforded to someone of your high station."

Rich was obviously testing him—seeing if he'd take offense at his needling comments. But Matt didn't take the bait. He concluded it was better not to mess with these people, especially after the tongue-lashing he'd gotten from the woman in the cube next to his.

"Where can I find the latest build?" he asked coolly.

Rich wrote down the location on the network and that was it. Matt walked back to his cube to begin his work. About a half hour later, the phone on his desk rang. It was Ruth, his boss, checking on him. He did his best to assure her that he understood what he had to do and was up to speed on everything.

"That's super," she responded. "I'm glad to hear that. If you need me, I'm in Building 35G. Otherwise, we'll touch base at the beginning of August to evaluate your progress."

Talk about hands-off management, Matt thought. "OK, I won't let you down," he continued. "I'm looking forward to this, Ruth—it's a tremendously exciting project."

When Matt put down the phone, he received a particularly caustic comment from his pink-and-blonde neighbor. "You're a great bullshit artist and a first-class ass kisser. You'll go far in this place."

Matt ignored the dig and went back to work. That night he called Rick, his graduate student friend, to get the scoop on the stewpot of hostility that was his office environment.

"Pay no attention to those people," Rick said dismissively. "They're just perma-temps."

"Perma-temps? What's that?"

"Permanent-temporaries, contractors with no chance of ever becoming Aggro Software employees."

"Why not?"

"Because they're from the wrong side of the bell curve. Because they only went to local colleges. Because they don't have health benefits, or sick days, or paid vacations. Because in the eyes of the company, they're just scum."

"But they're doing the same job I'm doing. Can't they work their way up?"

"Doesn't matter, amigo. Like I said, wrong side of the bell curve."

"So, there's nothing I can do to smooth things over?"

"Nope. They're going to hate you no matter what."

"I guess if I were in their shoes I'd hate me, too."

The next day Matt sat alone in the cafeteria eating lunch when Frank entered, surrounded by a group of Aggro employees. Frank had the employees in stitches with a whole batch of jokes which combined what appeared to be their two favorite subjects: *Star Trek* and Royster G. Pfeiffer.

"How is Roy like the Borg?" Frank shouted, in characteristic fashion.

The group paused, awaiting the answer.

"You will be assimilated. Macintosh is fu-tile!"

They really broke up over this one. And Matt was glad for his roommate—at least someone was making friends with the natives.

## *Shake Your Moneymaker*

Short of becoming a Frank or a Tad—which wasn't his style—Matt did what the typical NetSlave would do in such a situation: he shut up, kept his head down, and buried himself in his work. He arrived at the office every day at 9 a.m. sharp and kept working straight, without a single break, until he couldn't hold his eyes open any longer. The work itself was tedious, but he loved it. The code meant everything to him. The code was holy. He read through every line, interpreting and cross-checking its significance, as if it were a sacred text containing the secrets of the universe. Even his perma-temp cohorts were impressed with Matt's diligence, and Rich, the lead developer, even graced him with an occasional "Good job." Such praise took him off guard, because he wasn't trying to impress anyone. All Matt wanted was to live up to his own perfectionist standards and hopefully secure a position with Aggro Software in the process.

A month and a half passed—45 days of 14-hour days and 7-day weeks, when suddenly at 3 p.m. one afternoon, Matt looked at the code and announced to himself, "I'm finished. There really isn't anything left for me to do on this project." He immediately went to Rich with the news, and Rich's response was, "At the rate you've been going,

I'm surprised you didn't finish two weeks ago, as I had originally expected."

"Well, there were more problems with the toolbar linkages than projected in the technical specification. In any case, what do I do now?"

Rich laughed grimly. "Let me tell you something about Corporate America—when you've got no work to do, when you've got the downtime, you hang out and enjoy life. So go to a club, work out, go kayaking, or do whatever you want."

Matt nodded his head and took that as a clear indication to leave the office immediately and go to the gym. Matt repeated this ritual every day around 3 p.m., even though he knew it rankled the perma-temps, who never had a minute of downtime and were barred from Aggro's many clubs.

## *A Fateful Choice*

In the second week of August, Matt, sun-tanned and well rested, had his first and only meeting with Ruth. Ruth was the typical Aggro employee, in both looks and demeanor. Nonetheless, Matt hit it off well with her, because she was very impressed by his progress.

"Matt, you've done a terrific job. How would you like to work for us?"

"Well, it's been a great experience for me, too. To think that you'd save a position for me when I graduate is phenomenal."

Ruth smiled and corrected him cordially. "Matt, we seem to have a slight disconnect here. I'd like you to start working for us immediately as chief beta tester for Know-X. After its launch, we'd move you into bigger and better things—probably coding. Your starting salary would be 90K, plus stock options, health benefits, the whole shooting match. How does that sound?"

Matt's heart began pounding. "Ruth . . . I'm . . . overwhelmed. . . . I never expected such an offer. I'm only going into my senior year now, so I . . ."

Ruth smiled again. "I understand how you feel. I was in the same situation six years ago. Why don't you take the night to think it over?"

Matt left her office in a daze. He was so overwhelmed that he didn't wait for the shuttle to take him home—he needed to walk and clear his head.

By the time he arrived back at the townhouse an hour later, he was covered in sweat from the August heat. He found Frank, beer in hand, in his usual spot on the couch, with the volume on the TV blasting.

"Frank, I need your help."

"THE BEER'S IN THE FRIDGE," Frank screamed up at him.

"I said, I NEED YOUR HELP."

"SORRY, DUDE. I JUST USED UP MY LAST RUBBER."

Matt sighed and proceeded to turn off the TV.

"Frank, it's serious. I have a problem."

"All right, man. You've interrupted the game in the bottom of the ninth, tie score. This had better be good."

"OK, I'll make it quick. They offered me a job, starting immediately, 90K salary, plus stock and bennies."

"DUDE, for this I'm missing the game? . . . It's a no-brainer. They just offered me a programming gig, too—working on their browser—you think I'm going to pass up an opportunity like that? For what? Aggro Software doesn't come calling every day, my man!"

"You don't want to finish your education?"

"With the stock they've given me, I'll be a millionaire by the time I'm 28. I could retire and go back to school for the rest of my life! What's wrong with you? Take the job!"

Matt had the world by the gonads, but he felt terribly depressed. There was something foul about his prospect for future riches, something that didn't make sense. It was too good—too easy—it just didn't add up. It was against his parents' dream of having a son with a college degree. It was against nature. It was . . . Matt's brain had gone into overdrive. He holed himself up in his room with the door closed. He stared at the dark ceiling for several hours. Finally, he got up enough courage to call Rick, the only person who would understand how he was feeling.

"You have to ask yourself two questions," Rick began. "First, 'Am I a believer?' And second, 'If I'm not a believer, can I deal with it?' "

"What do you mean by 'believer?' "

"A believer is someone who has bought into the Aggro Software mind-set, hook, line, and sinker. Someone who thinks that they're changing the world with this software and would give their life for it."

"Well, I like it here, but I'm not sure I'm a believer."

"The only way to know is to figure out if you want to become one of them."

"But what if I'm not one of them and I don't want to be."

"That's where the second question comes in. You either get the hell out of there or you stay and fake it. A lot of them do."

## Getting Out/Getting In

Matt packed his bags and left a week later. After looking at the strangely overenthused faces of Aggro's employees and the way they lived, or didn't live—always working, the kayaks in their front yards never used—he decided he wanted more. What that was he didn't know, but it certainly didn't involve selling his soul to Royster G. Pfeiffer.

Matt returned to school and finished out his final year in relative calm. Although he toyed with the idea of following Rick into graduate school, he changed his mind, once the job offers, mostly unsolicited, started rolling in.

*We need someone with experience at Aggro Software to head up our development team,* read one.

*We are prepared to offer you $100K starting salary, including stock options,* read another.

The desk in his dorm room was piled high with such letters. He puzzled over them night and day and finally accepted the position with IntelliComp, for much less pay, because it satisfied his sense of purpose. IntelliComp was a small player, but it had a noble mission. Working there would let him attend to his sacred code, but without having to become a Moonie—a true believer or a one-dimensional corporate clone.

## Pushing the Button

It was now 3:31 a.m. As Matt stared at his explosive e-mail to Royster G. Pfeiffer, he realized that he hadn't escaped Aggro at all—a thousand miles away, they were still pulling the strings that jerked him like a puppet, as IntelliComp fought its last desperate battles against the behemoth.

"It's all about money. That's it. Just money," Matt said to himself. Then, in his last moments of consciousness, he hit the "send" key. His head grew heavy, his eyes defocused, and he collapsed into a deep, dreamless coma, with his head coming to rest on his mousepad.

Around 10 a.m. on Sunday, Matt's cell phone started ringing and ringing again. But this time it wasn't some developer trying to hunt him down, it was Dave Strike, the CEO of IntelliComp. Matt had never spoken to Strike, except for some brief, perfunctory exchanges in the hall.

"Swift, I just got off the phone with Roy Pfeiffer. He was mighty peeved at your e-mail, and forwarded me a copy of your, er, letter. He told me, and I quote, 'If that's the way you and your people think about us, we have no further recourse but to crush you.'"

"To crush me?"

"Us, you idiot. IntelliComp. What the hell do you think you're doing, goading Pfeiffer like this? He's already out to kill us all."

"I'm sorry, sir, I just couldn't help myself."

"Well, could you help yourself to getting your butt into my office at 10 a.m. on Monday, after the board meeting? I need to resolve this issue ASAP."

Matt knew that he was about to get canned. He staggered out of the office, got in his car, and drove home. He stuffed his cell phone under a pillow, disabled the ringer on his bedroom phone, and slept for 18 hours. When his execution came, at least he'd be fully rested for it.

## *Epilogue*

As things turned out, Matt was able to keep his job. But that was only because by 10 a.m. on Monday, IntelliComp's board had voted to remove the entire management team, all the way down to his boss, Marty. Matt wasn't sorry at all to see them go—they had screwed up the previous version of the software so badly by overloading it with useless features that the board had decided to trash the whole team.

Remarkably, despite such upheaval, a stripped-down version of SmartSpell 3.0 did ship on time, with an interim CEO in place. The new CEO couldn't save IntelliComp from continuing to lose market share to Aggro, but the company stayed afloat long enough for Matt to see his letter to Royster introduced as evidence in a much-heralded antitrust suit brought against Aggro for unfair market practices.

Matt knew that Aggro would never be stopped by one hysterical memo, or even by a boxcar full of evidence. And in truth, he hoped the Feds let Aggro continue their "scorched-earth, imperial stampede across the office productivity software space" forever. In a strange way that he could never have foreseen, Matt now owed a lot to Royster G. Pfeiffer. Because every time IntelliComp lost more market share, the company was forced to close another offshore office—London was the first to go, then Paris, and Hong Kong would certainly be next.

IntelliComp might be going to hell, but Matt's cell phone was quieter than ever, which meant that at long last, he could get some sleep.

LEVEL 2.0

# Cops and Streetwalkers

**Is That a Cellular Modem in Your Pocket or Are You Just Happy to See Me?**

## 2.1 Who Are They?

Are you disgusted by online porn?

Well, no matter what your personal views are on the phenomenon, you have to give it to its purveyors on two accounts:

1. They know how to make money (unlike most Internet companies).
2. Their no-bullshit attitude toward working the Web is remarkably free of the illusioneering propaganda that NetSlaves at higher levels in the caste system have to suffer through. (Example: Of all the people Steve and I spoke to, not one uttered those dreaded three letters "IPO.")

Said a young woman who called herself "Trixie": "I know what I do and why I do it–it pays." We put the same question to a Cyber-Cop named Ralph and his response was, "God knows, I'm not going to get rich doing this. But it keeps a roof over my head until I can find something better."

Our hearts truly went out to people like Ralph–when they weren't patrolling bulletin boards and chat rooms, looking for stalkers, racists, and pedophiles, they were being cursed out over the phone by crazed Social Workers demanding that a certain problem member be locked out. Worse, the Cyber-Cops labored without sick days, vacation days, or health benefits. For all the aggravation they had to deal with, they should have been receiving a lot more.

It was such sights that made our journey to the farthest corner of the Dark Side of the Web much different than expected. We'd looked forward to something juicy, only to walk away shaking our heads. Even the Streetwalkers, with their G-strings bursting with money, didn't seem to be having much fun. The johns on the other end of the peekaboo CUSeeMe cameras were flat-out creepy when they weren't predictable to the point of absolute boredom.

"And what are you doing now, baby? What are you doing now?"

And so it went, over and over again, guy after guy after guy, until Steve and I felt like we had sipped a bit too much NyQuil.

But hey, who are we to judge, right?

We promised back in the Introduction not to get preachy or moralistic and we're going to stick to it. We'll leave it up to you to draw your own conclusions. In the meantime, brace yourself. What you're about to read ain't pretty.

## 2.2 General Characteristics

*Where they can be found:* Chat rooms and bulletin boards—one patrolling, the other soliciting.

*Average age:* 23 to 30 (with Cops falling into the underemployed young slacker subcaste and Streetwalkers looking pretty as entrepreneurs).

*Average income:* $10 per hour (Cops); $10,000 per week (Streetwalkers).

*Mode of dress:* Jeans, sneakers, three-day facial growth (Cops); "Nothing at all, Sweetie" (so claim Streetwalkers).

*Living arrangements:* They either live at home with their parents (Cops) or are about to close on a waterfront condo (Streetwalkers).

*Percentage of NetSlave population:* 10 percent (reason? Being a Cyber-Cop or a Streetwalker isn't something you'll ever see on *Upside*'s "Top Tech Jobs" list.)

*Hours worked per week:* 50 to 60 (online sex—like its real-world counterpart—involves a lot more than lying on your back).

*How Cops and Streetwalkers feel about each other:* If you ask a Cyber-Cop, Streetwalkers are the purveyors of everything bad about the Internet, including abductions and meetings with "online friends" that turn into rape. On the other hand, if you ask a Streetwalker, it's the Cyber-Cops who are the purveyors of everything bad about the Internet: censorship, repression, the latest play of the Moral Majority, and the attempt by Corporate America to turn a vital, grassroots business opportunity into a G-rated shopping mall.

*Significant other:* Gillian Anderson and the babe on *Star Trek: Voyager* (Cops); "I'm all yours, honey." (again claim Streetwalkers).

*View the Internet as:* A way to get rich (Streetwalkers); a way to get by (Cops).

*Most recurrent nightmare:* Redbone the Great, a legendary online user whose favorite fetish involves goats and blenders (Cops); a cure for AIDS, in which case people would be having actual, honest-to-God sex, instead of getting their jollies by means of a computer (Streetwalkers).

*Chance of upward mobility:* Medium—the best and brightest Cyber-Cops can become high-priced digital spooks; Streetwalkers, if they play their cards right, can look forward to an early retirement.

*Chance of downward mobility:* High. All it would take is a breakthrough in content-filtering technology, along with government legislation, to put both these groups out of business.

## 2.3 The Story of Officer Kilmartin

*Kilmartin patrolled the mean streets of Synergy, the so-called family-oriented online service, from 1992 to 1994. He has since gone on to various other jobs in the technology business, but considers the time he spent chasing stalkers and enduring the abuse of a tyrannical boss "the experience that taught me everything I know about this medium."*

Kilmartin sat deep in the bowels of Synergy's White Plains headquarters, feeling a slight chill on his spine. It was 4:30 a.m., and his shift had just ended. All that remained was the dreaded ride home—those tense 50 minutes of twisting along dark Westchester highways, expecting something really bad to happen. It wasn't ghosts or aliens that scared him. His fear stemmed from more earthly dangers, such as drunk drivers, cops, and the flat-out crazies who claim the wee, small hours of the morning as their own.

What some call "paranoia" others view as a learned prescience. In the year and a half that Kilmartin had been working these hours, he had had more than a few near misses. Cars on the wrong side of the road, cops pulling him over and giving him tickets for being five miles over the limit, and, lest he ever forget, the woman who was running down the middle of the street naked and who screamed "Rape!" when he tried to help her.

All he wanted was to clear his head and to forget—to forget everything that had happened to him up to that point and to forget what might be out there in the night waiting for him.

He twisted the radio dial until he locked onto a jazz station. Sonny Rollins or Lester Young purred through the cheap dashboard speaker. A few months ago, back when Synergy still had some life in it, he'd listen to his favorite swinging sounds in a tiny cubicle near the center of what Synergy called "the Configuration," a great wheel of cubes housing Synergy's small army of online moderators, censors, and conversation managers. But ever since Synergy management had outlawed such minor pleasures, the only music Kilmartin heard was the steady percussive clicks of his own fingers as they reviewed, processed, and rejected thousands of electronic notes bouncing back and forth between Synergy's members each night.

Kilmartin was a Cop—a Cyber-Cop who patrolled the mean streets of Synergy from dusk to dawn in search of perverts, freaks, stalkers, and other undesirables threatening Synergy's carefully managed "family" image. It was tedious, tiring work, yet he kept doing it. He found the seamy underside of online behavior strangely intriguing. He had grown accustomed—in a sense, addicted—to a daily dose of deviance. He hadn't always been this way. The job had definitely changed him for the worse. He had become a strange nocturnal creature, surviving on the garbage of fetid minds while going without the basic creature comforts of the average job—holidays, vacations, sick days, to say nothing of the need to do something meaningful with his life.

Kilmartin made a quick right out of the garage. The streets of White Plains were calm and quiet. The City of Malls had closed down for the evening and a light snow had covered the gray and black pavement with a thin, glistening white sheet. He felt invigorated at escaping the place where he'd been imprisoned for the last 8.5 hours. He drove for a while, watching the homes drifting by, wondering how many of them concealed Synergy members chatting about bondage. It always amazed Kilmartin how perversity seemed to flourish amid well-manicured lawns and well-managed suburban lives.

He made a left onto the service road that led down a short hill to the Saw Mill Parkway. It was the same route he had taken for months, but tonight something about the road was different. He felt the car speeding up, and suddenly there was a lot of play in the steering wheel. Within seconds, Kilmartin realized that he had lost control of the car. He was skidding on black ice—heading straight for the guardrail.

A comet of red and white lights flashed across the windshield, followed by a jolting *thud*. When he opened his eyes, Kilmartin saw that the car was pointed lengthwise across the road with its nose buried in a snowbank from a previous storm. Shaken, but most definitely alive, he clutched his face and felt for a sticky river of blood. Nothing. He was lucky, very lucky. He sighed heavily and rested his head against the steering wheel for a long time. He listened quietly to the radio that was still playing. The low, unmistakable muted trumpet of Miles Davis—the Prince of Darkness—moved across his frayed nerves. It calmed him, and eventually gave him the courage to get out of the car and dig through the frozen mountain with his bare hands.

He made it home on three wheels. The fourth barely hung on, held in place by a single lug nut. For hours Kilmartin lay in bed, unable to sleep, replaying the accident in his mind. Once or twice, he drifted very close to unconsciousness, but never quite made it there. This was fortunate, because Synergy wasn't about to let him sleep.

## *Crackdown at Zero Hour*

The phone rang unexpectedly at 7:55 a.m.

"H-hello?"

"Kilmartin, this is Tom Harris. Get out of bed. We need you back in the office in two hours."

"W-what's going on? Is everything all right?"

"I don't have time for this now. Just be here in two hours." Harris hung up.

Harris was his supervisor. He was a real nasty SOB. On the outside, he looked friendly–sort of like Captain Kangaroo. Inwardly, however, his soul was tortured. Harris was a 50-something ex-VP of a bank who'd been banned from the Street for alcoholism, sexual harassment, and creative accounting. With two divorces behind him and four kids to support, he was a bitter guy who took great joy in making others miserable. Promoted to manager out of the despised ranks of Cyber-Cops, Harris ran the department like an electronic gulag. Nobody could be a minute late, they were forbidden to talk, and listening to the radio while working was a definite no-no. When Harris spoke, you listened or you were promptly shown the door. Kilmartin felt a mixture of hatred and pity for Harris: here was a man who had fallen so far from grace that Synergy was the only thing he had left. It was his last chance in a life of blown opportunities.

But Kilmartin had no time to reflect. He threw on his clothes as quickly as possible and, recalling his car's missing lug nuts, ran out into the snow to catch the 8:50 a.m. bus up to White Plains.

As the bus approached Synergy's enormous parking lot, Kilmartin could tell by the number of cars assembled that something big was happening–something very big. Inside one of Synergy's windowless meeting rooms, the entire cyber police force, day and night shifts, had been assembled–all 40 of them.

Standing at the back of the stuffy room, Kilmartin cocked his ears to monitor the flurry of wild rumors circulating in whispers–everything from "they're closing down the department," to "the company's being sold," to "Ross Fletcher, the president, is resigning." He discounted them all, reasoning that scum like himself were always the last to know.

Kilmartin looked around the room and eyed his fellow Cyber-Cops, who more closely resembled a gang of arrested adolescents than enforcers safeguarding Synergy's future. His fellow misfits lounged, yawned, and leaned against the walls, dressed in worn-out jeans and sneakers. They were by all accounts an unruly bunch, but they were by no means stupid. They instantly snapped to attention when Steve Tannenbaum, a senior manager, dressed in a dark blue suit and red tie, marched into the room and sat at the head of the long table. Tannenbaum smiled tightly at Harris, cleared his throat, and launched directly into his speech.

"As you all know, Synergy is a family service. And to that end, management has decided that a number of changes are needed, going forward. Effective at 6:00 p.m. tonight, all sexually offensive material, starting with the Frank Discussion bulletin board, will be taken offline. To minimize impact, we have not informed the members or the media and ask that you refrain from doing so. We also ask all content managers to begin rejecting any messages that, in your judgment, are even remotely sexual in nature and make a hard copy of any notes making reference to Synergy's change in policy. Are there any questions?"

Silence. Tannenbaum nodded, then continued. "We thank you for your time and consideration. The transition is not going to be easy. However, we know that you will continue your fine work in helping Synergy satisfy, retain, and grow."

Tannenbaum quickly disappeared through a hidden door at the side of the room into the ether of upper management. Every low-level staffer in the room longed to follow his vanishing act, but were stopped midflight by Harris, who raised both arms for attention.

"OK, OK. Listen up! We're gonna have a lot of pissed-off members tonight and I want you to be ready for them. I want all the canned response letters rewritten, I want the scan list updated, and most of all, I want you people to remember how serious this situation is. There will be no sex, no sex of any kind, tolerated on the service. I'm talking about the slightest innuendo, the least hint. It's gone, do you hear me? It's gone. No questions asked. And the new rules don't change your note counts. Every one of you meets your quota. Everything keeps moving or else. Am I making myself clear?"

It was more than clear to Kilmartin, who had long suspected that most of Synergy's paying audience consisted of pedophiles, adult babies, and White Power nuts. Somebody—probably high up at Data Magic or Handy-Home, the two companies that jointly owned Synergy—had been given a scare. Kilmartin wasn't so sure what would happen when Synergy's new directive collided with 2 million lunatics with modems. But he was sure that Harris was going to chop heads if the sacred quota—the number of notes that each Cyber-Cop had to read, approve, or reject each night–wasn't met. As he thought about it, he realized that he was reliving the last seconds of his accident, when the guardrail was rushing toward his windshield.

With zero hour approaching, Kilmartin decided that there was no point in going home for a few hours, just to return to the office at 8:00 p.m., and he resigned himself to a double shift. Although his gut told him that Synergy was probably making a big mistake, perhaps they could all ride it out. The problem was that Frank Discussion wasn't just a popular Synergy bulletin board–it was *the* most popular bulletin board on the service, being both a terrific moneymaker, and, at least in Kilmartin's mind, the key to Synergy's insane growth over the years.

Kilmartin's time on the mean streets had taught him that people went online for two reasons: sex and hate. If they were interested in family, they wouldn't be on a computer in the first place. If they were interested in values, they'd be in a church or a synagogue, instead of chatting about whips, chains, diapers, and swastikas. Still, Kilmartin figured that Synergy would ride out the storm–after all, the service had 2 million members and they couldn't all be perverts and psychopaths, could they?

The first hints of doom came at five minutes past zero hour. When the members realized that Frank Discussion wasn't accepting any new notes and was going to be deleted in a matter of hours, their reaction was shock, followed by anger and outright retaliation.

A flurry of obscenity-laden messages pelted the Cyber-Cops every time they downloaded editorial alerts.

"Are you people crazy? What are you doing?" read one. Another simply had "dickheads" written over and over again for six pages and was signed, "Hater of Dickheads."

Violent uprisings also erupted. There were "Synergy Sucks" threads everywhere and conversations flourished that were even more ribald, racist, explicit, and debauched than usual. Worse, they appeared on a variety of definitively nonsexual, G-rated bulletin boards (BBSs). A gang of fully diapered adult babies began appearing in the Parenting area, S&M people knifed their way into Radio Controlled Hobbies, and vampire pagan bestialists strutted their stuff in the Religion area. For eight straight hours, 40 Cyber-Cops raced from forum to forum, chasing the people displaced from Frank Discussions, attempting in vain to staunch the appalling flow of X-rated conversations. As panic set in, senior Cyber-Cops huddled around the Configuration to speed the censoring of messages, while frantic Cyber-Cops yelled out the contents of the notes as fast as they flashed on their screens.

"Somebody's saying, 'I have an ice cream cone. Does anyone have a cherry?'"

"REJECT!" the senior Cyber-Cop barked, after consulting his rulebook. 'Sexual solicitation.'"

"How about, 'I really love watching trains going into tunnels,'" somebody else called out.

"REJECT! 'Sexually explicit.'"

"How about, 'You bring the goat. Redbone's got the blender.'"

"REJECT! 'Grossly repugnant.'"

This desperate battle against the spreading stench of wanton messages went on for the rest of the night and didn't really abate for several weeks. Although Synergy was still pockmarked by obscenity, the antisex crusade was by all accounts a smashing success: Synergy was soon cleaner than Mickey Mouse, thanks to the tireless efforts of Kilmartin and the other Cyber-Cops.

But just as things seemed to be settling down, they found themselves facing an even more sinister problem—a problem that went to high school and had bad acne and a seemingly limitless appetite for online deviltry.

### Fun with the Huns

The Huns was an online gang that had sprung up out of nowhere to fight "the injustices of Synergy." Led by an unknown vigilante named White Knight, the Huns used the antisex clampdown as an excuse to wreak havoc. Their main weapon was spam, which they spread far and wide. More than anything else, they loved to target very serious, very highbrow boards, like Food & Wine, where on one occasion they completely covered the subject lines with "McDonald's RULES" and "Mad Dog 20-20" messages. Kilmartin and the other Cyber-Cops found it amusing to watch, especially as snooty, blue-chip members became enraged when their erudite conversational thread about Brie cheese and merlot wine was cut to shreds by some Hun shouting about the virtues of Velveeta and Pabst.

When Harris first heard about the Huns, he gave Kilmartin and the other Cyber-Cops orders to "shoot to kill," which meant they could permanently lock out anyone or anything even remotely related to the gang. This strategy seemed to work at first, but when the Huns kept returning under different IDs, Kilmartin concluded that White Knight probably had an endless supply of free accounts at his disposal—and the credit cards to go with them.

What was needed was a silver bullet. It was the only way to kill this beast that wouldn't die. But where to find it? The search for the Huns became an all-consuming obsession with Harris, who put both day and night shifts on alert for weeks. The chase finally ended when White Knight slipped up and used a legitimate credit card that Kilmartin traced to a member's address in Roslyn, Long Island. When police arrived at the Bronstein residence, they were shown to the bedroom of a 14-year-old boy named Jeff, whose parents were both psychiatrists. The boy, who claimed to have no idea that he was committing fraud and criminal mischief, was never arrested, although police impounded his computer for two weeks. The boy promised to "never, ever do it again," and the charges were dropped, because the last thing Synergy needed was another scandal.

With the Huns case solved, Kilmartin almost considered taking a vacation, but again, there was no time. In early 1993, Synergy launched a major ad campaign to promote the service in the public mind. There wasn't a TV, radio, or magazine that wasn't blaring out messages about how easy and safe it was to go online with Synergy, the "family" service, and Harris kept the pressure on Kilmartin's team to censor any messages that weren't sugar and spice.

Unfortunately, however, the masses weren't ready. Too many of them were running really old computers or didn't have modems or were just plain scared of going online, having heard about the legions of stalkers and perverts that were out to get them. The result was millions of ad dollars down the drain. Worse, the side effects of the anti-sex crusade began to haunt Synergy. The reduced member base hated and mistrusted the service and spread censorship horror stories from Cyber-America to Delphi to CompuTime.

By early spring, member erosion continued and usage plummeted, despite various good-will gestures on the part of management to loosen up the guidelines and run contests to make the service more "fun." Kilmartin knew that the only thing that would have packed them in again was the resurrection of Frank Discussion (its fans called it "Frankie D."), but he also knew that management would never let this happen.

With membership hemorrhaging, Kilmartin began to see the guardrail approaching again. Synergy was in bad shape, and Harris was firing people left and right for the most insubstantial reasons. Being two minutes late, talking, not posting your quota of notes per hour, not matching your socks correctly were all offenses likely to earn you that early morning call from the temp agency informing you that your assignment was completed. The only one who relished the slaughter was Harris. For the first time in months, he was smiling. He loved the purges because they improved his bottom line—reducing the department from 40 to 20 and then from 20 to 15 in a matter of months, while at the same time maintaining productivity.

## Fatcula's Revenge

For the Cyber-Cops, the situation was grim. With Synergy's membership in shambles, there were few notes to process and no editorial alerts to respond to, yet each Cyber-Cop was still expected to process his quota of notes. Huddled in groups of five per shift, their main job responsibility became devising new ways to justify their existence. Some logged onto two computers at once; others just held the "return" key down for five minutes at a time when they thought no one was looking. Harris knew what they were doing, of course, but he didn't care. It added to his efficiency scheme.

Any normal person would have gotten a different job. Problem is, Kilmartin and the other Cyber-Cops were definitely not normal. Nor would they ever be.

Many people in the beleaguered department were older folks, seasoned professionals who had been downsized out of Data Magic and other blue-chip companies on the ropes. Mostly male, these corporate castaways were 50 years old on the average, and the stricken looks on their faces indicated that most were still in shock over their changed circumstances. For these middle-aged warriors, the American Dream they had believed in, treasured, and devoted their lives to for 20 or more years had become a nightmare. Gone was the early retirement of swinging a golf club in Florida; gone the fat pension, the Cuban cigars, the expense account, the leggy secretary. The dream had ended suddenly, just as it was getting good, just as they were eyeing the corner office.

Kilmartin found this downsized crowd depressing and maybe even dangerous. When they weren't staring blankly at the computer screen in apparent shock, they seemed on the verge of going postal, of pulling a pistol from the pocket of their tweed jackets and shooting everyone in sight before turning the last bullet on themselves. Kilmartin knew their intense bitterness came from the nagging, lingering responsibilities left over from their former high-flying lives—the wives, ex-wives, mortgages, kids in college, the whole middle-class bit.

The downsizers kept themselves going by indulging in dark, vicious humor, often mumbled under their breath in the form of diabolical, sadistic jokes.

Downsizers formed about one-third of Kilmartin's team; the rest of them were young, overeducated, liberal arts idiots like Kilmartin. Because they had no reason to take the job as seriously as their older counterparts, they took every possible opportunity to make a mockery of it, especially on nights when Harris went home early or called in sick. They turned the radio up full blast, conducted chair races in the hall, played bumper cars with computer carts, and took extended dinner breaks to shop for CDs at the nearby Galleria mall.

Kilmartin instigated much of the absurd, adolescent activities and he liked getting people charged up to play "Truth or Dare," which had become a nightly routine around the Configuration.

"You're in a burning room, with a passed-out Nazi storm trooper and the *Mona Lisa*. There are flames everywhere. You only have enough time to save one. What do you do?"

He would then go around the Configuration to gather responses, which were more than predictable.

"I'd take the *Mona Lisa,* sell it and retire."

The dollar always seemed to win out. Perhaps it was because the people he was asking were too broke to afford ideals and ethics. In any case, it was a fun way to pass the time, with arguments between Kilmartin and his unsuspecting victims going back and forth on wild variations of already improbable hypothetical situations.

"You wouldn't do anything for a million dollars?"

"No!"

"What about five million dollars?"

"No!"

"Ten?"

"No!"

"Are you kidding me? You're already doing it for much less. Why not go for the big payback?"

The room erupted with laughter. Everyone loved it when Kilmartin cornered someone. But it was nothing compared to the screams of hilarious mayhem generated when he went head to head with Chris Mencken, a Desert Storm vet who probably knew more about computers than anyone in the company. Short and paunchy, Mencken had muttonchop sideburns, which he often topped off with a big cowboy hat. His intent was to look like a badass, but given his physical limitations, he came off more as a troll with attitude.

Equally curious was what Mencken was doing in the department in the first place. Although his technical skills qualified him for more prestigious and higher-paying positions, he had settled for a job as a Cyber-Cop because it was a better fit with his lifestyle and interests. Mencken was into hacking, running porn BBSs out of his home, gun collecting, motorcycles, and paganism. It was this final pursuit in particular that made him a target for ridicule, especially from Kilmartin, who was constantly ragging on him about it, calling him a "tree hugger" and a "devil worshipper," among other things.

Harris messed with Mencken in a completely different way. Instead of making smart-ass comments like Kilmartin and the rest of the Cyber-Cops, he said absolutely nothing to him, ignoring him completely, except for an occasional dirty look. This icy treatment bore in on Mencken, because in his paranoid mind, subtle gestures were evidence of a massive conspiracy against him. "That bastard's out to get me!" Mencken was fond of saying, although the statement was completely ridiculous, given that Harris was out to get everyone and anyone.

Kilmartin figured Mencken must have secretly enjoyed the mockery, or he wouldn't have constantly done things to make himself stand out as a freak. His behavior had become more bizarre of late, with Kilmartin privately suspecting that eventually something had to give. On Halloween night—almost a year to the date after the troll had joined Synergy—Kilmartin's fears were realized. Mencken showed up for the 11-to-7 shift in full warlock regalia, which included a long hooded black cape, a ruffled black shirt, black jeans, and black pointed boots. Harris wasn't there that night, so the comments starting flying immediately when Mencken walked through the door.

"Hey, who are you supposed to be—the Pillsbury Doughboy from Hell?"

"Didn't I see you in a movie once? I think it was called *Fatcula*."

Instead of taking the abuse, or else replying with a customary verbal shrug, Mencken responded in character. He pulled a long, shiny sword from a sheath at his side and began screaming at the top of his lungs: "CHRISTIAN OPPRESSORS, I WILL SMITE THEE FOR YOUR IGNORANT WORDS ON THIS HIGH-HOLY EVE!"

The Cyber-Cops sat there speechless. This nut is serious, Kilmartin thought. What a way to go: cut to pieces working the night shift for Synergy. The seniors, or sergeants, on duty tried calming Mencken down, but only made things worse, as he screamed even louder and directed his tirade at certain individuals.

"KILMARTIN, THE CURSE OF HECATE AND HECUBA UPON THEE!!!"

"STEIN, YOU LOOKIN' LIKE MR. SPOCK, DICKHEAD . . ."

Mencken advanced toward Kilmartin, but as he passed Stein's cube, Stein's fist suddenly flew up and knocked Mencken unconscious with a single hammer-blow punch. Pandemonium quickly broke out, as the remainder of the crew tackled Stein and dragged him into a conference room.

Before they could even set him in a chair, the half-crazed downsizer who hated being called Mr. Spock burst out crying. "I'm sorry. I don't know what came over me. My daughter might not be able to go back to school this year. The doctor bills, the goddamn doctor bills . . ."

Stein rambled on and on. Most of it was incoherent. From the few bits Kilmartin could piece together, Stein evidently had a tumor in his head the size of a grapefruit and had a 50-50 chance of surviving past the next weeks. Everyone listening was very disturbed and confused and seemed on the verge of tears themselves.

In the meantime, Mencken was just coming around. After several failed attempts, he finally made it to his feet and stood there holding onto a chair, groaning, still very unsure of himself. "Oh, Jesus. What hit me? What hit me?"

To make sure there wasn't any more trouble, Kilmartin rushed over to him, found him a chair in a vacant cube, and handed him a glass of water. "Hey, Chris, are you all right? We were just kidding around."

"I'm gonna kill that guy. I'm gonna kill him!" He threw the cup to the other side of room, the water splashing across one of the desks. "I'm gonna kill him, you hear me?"

Kilmartin held him in the chair, his hands clamped firmly on each of his shoulders. At first Mencken wouldn't listen to reason, but when Kilmartin told him about Stein's tumor he finally calmed down and was even ready to apologize.

"Geez, I'm sorry. I had no idea. This place is driving me nuts. In the army there were rules at least. And we knew who the enemy was." He paused to groan again. "I promise there won't be any more trouble."

That seemed to be the end of it. Months went by. No one breathed a word of that tumultuous evening to anyone until Stein, resigning for medical reasons, made an offhand comment during his exit interview about the "strangeness" of the department and of Chris Mencken in particular.

That was all Harris needed to hear. By the middle of the next day, a full investigation was completed and Mencken was dragged out of the building by a pair of burly security guards, who told him that if he was ever caught on the premises or mentioned anything to anyone about his time at Synergy, he would be prosecuted to the fullest extent of the law.

In the days following Mencken's departure, word got out about his extracurricular activities at Synergy. Among them was the fact that Mencken had been writing dirty e-mail to several female members for quite some time and had also been running an anonymous FTP server on Synergy's network that distributed porn and pirated game software. These revelations left Harris and Synergy upper management gasping. A misfit, pagan, cracker, ex-military freak had outsmarted them for months and, with even the slightest leak to the press, had the power to destroy their safe, family-friendly image.

Not a day passed that Kilmartin and the other Cyber-Cops didn't expect to pick up a paper displaying a front-page interview with Mencken and featuring a headline reading: VET NAMES SYNERGY AS SOURCE OF NAZI PORN or, short of that, a piece about Mencken's being found floating in the river with a self-inflicted bullet hole in his head. Although neither story materialized, Mencken didn't let them down. About three weeks after getting fired from Synergy, he was arrested for driving the getaway truck for a disgruntled ex-journalist who tossed a bomb at his editor's house and succeeded in blowing up a car that was parked in the driveway.

It was a magnificent turn of events, far beyond anyone's expectation. The result of Menken's spectacular exploits would be Synergy's first convicted felon, and he would go down in Cyber-Cop history as a legend and perma-temp saint. They could already see the story, written in a monk's hand, in a large leather-bound book with gold leaf: "After a brief incarceration, he continued his crusade against former employers by visiting Harris's house late one night with an explosive token of his affection."

Although this never came to pass, it wasn't a total loss because everyone got to see Harris scared around the time of Mencken's release, four months later. Keeping a very low profile, Harris became virtually invisible—he stayed in his office all night, left early, and communicated only indirectly, through e-mail or the seniors. His fear extended far beyond the nightmare of Mencken's planting a claymore mine in his car or jumping out of a bush with a broadsword. The question that really plagued Harris's mind was, "Who would be the next to snap?"

**Even** with Mencken on the loose, Harris regained his courage and reverted to being an even bigger bastard than ever, just to prove that he hadn't lost it. For starters, he forbade mention of Mencken, with the penalty of immediate termination. And as if that weren't clear enough, he launched an investigation to document all activities (divisive and otherwise) in the department over the past 12 months.

A loud, collective sigh went around the Configuration. The end seemed imminent.

## *Escaping the Inquisition*

Kilmartin watched the inquisition unfold before his eyes. Everyday someone else was called on the carpet and grilled for an hour and a half on past events, procedure, what-have-you. It was a hideous spectacle. People went into Harris's office shaky and sweating and came out practically on stretchers, the color completely drained from their faces and, in some cases, the tears dripping from their reddened eyes. A woman from the morning shift was so rattled that she had to cut her session short and make a mad dash to the ladies' room—only to vomit in the nearest water fountain.

By day three of the sessions, no one had been killed or fired yet, but paranoia was raging beyond control. There were rumors that the department was going to be eradicated; that the operation would be taken over by an outsourcing group in Grey, Tennessee; that Harris was going to dump the entire staff and start over from scratch. There seemed no limit to the negative speculation.

When Kilmartin's turn came, it was in the form of an early morning phone call instructing him to be in the office as soon as possible. The time was 11:06 a.m.; the date, June 12, 1994. Since no one talked about what had happened during the questioning, he didn't know what to expect when he got in his old car and headed up to White Plains.

It was the end, Kilmartin thought. It had to be the end. A big change was afoot. But what? He tried imagining what the next step would be. A return to academia? Teaching? A career in publishing? Mopping floors? Whatever lay at the endpoint of the terror in Harris's office, perhaps it wouldn't be as bad as what he had already been through. A slight chill passed over his body. He felt both happy and on the verge of passing out. It didn't help that he had had only three hours' sleep, after getting home at 5 and watching TV until 8.

Turning in to the parking garage, he felt everything slowing down, as in a dream in which the dreamer desperately tries to run from an inescapably looming tidal wave. He smiled faintly. He thought of the night on the black ice. It was the same thing. His luck had finally run out. The gods had grown tired of helping him. Or so he thought.

Harris sat at his tiny desk in his cramped office, going through a large pile of papers directly in front of him. At first, he didn't notice Kilmartin standing at the threshold and seemed preoccupied with reading and rereading the papers, writing comments on some of them, circling words on others with a bright yellow marker.

Kilmartin knocked lightly on the opened door and Harris looked up and smiled. It was the last thing he expected. He assumed the worst until Harris began speaking.

"Although I had originally set aside this time to comb through and evaluate all the notes you processed over the past year and give you a hard time over some of them, the fact is, we suddenly have other plans for you. As you probably know, usage on the system is up and we want to set up some new bulletin boards to stimulate further growth with . . ."

"Yes?" Kilmartin interrupted suddenly, unable to contain his excitement and nervousness.

Harris didn't appreciate the interruption, but continued, with an uncharacteristic calm. "Would you be interested in heading up a few of these boards? The salary would be twice what you're making now; you would work from home and if you're successful, you might be able to get a full-time job in this place; although at this point, I don't see why anyone would be crazy enough to want one."

"Uh, what's in it . . . for you?"

Harris laughed. "I brought you up good. I've made you a cynical bastard as well! What's in it for me? Why, I'll have a toehold in a completely new department."

The translation was that Harris would be calling every chance he got. But everything comes at a price. At least there would be distance between them.

Kilmartin danced out of the office holding a signed contract. He couldn't believe what had happened. He passed the Configuration for the last time, waving and smiling to his colleagues, who already knew the deal. It was sweet. Sweet victory. Although he still would be electronically tethered to the madness, the wheels had stayed on. The lug nut had held. He had made it home again, after all.

## *Epilogue*

Kilmartin worked as a moderator for Synergy for another year and a half. The "personality" behind bulletin boards such as Arts and Singles and Lifestyles (the successor to Frank Discussion), Kilmartin found it an ideal job, the complete opposite of being a Cyber-Cop. Not only could he enjoy sunlight and holidays and days off, but with the extra money he was earning, he could finally move out of his parents' house and buy a new car with four fully functional wheels. Most important, however, working as a moderator let Kilmartin polish his writing skills. He was always an English major at heart and the constant wordsmithing at the keyboard opened up new and totally unexpected opportunities.

By 1996, Synergy had fallen from premier online service to its current state of Internet service provider obscurity, collapsing Kilmartin's literary soirees. But with his enhanced skills and reputation as a survivor intact, he was able to become a well-regarded Internet analyst, with articles appearing regularly in a host of technology publications and Web sites. Today, he rarely thinks about Synergy anymore, except on nights when he's driving home very late and the chill of a coming snowstorm recalls the events of a few years ago with an icy clarity—the smut, the hours, the constant fear of being fired, the lack of doing something meaningful with his life.

On particularly bleak winter evenings, he even thinks about Harris, who was forced to leave Synergy after suffering a sudden nervous breakdown. And he sometimes wonders where Mencken is. In his mind, he can see the troll marching through the snow in his Halloween costume, carrying a scythe and a velvet bag of runes. Beneath his great hood, the troll is smiling peacefully and humming a tune—something by Miles Davis. Kilmartin isn't sure what this vision means, but he always draws comfort from it.

# LEVEL 3.0

# Social Workers

### Click Here for a Clean, Well-Lighted Place

## 3.1 Who Are They?

The longer Steve and I spent on the Dark Side of the Net, the more we realized that Cops and Streetwalkers of Cyberspace were not its only inhabitants. There was also this strange and overly friendly group of individuals calling themselves "Social Workers"–although at first glance their mode of dress and their duties seemed more reminiscent of missionaries.

From colorful tents pitched inside chat rooms, bulletin boards, and special-interest Web sites, these tireless souls did everything from solving marital problems and providing sustenance to weary surfers to serving as hosts and liaisons for celebrities and other notables visiting the electronic community.

What's more, the members of this caste all seemed to be experts in their particular field of interest. There were Social Workers who could rattle off the chronology of all German Expressionist films made between 1919 and 1929. Others were authorities on model railroading. Still others could tell you how to survive in the desert for months at a time with only a tuning fork at your disposal. Steve and I learned a great deal from talking to the Social Workers. And it was quite entertaining to watch the emotions fly fast and furious as people argued so passionately about the most obscure subjects. While we maintained a professional and scientific demeanor for the most part, we had to excuse ourselves whenever the conversations veered toward "Wiccan investment strategies" or "the metaphysics of polka."

Our restraint was due to fear, rather than any excessive politeness. In such tightly knit communities you are either an insider or an outsider. And to be the latter is often dangerous to your digital health. Social Workers are by definition understanding types, but instantaneously transform into modem-wielding Furies whenever they feel their territory is being threatened. Imagine the Incredible Hulk with fly-fishing fever and you've only begun to scratch the surface of the horrors awaiting the smart-ass outsider who starts joking about zippers and oral sex.

Steve and I don't begrudge Social Workers the urge to protect their communities. We know it's their job to keep the conversations lively and on-topic and to imbue their communities' inhabitants with a sense of safety, of having a place to go to escape the stresses of their everyday lives (see Sublevel −1.0 at the end of the book for details). In this respect, the Social Workers of cyberspace have more in common with their real-life counterparts than any missionary sect, who, at bottom, care about the culture of the natives only as much as they can undermine and "convert" it.

## 3.2 General Characteristics

*Where they can be found:* At the other end of any celebrity chat, in the thick of bulletin board discussions, below the banner of any interest-specific hub ("Welcome to the Midget Tossing Alchemist's Forum! My name is Hieronymous Smith and I'll be your guide!").

*Average age:* 25 to 35. Since being a Social Worker implies a certain level of maturity, members of this caste are slightly older than the average person you'll find trolling AOL's chat rooms at one o'clock in the morning.

*Average pay:* Varies. Many social workers provide their services in exchange for free accounts or server space. Others do it as a second job to supplement their income. Wages are nominal at best ($10 to $15 per hour), but in the eyes of Social Workers, dealing with the bitchy members on the Plant Cultures topic beats taking a bullet on 7-Eleven's graveyard shift.

*Marital status:* Married (last time they checked).

*"Official" Social Worker attire:* Pink fuzzy slippers, cigarette-burned undershirt.

*Psychological profile:* Obsessive. They know a great deal about their particular (some say, "peculiar") area of interest and very little about the world at large ("Monica Lewinsky? Who's that?").

*Hours worked per week:* 20 to 30. (So reads their contract, but given their obsessive nature, most Social Workers put in upward of 60 to 70 hours, gratis.)

*Percentage of NetSlave population:* 40 percent. If you've ever been to GeoCities, theglobe, or About.com, you'll know why this number is so high.

*Unsung abilities:* Social Workers are the emoticon kings and queens of the New Media Universe. Not only do they possess an encyclopedic knowledge of every possible facial expression and abbreviation (VBG, LOL, IMHO, SEG), but they wield them with the skill and grace of concert pianists. Also, being negotiators at bottom, they can resolve electronic disagreements quicker than you can say "Henry Kissinger."

*Other talents:* Social Workers who do celebrity chats should be awarded the Real-Time Medal of Honor for putting up with the immense egos of our modern-day gods and goddesses, who have been known to storm out of events midway, not show-up at all, or otherwise act like such royal pains in the ass that Social Workers have had to make up their responses on the spot. (Yes, that's right, boys and girls. Odds are that the big-time actress you thought was gracing the same chat auditorium with your humble selves was probably just a Social Worker doing an electronic puppet show. Think we're kidding? See the following story.)

*Chance of upward mobility:* Unlikely. Most Social Workers putter away in their little fiefdoms in relative peace and harmony as compared with other NetSlaves. However, on the off chance that they befriend a disaffected teenager (who just hacked Fort Knox) or something equally wacky happens, the sky's the limit—book deals, venture capital, the lecture circuit, you name it. (Think Howard Rheingold.)

## 3.3 The Story of Cindy

*Cindy became the Celebrity Chat Queen for Cyber-America literally overnight, but just as fame has its price, so did working with* Fame *magazine and its seemingly endless supply of strange and often obscure "guests"—the oddest of whom was a certain burned-out '60s rock star, who didn't know a modem from a mandala.*

Cindy Angstrom ran barefoot down Sunset Boulevard with her Think-Pad in one hand, her high heels in the other. It was 105 degrees, the hottest day of the year so far, and Cindy was about to be late for the most important event in her online career.

In exactly 40 minutes Cyber-America, the nation's preeminent online service, would present the biggest, most widely promoted celebrity chat in the service's history. Phil Garland, the fabulously reclusive rock singer and songwriter, was the guest, and he'd be taking questions in real-time from thousands of adoring fans. The whole world would be watching—the event was all over the press, and Cyber-America's entire member base of 2 million strong had been whipped into a wild state of enthusiasm by a month-long mass e-mail campaign that spared no user the breathless news that *Phil is back and wants to chat!*

Now the only question was would Cindy—the person in charge of producing the event—be able to deliver? To see her running at full speed from the overheated, disabled Honda four blocks behind her, her stockings in tatters, her hair hanging in clumps, would any L.A. grease monkey believe her story, or would he just laugh in her face?

"Phil Garland?" the big mechanic asked, as Cindy stood sweating by the Argo gas pumps. "Never heard of him. But I'll pick your car up for you, and you can get a loaner across the street at Dave's Rent-a-Wreck."

"Thanks," Cindy said, and walked away, limping.

Cindy's rented Taurus glided through the electronically controlled gates of the Garland Estate, and she checked her watch—15 minutes to spare. Time enough to plug in her laptop, log on, and calm down sufficiently to get Phil warmed up. She parked the car by the guesthouse and checked her face in the rearview mirror—not bad, a little flushed, but still young-looking, bright, and hopeful.

### *Empty Nest*

Ninety days ago, Cindy wouldn't have believed it if Jeane Dixon herself had predicted that she'd soon be L.A.'s busiest celebrity chat maven.

Cindy was 48 years old, a mother of three grown children, and she hardly matched the profile of a typical computer geek, much less someone destined for a high-flying career in L.A.'s fledgling online industry.

Like most things in life, it had happened by accident. On the day her youngest son Elmer was packing his things before leaving home for UCLA, she sadly asked him to stay in touch, to speak to her more frequently than her older sons did—two lousy calls each year on her birthday and each Christmas. "Get a computer, Mom," Elmer urged her. "That way we can be in touch all the time."

But Cindy didn't like computers—she'd used them 20 years ago when she was a reservation clerk at Pan American Airways and didn't understand how they could possibly substitute for the heart-to-heart communication of a phone call or a sit-down dinner. Cindy's husband, from whom she was feeling a bit alienated these days, did have a computer—a big, beige box that he'd set up in their laundry room/study a year ago. Since he'd gotten it, Cindy had seen less and less of him, and she'd often fall asleep alone in their upstairs bedroom with the television on, while he clicked away in the darkness at the other end of the house.

"What exactly do you do down there that keeps you up so late, Hon?" Cindy would ask at the breakfast table.

"Research," said her husband, with a slightly annoyed look on his face. Then he'd kiss her lightly on the cheek and head off to his job at Applied Dynamics.

Late one night, Cindy awoke to gales of laughter booming from the laundry room/study, so she put her bathrobe on and went to find out what all the ruckus was about. She opened the door, and there in the blue-lit darkness, her husband was collapsed in hysterical laughter in front of his PC.

"Joe, what's going on?"

"It's this dead sheep movie. I just can't get over it."

"Joe, you'll wake the kids...," Cindy began to say, but then stopped, remembering the kids were sleeping somewhere else tonight and every night.

"Speaking of the kids," Joe said, "I heard from Elmer."

"What's he say?"

"He's worried about you. He wants you to get a computer. You know, I think it's a pretty fair idea, Cin. You've been moping too much recently."

"Come to bed," Cindy said.

"I'll be along," said Joe, and refocused his eyes on the glowing screen.

## ThinkPads and St. John's Wort

Her husband was right—Cindy had been moping ever since Elmer had moved out. In fact, it had been a long time since she'd felt any zest in her soul. Every day was very much the same—another day of California sunshine whose brightness mocked the darkening interior of her world. "So this is depression," Cindy mused, staring out at the hummingbirds flitting gaily among the honeysuckle in the garden. After a long sigh, she padded into the kitchen and gulped down two St. John's Wort tablets. The herb would cheer her up, but it made her skin so sun-sensitive that she didn't dare go outside the house for the rest of the day.

Because of Elmer's repeated proddings, Cindy finally did buy a laptop PC at a local computer superstore, but only after her son agreed to accompany her so she wouldn't buy the wrong thing. They settled on a 486SX IBM ThinkPad—it was expensive, but Elmer talked up the fact that it had the best typing "feel" and a beautiful active matrix display his mom wouldn't have to squint at. Elmer unpacked the box, showed her how the mysterious ThinkPad worked, and set the compact black machine up on the dining room table, which she and Joe never used anymore (Cindy usually ate in the kitchen, Joe in the "computer room"). Then Elmer installed a Cyber-America account from a pack of free disks that had been sent to his dorm.

Within days, Cindy began to explore the strange, colorful world of Cyber-America, and her depression began to lift. She discovered how easy it was to e-mail Elmer and wrote him just about every day. Within a week, she realized that she could read her hometown newspaper in Dayton, Indiana, and even experimented a bit with chatting, although the screens moved so quickly that she had trouble following them. Soon, she settled into the service's bulletin board area and made herself at home there. Boards, unlike chat, give people a chance to compose their thoughts before committing them to strangers—it's a nice way for people to say what is on their minds in a deliberate, intelligent way.

Cindy's favorite forum was Adult Relationships because she found so many kindred spirits there—women in their forties and fifties with empty nests, who were grappling with midlife crises and inattentive mates. She quickly struck up relationships with a few of these women and exchanged heart-to-heart e-mails. She read books they recommended, such as *Passages*, *Life Begins at Forty*, and *Refeathering the Nest*, and she posted thoughtful reviews of each book to the forum, which soon blossomed into the most popular message threads on the board.

Six weeks into her online odyssey, Cindy received an unexpected e-mail from the manager of Adult Relationships, asking her if she'd like to help manage the board on a volunteer basis. She jumped at the chance. Although she was already a respected member of the board, she felt honored that the manager thought so much of her that he'd let her work "on the inside."

## The Gift of Gab

Keeping the Adult Relationships discussions on topic and free of clutter was a bit too much like housework to be a lot of fun, but Cindy accepted her chores without complaint. She ran the board with a caring spirit and a bright e-mail manner that made liberal use of "smiley" emoticons, even when she was politely chastising a teenager for confusing menopause with masturbation. Traffic on the board was increasing, and back in Cyber-America's East Coast headquarters, managers were beginning to take notice. One day, she received a call from Peterson, a manager with hiring authority.

"Cindy, we'd like you to think seriously about doing what you're doing with Adult Relationships on a new board that we're going to launch in a month. We like your work a lot and really need somebody who can keep things moving. We don't have a budget to hire you full time, but I can pay you, say, $500 a month to manage the board. Does that sound fair?"

"Of course, it's fair, Mr. Peterson," Cindy said. "What's the board about?"

"Celebrities," Peterson said. "I'll follow up by e-mail when I know more about it."

Cindy didn't have any experience with L.A.'s celebrity power set, except for the fact that, years ago, she'd helped Sammy Davis Jr. check his bags in at LAX, and a man resembling Warren Beatty had once wolf-whistled at her from his sports car while she was waiting for a bus on Vine Street. There was something scary about celebrities—the way they didn't seem to be real people with any feelings; they came off as remote types who shunned any contact with the "little people" of Los Angeles. On the other hand, Cindy reasoned, celebrities might just be regular people who had gotten lucky—plain folks suffering from the same kind of problems she had been suffering from before she discovered Cyber-America: loneliness, boredom, and a sense that life was passing them by.

When Cindy heard from Peterson a week later, he seemed a little flustered, almost embarrassed. "Cindy, we've changed the approach of the board a little bit, and I hope you'll agree that it's a good idea. Basically, we're not going to have a board—I mean, there will be a board, but Cyber-America won't really be running it. You see, we're doing this whole thing jointly with *Fame* magazine, and they feel, justifiably of course, that they'd like to run it—it's kind of political."

"So does that mean you're not going to need me?" Cindy asked.

"Oh no. We really want you, Cindy, but we need you to do something else for us—something much more important. See, *Fame* is New York–based and doesn't really have anyone in L.A. right now who can do celebrity chats—you know, remote conversations with celebrities. It's the hot new thing now—getting the membership to talk to movie and TV stars and such. We've done some tests here and it's definitely something that people want. So I'd like to make you a slightly different offer..."

"You want me to go out and chat with celebrities?" Cindy asked.

"That's our thinking, yes," Peterson said.

"I suppose I can do that, Mr. Peterson," Cindy said.

"Oh that's great, just great," Peterson said. "Now the money will have to be a little different, too. We don't have guidelines for this, but we can pay you, say, $15 an hour."

"How long are the chats?" Cindy asked.

"Well, an hour or less, but we'll pay you to prepare, you know—pay you for any time you spend researching the celebrity, or driving to the event, or making up questions. Does that sound fair?"

"Yes, Mr. Peterson, I think so. Oh, who tells me what to do, I mean, where to go and who to chat with?"

"Well, that's up to someone at *Fame*—Andy Miller, he's a senior editor there. I'll put you in touch with Andy, and send you both e-mail so you can link up."

Cindy put down the phone and stood there in a daze. Things were moving so fast.

## *Have Modem, Will Travel*

Cindy's first celebrity chat was with an animal trainer known as Mr. Marvelous, an event set up by *Fame* to serve as a tie-in to its annual "Hero Pet Celebrities" cover story. The chat took place in Mr. Marvelous's hotel room and, considering that it was her first chat live in the field, it worked out fairly well—no dropped connections, no lost transcripts, and a healthy audience of some 300 online people who crowded into Cyber-America's Celebritorium. After the event was over, as Cindy was packing her cables, Mr. Marvelous and his manager seemed to be arguing about something, but Cindy stayed out of the way.

"I just don't get what the value is in pouring out your guts for a lousy 300 people," the manager said. We pack 300 people into the front rows of the Vegas show every night—this is bull."

"Still, they're my public," Mr. Marvelous said in a thick Romanian accent. "I owe something to them, don't I?"

"You've wasted an hour that you could have been on television," the manager said, turning to Cindy. "Am I right or am I right?" Cindy smiled feebly, zipped up the case of her ThinkPad, and slipped through the door without saying a word.

A week later, *Fame* sent her to the offices of Jay Howard Eyck, a Beverly Hills plastic surgeon who'd recently written a book about celebrities whose faces he'd worked on in the past 10 years. About 600 people showed up, and Eyck was happy to chat—in fact, he spoke so quickly that Cindy had trouble typing fast enough to keep up with his answers. By the time the one-hour chat was over, her wrists and fingers ached terribly.

"Carpal tunnel, eh, Sweetie," Eyck mused, noting Cindy's swollen wrists. "You should squeeze a tennis ball."

"It's temporary," Cindy answered, unsure whether Eyck (who had tennis trophies all over his office) had just made a pass at her.

"You know, I could do a lot with a face like yours," Eyck offered, lighting a cigarette.

"I think you should start with your own face, you big creep," Cindy said, referring to the doctor's own countenance: a strange shade of orange that had more lines on it than a map of Burbank. Cindy drove home in tears, but also deeply afraid that Eyck would call someone at *Fame* (which was running its annual "Celebrity Makeover" issue) to complain about her unprofessional conduct. Fortunately, Eyck didn't bother—he was too pleased with the chat, which had resulted in a flood of online orders for his book.

Over the next few weeks, Cindy visited an obscure, ragtag bunch of L.A. celebrities, who, it seemed, weren't much more famous than herself. With ThinkPad and modem cable in hand, she met with third-tier daytime soap stars (for *Fame*'s "Soap USA" issue), personal trainers (for the "Celebrity Fitness" issue), and even a group of grown-up former child stars (for the "Where Are They Now?" issue). She even showed up to chat with a former CIA agent who was peddling a screenplay from a recently penned memoir. The experience left her feeling extremely paranoid, especially when the agent gave her an autographed copy of his book and wrote, "They're watching you," below his signature.

As another month passed, Cindy was beginning to feel that *Fame* was deliberately sending her around to visit with the very dregs of L.A.'s celebrity circuit, and she complained about it in a phone call with Peterson.

"I don't mean to sound ungrateful, Mr. Peterson, but I kind of thought that I'd be interviewing people who were, well, a little more famous than the people I'm seeing. I mean, are online people really that interested in Beverly Hills locksmiths and trainers of surfing parrots? Couldn't *Fame* send me around once or twice to talk to, I don't know, Roddy McDowall or Dick Van Dyke, or somebody?"

"Cindy, I can't speak for *Fame,* but my guess is that they're probably finding that it's tough to get top-caliber celebrities to commit to them. See, online chat is very new, and I'd imagine that a lot of the celebrity handlers—you know, managers and such—just don't see the value in it right now. My bet is that this perception will change, and believe me, when it does, you'll be right there on the ground floor."

"Sure, Mr. Peterson."

"Cindy, there's something very big that's coming up, and I'm going to be putting in a good word for you with Andy Miller. It's the grand opening of Planet LA—a really big event that *Fame* has an online exclusive on. If I can get Miller to agree, you can cover the event with him—what do you say?"

"Sure, Mr. Peterson. No surfing parrots?"

"You have my word, Cindy."

## Planet LA

Andy Miller was one of the founding editors of *Fame,* and he'd single-handedly engineered the magazine's alliance with Cyber-America. Miller had overcome considerable opposition among *Fame*'s editorial board, who acknowledged that the online medium was growing nicely, but didn't want to commit editorial resources to something that wasn't really in their target demographic—housewives who picked up *Fame* from the racks placed at supermarket checkout counters across America. But Miller had fought hard, and when he got Cyber-America to pay the princely sum of $100,000 for a one-year exclusive distribution deal, the board had caved in.

Miller was in his late thirties and bore a slight resemblance to Michael Caine. Unlike Caine, Miller had the reputation of becoming an angry, destructive drunk once he'd consumed more than six Cosmopolitans, a fact that so threatened to damage his career that his wife had presented him with an ultimatum: either join AA or she'd leave him. Miller had agreed to join, and was about to celebrate his first year of sobriety the night of the Planet LA opening.

But Miller had started drinking on the plane. Perhaps it was because cocktails in first class were free, or because he needed something to alleviate his well-known fear of flying. Miller wasn't raving drunk when his plane landed at LAX, but he stopped off at the airport bar to have two more quick ones while waiting for his luggage. Then he walked out to the exit ramp, where Cindy had prearranged to pick him up in her Honda.

"So you're the one that's been complaining about chatting with the animals?" Miller slurred, as he got into Cindy's car and tossed his travel bag in the backseat. "You know why I like animals?" he asked, slamming the door.

"Why's that, Mr. Miller?" asked Cindy, pulling the car away from the curb and merging into the heavy airport traffic.

"They don't complain," Miller said, and hiccuped.

"You mean they don't bite the hand that feeds them?" asked Cindy.

"Exactly. They're grateful, not like some people I know."

"I'm grateful, Mr. Miller," Cindy said, keeping her eyes on the road.

"It's 'Andy,' " Miller said, looking at her in profile. "Hey, were you ever an actress?"

## *The Big Snore*

Cindy steered the car into Planet LA's driveway, already packed with cars and a big flatbed truck whose two large klieg lights raked the purple sky overhead. Cindy and Andy were both on the guest list and were ushered to a small VIP lounge overlooking the room. They had a full hour before the big chat began at 9 p.m., and Cindy unwrapped a 50-foot roll of phone cable, ran it into a nearby office, and taped it down with duct tape. When she looked up, Andy had disappeared, but Cindy was too focused on trying to establish a connection with Cyber-America to panic.

The room below was crowded with celebrities, and Cindy began to type the names of notable people and what they were wearing into her

Notepad. This way, she could keep the back-and-forth banter between herself and Andy moving along, by pasting in spicy tidbits such as "Oh, Andy there's supermodel Luxa with her beautiful red dress, standing just next to Jack Nicholson." By 8:50, with Andy nowhere in sight, Cindy began to perspire, fearing the worst: that she'd have to conduct this chat on her own, faking Andy's comments, as well as her own, to simulate an actual conversation.

Finally, at 8:55, Andy staggered into the lounge, fresh from the downstairs bar. Cindy smiled at him; Andy smiled back, then passed out cold on the leather sofa next to her.

"Andy, wake up!" Cindy, said, nudging his arm, first gently, then firmly, with her elbow. But when he began to snore at 8:59, Cindy gave up trying to revive the jerk. For the next three hours, as Andy slumbered, she typed in what she figured he'd have typed in—lines such as, "From the looks of it, Cindy, Universal might seriously be courting the indies for some overseas distribution, if my sources are correct," and other such industry nonsense, followed by her own inane dish, "Andy, did you see that crazy halter Drew Barrymore is wearing over by the soundstage?" Her electronic fakery appeared to be working: more than 1,000 Cyber-Americans crowded into three linked Celebritoriums, and each seemed to be hanging onto every word she typed.

She closed the chat down at midnight, by typing "Well, Cindy, it's been a wonderful evening here at Planet LA, and I'd like to thank all of you wonderful users—you've been a terrific audience and, Cindy, you've been wonderful, too. I'm Andy Miller, your cyber-host—goodnight, now!" As she typed these final words, Cindy realized to her horror that she hadn't engaged the autorecord feature that archived a transcript of the chat to her hard drive. But she kept her cool and quickly e-mailed Elmer, who, she knew, had logged onto the event to watch his mom in action. She heard back from him before 1:00 a.m. and, thank goodness, Elmer had recorded it in its entirety. He would e-mail it to her the next day.

"Wake up, you big lunk!" Cindy said, poking at Andy's shoulder again. This time, he came round, looked up, and asked her, "Who the hell are you?"

"I'm the woman who just saved you," Cindy said. She packed up her cables and her ThinkPad, and was soon on her way downstairs, followed by a reluctant Miller, who seemed shocked and disoriented by the unfamiliar surroundings.

After driving for miles in stony silence, she dropped Andy at the Hollywood Hilton. He retrieved his bags from the car and started to get out, but held the door open. "Look, I'm very grateful for what you did back there. I really can't drink anymore—I know that. I've been sober for a year now, and I'm sorry—I'll try to make it up to you."

"Forget it," Cindy said.

"No. I mean it. If you ever need anything, call me. I might be able to help you. Here's my card—it's my personal card, with my home number. Call me if you ever need a favor—I already owe you a big one."

"Thanks," Cindy said, and with that, Miller closed the door and walked slowly into the lobby.

## *Mr. Rock and Roll*

Cindy didn't get home until after 4 a.m. She was so exhausted after her long night of online fakery that she didn't even try to climb the stairs; she just collapsed on the living room couch, fully clothed, with her shoes still on. When her husband emerged from the shower at 7:30, he took one look at her, shrugged, and went into the kitchen to make his own breakfast.

At 9 a.m., the doorbell rang. It was FTD with a big bouquet of roses, which she set up on the dining room table next to her ThinkPad. Then she opened the card. It was a message from Peterson, saying merely, "Big news: call me!" and Cindy promptly did.

"You were terrific at Planet LA: the usage reports are off the map. Everybody's talking about it—how was Miller to work with?"

"Oh, it was all fine," Cindy lied. "It was really a lot of fun."

"Well, I've got something much bigger for you. You know Phil Garland's got a new CD coming out—the first one he's recorded in almost 20 years—and he wants to kick off the campaign online, in a way that shows everybody that he's up to date, you get it?"

"Wow, Phil Garland—I grew up with his music."

"Now, you probably know that Garland—well, a lot of people don't know what to make of him. He's been through a lot of changes, and, well, he might be a bit unpredictable to work with."

"That doesn't bother me," Cindy answered.

"Good. We're rolling out the big guns for this one. The whole usage base will get messaged—I hear there's even a TV ad in the works. So, do your research, get to know this guy real well, and go for it—this will put you on the map, guaranteed."

"I'll do it," Cindy said. "I'll really do it."

Cindy spent part of the next week in the library, looking over old copies of *Rolling Stone,* trying to fully understand the mysterious, reclusive Phil Garland. In a brief, five-year period, from 1969 to 1974, he had shaken up the rock world with his beautiful, enigmatic compositions that, even today, were a steady staple of oldies radio across the country. But then something happened to Garland and he stopped producing records, stopped touring, stopped doing press interviews, and dropped out of sight. She had always been a Garland fan and picked up a Greatest Hits cassette at Sam Goody just to listen to in her car.

On the Friday of the Garland chat, her body was decked out in her hippest L.A. clothes, her ThinkPad's battery was juiced, and her Honda was freshly washed, and she backed out of her driveway with her heart as light as a hummingbird. She rewound the tape, closed her windows to the gassy, overheated freeway air, hit "play," and boosted the gain until her speakers squawked with distortion. She felt young again, a fast chick in a fast car, and Garland was the magic mushroom that made her, and an entire generation, want to gather together and sing about a better world.

Now Cindy sat in Garland's driveway in the Taurus, feeling like she had reached the end of a spiritual quest. With the crisis of the overheated Honda behind her, she thought she'd overcome the last obstacle to entering the big time and felt a glowing sense of inner peace and confidence she hadn't felt in years.

"You go, girl," she told her reflection in the rearview mirror, then grabbed her ThinkPad, and walked between the mansion's massive Doric columns into the temple of the God of Peace and Love.

## *Satori*

Cindy was greeted by a burly man with long hair and a cheerful, ruddy face. "You made it," he said to her, and Cindy instantly got his double meaning: at long last, she'd really "arrived." The two of them walked across the white marble receiving hall and up a grand, sweeping staircase to the second floor. The ruddy-faced man ushered her to the right, into a massive, carpeted room that was flooded with light, and there, on a white Naugahyde sofa, sat Phil Garland, looking out through tall windows at the birds that flitted among the forsythia blossoms.

"Cyber-America's here, Phil," the ruddy-faced man said, and Phil Garland turned around slowly to face Cindy, beaming with a happiness that seemed to channel all joy into a single focal point of bliss.

"I'm very pleased to meet you, Mr. Garland," Cindy said, and waited for Garland to offer her his hand. But he didn't—he just kept smiling at Cindy, until she broke from his benign stare with a cheerful, "Well, we don't have much time, so I'd better get to work." She proceeded to unpack her ThinkPad and lay a short length of RJ-11 cable into the nearest phone box. She set up at a table along the wall, close to the phone jack, and dialed in to Cyber-America. She quietly breathed a sigh of relief—it was a good connection. The ruddy-faced man sat down next to her, and she shifted the notebook a few inches so that he could better see the screen.

As planned, the Phil Garland chat would consist of two parts: 30 minutes of prepared questions, followed by another 30 minutes of user questions that Cindy would selectively relay to Phil.

She launched a Notepad document, which contained an introduction and the list of prepared questions that she'd come up with from her research. She flexed her fingers, ready to type sure and accurate responses from the Great Man. She watched Cyber-America's complete list of 50 linked Celebritoriums light up their "maximum" lights—this meant that 5,000 people were now online. The biggest chat in history was about to begin.

"It's almost time, Mr. Garland," Cindy said. "Would you like to come closer, or would you like me to move closer to you?"

The ruddy-faced man waved his hands at her. "Phil likes to sit there," he said. "And he wants you to sit where you are."

"So, would Phil like me to say the questions out loud, d'ya think?" Cindy asked.

"That sounds good," the man said.

At exactly 12:01 p.m., after Cindy had engaged Cyber-America's autorecord feature to preserve a transcript, she pasted in a long introduction that detailed Garland's accomplishments, and then she carefully pasted her first prepared question in and read it out loud.

"Phil, among your many musical compositions, what is the single song you're proudest of?"

Garland sat a long time, reflecting. Either he couldn't make up his mind or he found the question nonsensical, as if he were processing all possible permutations of the word "proudest" in his mind. Ten seconds stretched to twenty, then to twenty-five.

"He's proudest of 'Endless Highway,'" the ruddy-faced man broke in, and Cindy rapidly typed in the answer.

"Phil," Cindy asked, "why have you waited 20 years to record a new album?"

The expression on Garland's face changed slightly, as if he was trying to solve a nettlesome puzzle. His eyes narrowed a bit, and Cindy was sure that he was trying to say something. Fifteen seconds became twenty, then thirty, but Phil seemed no closer to an answer.

"It's taken a lot of time for me to rediscover what music really means," the ruddy-faced man said quickly, and Cindy typed this into the chat box.

"Can't he talk?" Cindy whispered to the man.

"Of course he can talk!" the man snapped angrily.

"Can you get him to talk now?" Cindy asked.

"It's completely up to Phil," the man answered.

After firing off five more questions and having the ruddy-faced man step in each time, Cindy resigned herself to dealing exclusively with Garland's handler, who seemed to know enough about Garland's inner state to serve as an effective personal proxy. It was an utter sham, of course, but it kept the conversation moving, and that was the important thing. Not one of Cyber-America's thousands of users would ever know that Garland never once uttered a word throughout the entire event.

When the chat concluded, Cindy looked back one more time at Garland and felt genuinely sorry for him, but strangely envious, too. Locked inside a cocoon of blissful, peaceful silence, surrounded by stone and a beautiful view, he'd forever remain a man of mystery—an untouchable enigma who had given everything he had to the world and kept giving until there was nothing left.

Cindy could just as well have been talking about herself. After she picked up her repaired car at Dave's Rent-a-Wreck, she drove back to Orange County in silence and never played the Garland cassette again. She parked the Honda in her driveway and sat for a long time in her car, staring at her reflection in the mirror. She realized, a bit sadly, that there was no "Endless Highway" that would ever take her home—it was all just a freeway of lies, and she was just a small part of the machinery that kept it all running.

## Epilogue

Although the Garland chat was a fabulous success and, by all rights, should have propelled her into a position where she'd never again have to chat with another sleazy plastic surgeon or failed child star, Cindy soon lost her part-time job when Cyber-America, facing forecasts of reduced usage due to Web competition, slashed its budget for chat freelancers. Cindy tried calling in her favor to Andy Miller by contacting him on his private line, but Miller claimed not to remember her—nor the fact that she'd saved his reputation the night of the Planet LA fiasco. Unemployed for a painful year in which she'd grown increasingly distant from her husband, Cindy finally divorced him and moved into a sparse one-room apartment in Westwood to be closer to Elmer. From there, she started to eke out a living by managing the bulletin boards of a Web site devoted to women who'd lost their mates to Internet addiction. Phil Garland's comeback album, for all the promotional fanfare, didn't crack *Billboard*'s top 100 charts, and he's not been heard from since—in cyberspace or elsewhere else.

# LEVEL 4.0

# Cab Drivers

## Another Day, Another Startup

## 4.1 Who Are They?

Like the sneakers on your feet, the Web sites you use to check your stocks or make airplane reservations have a strange and often slave-like origin. No, they're not built by 13-year-old girls in the Philippines—not yet at least—but they are the products of people who have much in common with Robert De Niro's character in *Taxi Driver*.

"How so?" you ask.

Well, let's put it this way. Most Web sites are designed by itinerant, restless young people who have given up the constraints of working for one company in particular, in exchange for the self-determination of pursuing their own path. The rationale is that they can earn a higher hourly rate and pick and choose their projects. The reality, however, is that these Cab Drivers have to constantly hustle for work and their passengers, or clients, who are also cash-crunched, are notorious for skipping out on their fares. Added to this is the lack of health benefits that Cab Drivers face—a plight which has forced many to simply neglect themselves.

But beyond the daily hassles is the work itself, characterized by completely unrealistic deadlines ("Can you have the site up by Monday?"), 16-hour days, and an utter lack of job stability. Of course, some companies try to put a good face on the situation by allowing the cabbies to drink beer or bring their dogs to the office—in short, to make themselves at home. For many, these token acts have only added to the discontent burning inside them. So much so that there has been serious talk recently of unionization.

The image of angry hack NetSlaves flinging huge PERL and HTML manuals through the windows of oppressive dispatchers struck Steve and me as ludicrous, but it didn't stop us from devoting the next leg of our journey to talking to these people and seeing if much has changed since we were in similar circumstances.

What followed was a series of visits to Web design firms, which led us to the conclusion that, if anything, things have gotten worse. There was an anger and a lunacy in the eyes of these people—we didn't see any guns, but if anyone asked us the eternal question, "You talkin' to me?," we would definitely have jumped out of our skins.

A warning before you continue: Don't ever, ever, tell a Cab Driver that he or she is cruising down Easy Street, in Cyberville or anywhere else for that matter. And a good tip wouldn't hurt, either.

## 4.2 General Characteristics

*Where they can be found:*  Cab Drivers lead a feast-or-famine existence. When they are working, it's in the most primitive of circumstances—crowded in underlit, poorly ventilated back offices for days and weeks at a time, doing whatever's necessary to complete a project that's already past due. In times of unemployment, which are frequent and are often the only reward for a job well done, Cab Drivers can be found slumped on lumpy old couches watching daytime TV with blank, defeated expressions on their faces ("Hi, Ricki!").

*Average income:*  Lower by the second. In 1995, when the Internet was the new thing, Cab Drivers could pass themselves off as Private Car Services or even Limousine Operators—their sharp hand-eye coordination skills in working through the then-mysterious lines of <p> tags and image maps commanded upward of $70 per hour. These days, however, with heavy competition from unlicensed Gypsies who think their internship will lead to big bucks in the next IPO, many Cab Drivers are lucky if they get $15 per hour. Other factors that have hurt the pocketbooks of the Web's workaday hacks include the rise of WYSIWYG (what you see is what you get) tools and the consolidation of design firms into a short list of key players owned by advertising conglomerates intent on keeping production costs as low as possible, while charging their still-clueless old media clients higher and higher fees.

*Percentage of the NetSlave population:*  50 percent (but falling with a bullet). As prospects for Cab Drivers grow worse by the second, many are taking civil service exams or forgoing the workaday world altogether and running back into the maternal arms of academia.

*Psychological profile:*  Cab Drivers always seem about a block away from the nuthouse. While they would like to think that their mental state is due to the horrors they've experienced as Internet drones, the truth is that being highly excitable liberal arts types at heart, they were always pretty wacked. (Favorite bands in high school: Bauhaus, Joy Division, Depeche Mode.)

*Average age:*  28 going on 72. Internet Time unfolds even faster than dog years, which has the effect on people in the business (especially the ever moving Cab Drivers) of 20 years for every calendar cycle.

*Career aspirations:*  To start their own Web design company and sign up a few sugar-daddy clients, which would allow them to live a free and economically secure existence, on their own terms.

***Likelihood that their career aspirations will come true:*** Slim to none. Without rich parents to bankroll them, Cab Drivers have as much a chance of getting seed money from venture capitalists, or landing sugar daddies, as your grandmother's latest Internet play has of being successful.

## 4.3 The Story of Jane

*Like many Cab Drivers in her position, Jane was hurting for cash. When she accepted a freelance position with Edler-Watson's Challenger, she had no idea that she would have to run the gauntlet past O. J. Simpson and the jury that wouldn't convict him. But Jane would do anything for Mr. URL.*

Jane Dantzig thought she had seen it all. She'd worked in New York's fast-paced New Media industry for over a year, and paid her dues in high-tech sweatshops from Chelsea to Broad Street. Jane was a freelance HTML coder—a production grunt, one of the thousands of invisible people whose job it is to build, maintain, and refresh commercial Web sites so that the titanic dreams of their visionary masters can be realized, instead of sputtering to a halt on a broken link or a badly placed <DIV> tag.

Jane liked the impersonal exactness of doing HTML—it would never make her rich, but it paid the bills. And she liked the independence the freelance life gave her even more. By being able to choose her clients, she could regulate the bull in her life and control her destiny in a way that no full-time NetSlave, chained to the fate of her company, ever could.

Jane worked hard, didn't goof off, rarely messed up, and never kissed ass. But the mere fact that she controlled her destiny didn't mean that she ruled fate. And when fate, in the guise of Challenger, Edler-Watson's gigantic Web site, offered her a three-month production assignment in the fall of 1995, Jane took the job.

It was a decision that led her into the stygian depths and culminated in the single greatest disaster in the annals of New Media. For a brief 15 seconds that shocked the world, technology, human will, and reality itself suffered a simultaneous, cataclysmic failure whose ramifications are still being felt today.

It was the Day the Web Stood Still.

### *Hands On*

Jane's long road to disaster began when she accidentally injured the left foot of her African Gray Parrot, who had let himself out of his cage and mischievously alighted on the top of her bedroom door. The door closed, the bird howled with pain, and Jane immediately rushed the parrot, whose name was Mr. URL, to the Animal Medical Center on 92nd Street. X-rays proved the bird's mashed leg wasn't broken, and Mr. URL was released within two hours, which made Jane, who had a huge guilt complex, feel a bit better. But Mr. URL's emergency treatment would cost Jane $320, and this was enough to send her carefully calculated personal economy into disarray, because she just didn't have the money.

Jane blamed herself for always being short on cash, but it was part and parcel of the freelance life she'd been living. Formerly employed as a full-time professional typesetter, Jane had given up the steady life of twice-monthly paychecks to pursue a Web builder's career at age 28. Because she knew page design inside and out and had figured out that HTML was a much simpler page description language than the cryptic markup tags she'd been using for years to compose business forms, she quit her job and set up her own design shop, called Rational Bits, in early 1995.

Although freelance site building provided Jane with a much higher hourly income than she'd made as a typesetter, she still found it difficult to make ends meet. Jane didn't spend extravagantly, nor did she pay more than $1,000 a month in rent for her one-bedroom on Waverly Place. The problem lay on the supply side of the equation: many of her clients held onto her invoices for months or sometimes didn't pay at all.

By the fall of 1995, Jane's accounts receivables were about $9,000– about half of which was past due from a slick uptown design house that built Web sites for several international petrochemical companies that, as far as Jane knew, weren't hurting for cash. She'd hassled her debtor for two months and received plenty of promises, apologies, and assurances–but no check.

Another small startup for which Jane built sites went belly-up after its largest client canceled their contract and went with another design firm. Thirty people lost their jobs in this minor catastrophe and Jane bid a not-so-fond farewell to the $5,000 she was owed. With her quarterly self-employment taxes coming due September 1, Jane's bank account was approaching zero, and she feared that she'd soon be unable to afford even parrot food, which meant she'd have to keep Mr. URL alive on pizza crusts.

"That's not going to happen, Sweetie, don't you worry," Jane said, as the parrot balanced on his good leg and made clicking noises that sounded exactly like her keyboard.

## Scanning the List

In the following days, Jane tried hard to drum up some business by continually monitoring the job postings that scrolled across the New York World Wide Web Workers e-mail list. The WWWNY (or "Winnie") list circulated among 2,000 Web professionals in New York, and it was a good place to hunt for freelance assignments. The Winnie list also provided a forum for a lot of quirky blowhards to rant endlessly about Aggro Software's browser or attack NetScathe's flaky table support, but Jane tolerated the noise. She didn't give a damn about the fate of VRML or the future of interactivity—she just wanted to find a short-term job to pay her bird's medical bill.

Unfortunately, most of the jobs posted to the list that week advertised intern positions for which Jane was overqualified.

"The idiot interns are ruining the job market," Jane would complain.

"Oh no," Mr. URL answered back.

On Thursday, one listing did appear. It read simply:

### HTML Production: Challenger

Long-term freelance opportunity. Must have extensive knowledge of HTML. Must be familiar with cross-platform, cross-browser compatibilities. Opportunity to expand your knowledge. Send e-mail to production @challenger.com.

Jane usually didn't apply for long-term assignments because most didn't pay out until the project was completed. She'd already been burned twice speccing her time on long-term projects, and she needed some instant cash.

She'd also heard weird things about Challenger from other HTML grunts who'd worked there.

"It's chaos," said one.

"Don't go there. It's a sick building," said another.

"They use image maps for everything," said a third.

But, desperate for money, Jane fired off her résumé anyway—she didn't want to feel that she'd left a stone unturned in her search for work.

The next day, Jane was going over her $239 Bell Atlantic bill, when her mother called from Cincinnati. She hated to hit her mother up for money, but she realized that if she didn't, she'd be relinquishing her best shot of making it through the next week.

"Have you ever thought of trying to find a real job?" Jane's mother asked.

"Mom, I've got six jobs. I'm making more money freelancing than I could at a real job."

"If you're making so much, why are you asking me for a loan?"

"InterPetrol owes me $6,000. They've got to pay me—I just don't know when."

After wrangling for a few more minutes, Jane's mother agreed to mail her a check for $600, a sum that would go a long way in Cincinnati.

"Well, it's something," Jane said, somewhat unconvincingly.

## *Picking Up Fares*

Jane's luck began to change the following week, when she got a call from LaserCrab, an ultrahip downtown design house, asking her to come in for a couple of days of HTML coding. She'd worked at Laser-Crab before and had profoundly mixed feelings about going in because its rarefied, design-driven atmosphere was, as she put it, "all sizzle and no steak."

Jane also felt out of place among its pretentious, bohemian crew of 20-something design mavens, who drank endless amounts of coffee, discussed Foucault and Hegel for hours at a time, and were openly hostile to anyone they deemed "bourgeois." With her plain midwestern appearance and nonblack attire, Jane fell directly into this category and was the victim of upturned noses and more than a few snide remarks. Jane didn't care what these people thought of her, but their attitude made the job harder than it needed to be, especially when she had to tell them that their top-heavy, Java-dependent prototypes crashed every browser except the latest Mac version of NetScathe. Jane did her best to ignore the bull and wound up her three days there without killing anyone. To Jane, this was a remarkable achievement.

The next week, she landed a two-day gig at Hedge-Downs, a computer publishing company that had recently fired 30 percent of its workforce in a bloody restructuring, but still needed to crank out Web pages with gigantic tables comparing hundreds of components and other widgets. Unlike LaserCrab, whose SoHo loft space was a packed, dingy sweathouse of activity, Hedge-Downs's plush Park Avenue South offices were practically empty—either the editors were all at Comdex, or they'd all been fired.

Jane took Thursday and Friday off—her hands and wrists were hurting her, not so much from typing, but from clutching the crappy, non-ergonomic mouse that Hedge-Downs had made her use. Living with pain was something that Jane had grown used to, but as long as she gave herself a few days of recuperation from frenzied clicking, it seemed to disappear. She hoped she wasn't doing permanent damage to her wrists, but she really didn't know—she hadn't seen a doctor in a year, because she had no health insurance coverage.

She e-mailed her two invoices: 32 hours of work, at $30 an hour—a grand total of $960 billed to two solvent clients who'd been pleased with her work. This was the going rate for HTML production people of Jane's caliber—fast coders who checked their work, proofread and corrected mistakes (even if they weren't theirs), and made sure that all was safe and sound on the servers before clocking out for the night.

## *Short-Timer*

Jane knew that neither LaserCrab nor Hedge-Downs would be likely to call her back soon—both companies were looking for a full-time coder who would work for next to nothing, and they'd probably fill the position in the next day or so with an intern or someone even more desperate than Jane.

New York was full of New Media talent, young men and women eager to get in on the action—and get rich in the next big IPO. The companies knew and exploited this mind-set to the fullest, offering these NetSlaves meaningless stock options in exchange for 14-hour days. It was a very good trick—it worked for the most part, except when one of these people unexpectedly burned out and the companies had to call in Jane at the last minute. In Jane's experience, burnout was becoming a more and more common occurrence, plaguing full-timers who were forced to do HTML and nothing but HTML for months without a break.

Jane was quite adept at producing massive tables, cleaning up crappy code, and handling all the other minutiae associated with hand-crafting Web pages. But she couldn't bear the thought of doing HTML all day, every day. Beyond the torture it inflicted on her extremities, Jane also suspected that too much production could actually drive one crazy. After a certain point, it became like Chinese water torture—a sinister thing whose evil lay in the fact that none of its victims ever believed that innocent little drops of water could be capable of inflicting such crippling psychic pain.

The fear of mindless repetition, beyond any other reason, lay at the root of Jane's hatred for permanent jobs. It wasn't, as her mother suggested, that Jane was "afraid of commitment," or "suspicious of long-term relationships." Jane had nothing against men, beyond the fact that most were hopelessly messy creatures who felt they'd been granted an inalienable right to interpose themselves in Jane's life and talk for hours—usually about themselves. In this respect, they were like Mr. URL, but they took up much more space.

If Jane had had the time to see a shrink, he might have advised her that her strong bias toward independence might be causing her to miss out on things that only long-term relationships bring: security, a family, a sense of being more than a nomad who lived by the clock. But Jane had no desire to change her life—whether it meant hitching her chain to some flaky man or to an even flakier Internet startup. Jane's reluctance to commit to long, drawn-out affairs of the heart—or of the workplace—actually stemmed from the simple fear of boredom—the dreary, mind-numbing sameness that, like water torture, ultimately became unbearable.

## *The Challenge*

On Saturday around 6 p.m., the phone rang. It was Challenger's production head calling about the résumé she'd sent in a week before.

"I need coders," the voice said. "Your résumé looks good. What's your availability?"

"Well, this week is clear."

"Report to 3724A. You'll need a visitor's pass. Be there at 10 a.m."

"But I . . ."

The phone clicked. It was the shortest conversation Jane had ever had.

"Oh no," said the parrot.

"Well, we do need the money," Jane answered.

On Sunday, Jane was sleeping late, when the phone rang again.

"Where are you?" the voice shouted, and it took a few seconds for Jane to properly associate it with Challenger.

"I thought you were talking about Monday," Jane said.

"I'm talking about now," he said. "Can you make it in or not?"

She looked at her clock radio, which read 10:20. "I'll be in as soon as I can," she said.

Jane took the 6th Avenue subway up to the Edler-Watson building, a 50-story, modernistic slab of concrete in the low 50s. She got a visitor's pass from a sleepy guard in the visitor's center and waited for the elevator. The lobby was empty and echoic—a mournful mausoleum to 1950s modernism. But when she stepped out on the 37th floor and was buzzed through Challenger's security system, Jane entered a scene of bustling activity—people were darting back and forth in a long corridor of cubicles that stretched the entire length of the building's east wall.

Jane began to sweat—it was hot in the massive room, and clouds of condensation had formed on the inner services of the sealed-pane glass windows. She wandered through the bullpen of cubes and circled back to the entrance, disoriented and confused. At last she found Room 3724A, a small, windowless office that she'd walked right by when she came in, mistaking it for a utility closet.

"I'm Jane Dantzig," she said to a man in his late twenties hunkered down behind two gigantic monitors on a cluttered wooden desk.

"Good," he said, without looking up. He rustled some forms and handed them to her. "You need to fill these out, and these, and these. Your rate is $20 an hour. Fill out the time sheet when you're done."

She filled out the tax forms and waited for more instructions, but the production head was busily clicking away at something behind the pile of debris.

"It's pretty hot in here," Jane commented, trying to strike up a conversation.

"Building services doesn't like running the air conditioners on weekends," he said.

"What would you like me to work on?" Jane asked.

"We're redesigning the site today," he said. "I need a report on broken URLs. Find a vacant cube."

"Do you want me to fix them?"

"No. Just a report."

Jane found an unoccupied office near Challenger's coffee machine and logged onto the network. She launched NetScathe and began tooling around the Challenger site—a huge collection of content from about 80 of Edler-Watson's magazines. She explored the sites's top-level pages and, although they were slow-loading, image-mapped monsters, none of them were actually broken.

But when Jane began exploring the pages of the magazines themselves, she found hundreds of errors and had soon filled up an entire page with notes on their locations. By the time she was ready to leave, around 8 p.m., she had accumulated a list of about 1,400 bad links.

The production head studied her printout. "That's good. That's very good," he said. "Can you come back tomorrow?"

"I'd like to, but I usually get $30 an hour," Jane said.

"You're just checking links. This isn't rocket science."

"Yes, but if I do this gig, I can't do my other jobs, which do pay me $30 an hour," Jane shot back.

"Well, I could probably use someone on PowerStager. It's rolling out next week. I tell you what—I'll pay you $25 an hour, but we'd have to train you, so you'd have to agree to stick around to make it worth our while."

"All right," Jane said.

## *Feel the Power*

The next day, Jane began to learn how to operate PowerStager, an elaborate piece of software designed in-house by Challenger's software engineers to streamline the way content was uploaded to the site. PowerStager was built to correct a problem that had plagued Challenger from the beginning—a problem known as "update gridlock."

Challenger, like many large Web sites, used two physical machines to store its massive collection of content: a public server and a staging server. Editors would "fetch," or FTP, new content to the staging server, and then, after a period of time, the staging server would refresh the public server, so that users could see the new stuff.

Unfortunately, as Challenger aggregated more content and refreshed content more frequently, the staging queue often backed up, causing the time lag between server refreshes to grow to a point where it might take three or more hours for a fresh news item to appear on the public servers.

Challenger's editor in chief, Jeff Marshall, yelled and screamed about update gridlock because it caused Challenger to get scooped on breaking news stories. Others were screaming, too—sometimes the site's hopelessly slow content queue would actually cause the staging server to fail, which in turn caused a wave of hair pulling and subcritical brain embolisms to sweep through Challenger's short-tempered crew of editors. They all knew that in a matter of moments their phones would light up and they'd be treated to obscenity-laced tirades from their content partners, who couldn't update their sites.

PowerStager, on the other hand, was designed to selectively bypass the staging server, so that Challenger's editors could write content directly to the public server—a very powerful, but very dangerous, capability that filled the tech team with dread. The potential for disaster—through accident, miscalculation, or madness—was very real, because PowerStager provided a way for technically inept editors to inadvertently overwrite the entire site–the equivalent of typing "FORMAT C:\" in a DOS window. If this happened, the technicians' only recourse would be to restore Challenger from an archived tape drive, a maddening process that took them three days to finish in their dark, subterranean server farm complex across the street.

To prevent any unauthorized overwriting, PowerStager's Web-based interface was deliberately made very complicated, to mislead Challenger's editors into believing it could update only a single file at a time. As a secondary security measure, PowerStager included a feature which forced editors to click through three separate "Are you sure you want to do this?" screens before they could update anything. As a final line of defense, PowerStager automatically created a log file capturing the Internet Protocol (IP) address of the updater, and, it was rumored, "did a lot of other things" to identify editors screwing with the public servers without permission.

## *Bugs*

While Jane had no trouble understanding the theory behind PowerStager, she found its practical operation somewhat erratic. When she tried using the software to move some noncritical test files to a test directory, she observed that it worked only about half the time. Sometimes the Graphics Interchange Format (GIF) file would arrive corrupted; HTML files didn't always arrive intact either. PowerStager also seemed to slow down at certain points in the day, which meant that Jane had to wait around for 10 minutes before she could get through all the "Are you sure you want to do this?" screens.

She called up her contact on the tech side about this.

"We know all about the bugs," he said.

"Is it something I should worry about?"

"When it launches, they'll be gone," he said.

By Wednesday, Jane noticed that some of PowerStager's bugs had been eliminated, but others were mysteriously appearing. Sometimes PowerStager would "hang" in the middle of an operation, forcing her to reboot her machine. Sometimes her hard drive would spontaneously start spinning by itself–Macs had a tendency to do that, of course, but it still seemed peculiar, and Jane wondered if PowerStager wasn't probing her machine for reasons of its own. Later in the afternoon, Jane received a real scare when a file she was working on completely vanished from her desktop, even though she hadn't deleted it.

"That's a new one," said the engineer. "It may have something to do with the resolver."

"Sounds a lot like rocket science," Jane said.

## The O. J. Files

Before Jane left for the weekend, the production head specified that she make a special attempt to arrive early on Monday—something important was going on.

"Another redesign?" Jane asked.

"No, it's this O. J. thing," he said.

"What's the O. J. thing?"

"Aren't you following the trial?"

"No."

"Well, forget about it. Just be here early. It's probably going to be a killer day."

"OK," Jane said, signing her time slip.

Jane spent a quiet weekend at home and didn't think much about O. J. Simpson, Challenger, or PowerStager. She was aware that O. J. had been on trial in Los Angeles for months, but she had more or less blanked it out. The whole thing seemed to have very little to do with her life—it happened far away, in a city that she didn't know or like very much.

But Challenger felt very different about the fate of O. J. Simpson, and one of its most popular subsites, O. J. Central, had served as the Internet's greatest single touchstone for Web users, who, in many cases, seemed obsessed by the whole saga. O. J. Central provided an interactive map of the murders, daily trial transcripts, and a message board, which teemed with thousands of ranting, raving, and hand-wringing opinions on what the whole mess meant to the future of the western world.

Like the networks, Challenger was making big bucks off of O. J. and knew, as Jane did not, that the Simpson trial would likely reach a verdict on Monday, October 3. So to capitalize fully on their expanded O. J. coverage, Challenger had made it known to O. J. Central's users that it would be the first site to announce the verdict, within minutes of its rendering.

Over the weekend, an emergency O. J. team camped out in the overheated confines of Edler-Watson's 37th floor, planning the best way to make sure that nothing went wrong. Although everyone on the O. J. team believed that Simpson would surely be found guilty, they didn't take any chances, so the art department was instructed to prepare two different, image-mapped GIFs to replace Challenger's default home page. One read "O. J. Guilty!" and showed a dour, depressed O. J. Simpson appearing to scream at the judge. In an inspired flourish, the GIF also included within its sidebar the ominous notice that said: "L.A. Police on Alert."

The second home page, "O. J. Innocent," showed O. J. Simpson in a completely different pose: quiet, somber, and beatifically grateful to the jury that had just let him off the hook. Obviously, no reports of the L.A. Police Department's alert status were included in this image. Temporary pieces of ersatz text reportage were hammered out by Challenger's news editor, to serve as placeholders until someone could grab enough text from an incoming Reuters wire report to flesh things out in more detail.

By late Sunday night, all of the new O. J. content had been finished, the weary team had retired for the night, and all the O. J. files were plopped into two folders, named "Guilty" and "Innocent," which sat on Challenger's local area network (LAN).

## *Apocalypse*

At 8:30 a.m. on Monday, Jane took position in her cube and waited for instructions from her masters. It was quiet in Challenger's massive bullpen, but things came to life when its staffers started appearing around 9:30, with members of the O. J. team looking sleepy and unkempt. A large, 21-inch television mounted on the wall was turned on at 10:30, and Jane listened in on the preverdict coverage on CNN. The O. J. jury had been sequestered all weekend, and reliable sources said that they were finally ready to pronounce a definitive verdict on the ex-football player's crime.

At 11:30, a small crowd began to gather around Jane's cube, which was right below the big TV. Minutes later, Pathfinder's production head appeared at Jane's cube, and showed her where the "Innocent" and "Guilty" folders resided on the LAN.

"OK, all you have to do is make sure that the right files go up," he said. "Just select the right folder. When I say 'Go,' get through those damned confirmation screens as fast as you can."

"Right," Jane said.

At 11:59, all of the major networks preempted their normal programming and switched to a live satellite feed from the L.A. County Courthouse. The O. J. jury filed out of its deliberation room, and the foreman began speaking into a microphone. "We find the defendant, O. J. Simpson, . . . not guilty of the crimes . . ."

"Go," said the production head.

Jane dragged the "Innocent" folder into PowerStager's "put" window, and hit "OK." She rapidly clicked three times more, to get through the confirmation screens. She then switched to Challenger's home page and hit "Reload" on her browser.

It was a moment that was just like the expanding, slow-motion, head-through-the-windshield impact of a car crash. All the moments of Jane's life seemed to pass through the terrible funnel of that frozen five seconds. Time stood still, and there for all the world to see on Challenger's public servers, was the wrong home page–the one that said "O. J. Guilty! L.A. Police on Alert."

Jane had just uploaded the wrong file.

The production head screamed. "UPLOAD IT AGAIN. AGAIN."

Jane repeated the steps in PowerStager. She hit "Reload" again. An interminable moment passed as the browser's cache refreshed.

"Oh, thank God. Thank God. It's OK. It's the right one," said the production head, with a tone of relief in his voice.

A relieved murmur rippled through the room. People started to return to their cubes, although they remained in a state of shock, because few among Challenger's staff believed that O. J. Simpson was innocent of murder.

But within an hour, there was more bad news. Although the "O. J. Guilty!" GIF had been on the public servers for less than 15 seconds, a user in the Far East had retrieved the file from his cache, posted it to a Web site, and was spamming Usenet with news of Challenger's mistake. Throughout that terrible afternoon, "O. J. Guilty!" mirror sites sprang up all over the Web. By five o'clock, Rupert Klintoch's own site, iView, was running a headline story comparing Challenger's journalistic fumble to the legendary "Dewey Defeats Truman" newspaper debacle of 1948.

"Jane," said the production head. "We're going to have to talk about this." And with that, he called her into his office and closed the door.

"What do you mean, I've got to appear at a hearing?" Jane asked the production head.

"It's not a hearing–it's more of a fact-finding conference," the man said.

"I don't think I want to get involved in this."

"Well, the editor in chief wants to get to the bottom of what happened. There's a lot of finger-pointing going on here–the editors are blaming the art department, the art department is blaming the tech side, you're blaming the software, and some people are blaming you."

"I know the difference between a folder called "Innocent" and one called "Guilty.""

"I believe you, but can you convince them?"

"Look, mister. If you're going to make me the central figure in some kind of an inquest, you're going to have to pay me a lot more than $25 an hour."

"What's your price?"

"$50."

"It's high," he said, "but I'll pay it."

"Yeah, well, I've got better things to do," Jane fumed, and stormed down the corridor toward the elevator. She never came back.

## Verdict

Jane was the only one of the various participants in the Great O. J. Disaster who refused to attend the grueling, day-long inquest that was held to investigate the incident. As a result, she was fully blamed for the whole thing. One editor speculated that Jane, being a woman, couldn't bring herself to believe that O. J. Simpson was really innocent of murdering his wife. Instead, in a "trancelike state of denial," she'd acted reflexively, without thinking, and grabbed the wrong folder. One woman at the inquest objected to this interpretation and suggested that Jane was probably a closet racist who just couldn't handle the truth.

But the inquest's final report rejected both of these interpretations and simply concluded that Jane was an incompetent who should never have been hired in the first place. She was quickly removed from Challenger's list of approved freelancers and was never called back.

## Epilogue

Although PowerStager's role in the Great O. J. Disaster briefly surfaced at the inquest, no one seriously believed that such an elegant piece of software could possibly have mixed up the "Innocent" and "Guilty" files, and it was placed in service the next day. All ran well for a couple of weeks, until, one morning, Challenger's entire site disappeared from the Internet, just after the news editor updated a small, insignificant file to the public servers. After technicians spent a week restoring the massive site, PowerStager was taken down for "routine maintenance" and was quietly retired.

Jane, on the other hand, is still in service, and continues to live with her parrot on Waverly Place. She still builds Web sites in New York, and still makes about $30 an hour. She rarely thinks about O. J. Simpson or the Great O. J. Disaster, but admits that if she ever saw another copy of PowerStager, she'd drive a stake through its heart.

No jury would convict her.

# LEVEL 5.0

# Cowboys and Card Sharks

**Turnkey Solutions Traced in Blood**

## 5.1 Who Are They?

If Cab Drivers are the Silicon Schmoes who hack together the HTML for Web sites, Cowboys and Card Sharks are the "geniuses" responsible for the high-level programming that goes into software and systems.

Sounds like the same thing, right? Well, yes and no.

Yes, in the sense that both are involved with code; and no, in the sense that because their skills are so much more "advanced," Cowboys and Card Sharks can and often do get away with murder.

In the Old West, it was a quick gun that counted. In the Internet Age, it's the ability to churn out C++, Java, SQL, and other such languages at a lightning-fast pace that puts cyber-studded Cowboys and Card Sharks above the law.

You could be a pedophilic, junkie, serial killer with dead bodies buried under your house, but if you're a whiz with code, you'll get hired and paid very well; in fact, you'll probably make even more money because such baggage adds to your genius mystique.

Are we cynical? You bet. And with good reason.

While most NetSlaves are just scraping by, the members of this caste use their considerable clout in the most mercenary fashion. They command such exorbitant fees for their services that they hurt everyone else and more often than not upsell themselves so shamelessly that they take twice as long as they should to complete projects and have been known to flat-out lie to clients in order to improve their own bottom line.

This is not to say that all programmers are evil, but from the ones we talked to throughout our journey and the ones we've encountered in our own experience, it seems like many are, shall we say, "morally challenged." It's not their fault, really; they've been given such power (as demigods of the Digital Age), that in similar circumstances, almost anyone would be tempted to capitalize on the situation.

As far as Steve and I are concerned, Cowboys and Card Sharks belong in the same circle of hell as professional athletes and celebrities–they are a bunch of overhyped, overpaid nobodies who are screwing the rest of us. Steve and I haven't decided what would be the appropriate torture for them just yet, but we are open to suggestions from anyone who can identify with the following profile and story.

## 5.2 General Characteristics

*Where they can be found:* The most skilled (and unscrupulous) Cowboys and Card Sharks work for consultancies; the rest are virtual consultants (hired guns) in the sense that they would drop their current employer in a second for the chance to make more money elsewhere.

*How Cowboys differ from Card Sharks:* Cowboys will charge you twice as much for a simple application. Card Sharks will charge you 10 times as much and will justify themselves by covering every whiteboard in sight with complex data flows—even before you've finished describing what you want. ("An intranet? Sure, no problem. But you're going to need an object-oriented database, which will take 24 months to build.")

*Average actual hours worked per week:* ???. (No one is quite sure what these people do, so it's equally difficult to determine how much time they're putting in.)

*Average age:* 35 (in Dick Clark Time).

*Average salary:* $60K. (The reason this number is so low is that many Cowboys and Card Sharks are immigrants from Russia, India, and Taiwan, working for much less than market rate in exchange for citizenship.)

*Favorite offline activities:* Pretending to know the difference between an overpriced cigar made in Cuba and another made in the Dominican Republic; bitching about their stock portfolio; bragging about their "great time out on the links last Saturday" with fellow Cowboys and Card Sharks, too stupid to realize that golf is really the rich-guy and rich-guy-wannabe equivalent of bowling.

*Number of jobs held in the past three years:* 336 (all at once, for the entire period . . . and counting).

*Mode of dress:* Tan Dockers, penny loafers, sky-blue dress shirt, argyle socks. Note: Cowboys and Card Sharks have no time to think about what to wear in the morning and therefore their entire wardrobe consists solely of the aforementioned.

*Current technical fetishes:* Because it is the stock in trade of Cowboys and Card Sharks to appear to be on the cutting edge of technology, they are the early adopter's early adopter. They own everything from wireless modems to global satellite phones to upward of 12 personal digital assistants (PDAs), which they flash whenever possible.

*Outside interests:* None. Cowboys and Card Sharks can shoot a Java compile off a Garbageman's head at 100 yards, but they are often very uninformed about current events ("NATO's fighting the Germans? What for?") or what particular day it is.

*Marital status:* Unknown. It's not that this information isn't available; rather, it's that Cowboys and Card Sharks are so busy writing code or scamming for dough that they themselves have forgotten.

*Psychological profile:* 01000111 = $$$$$$

*Career aspirations:* To be cloned.

## 5.3 The Story of Zorn

*David Zorn's experience at BDS Consulting was very much like a mechanical bull ride–short, fast, intense, with lots of jolts and gyrations. To his credit, Zorn turned out to be a really good Cowboy. He held on with an iron grip and never got thrown, although there were times when he was tempted to use his six-gun on the Card Sharks who were supposed to be his friends.*

David Zorn tapped his pen nervously on the mahogany surface of the conference room table. He wanted to get up and leave, but was prevented from doing so by an ingrained professionalism and a strong moral sense that told him he was getting exactly what he deserved, right down to Chip Meyers's last sputtering curse.

Under different circumstances, Meyers was the ideal client. The chief technical officer (CTO) of Global Pacific Securities, he paid well and he paid on time, and if you treated him right, you were on the gravy train for years. But that was all out the window now. The project he had hired BDS Consulting for was months behind schedule–so badly botched in fact that the only chance Meyers saw for a speedy resolution was to get everyone in a room and "make his expectations clear."

Although the meeting had begun with whiteboards filled with flowcharts and other earmarks of a serious strategy session, it was quickly derailed when Zorn's T-shirt- and jeans-clad team started making jokes about their progress (or lack thereof). It was a degree of levity which Meyers was in no mood for and caused him to launch into a 30-minute nonstop tirade, which he punctuated with a threat.

"I've written a memo that has the project rolling out on May 28. If it's not completed by then, there's going to be serious consequences." Meyers took a piece of paper out of his leather briefcase and waved it over his head. "This is the memo–it's dated two weeks from now. I don't know what you have left to do and frankly I don't care. I want this project debugged and delivered, as advertised. No more messing around. No more bull. Got it?"

Meyers paused for a reaction and saw nothing but a roomful of lifeless, dour faces. His own face turned beet red, and he finally screamed, "Are you guys listening to me?"

Zorn was about to say something to ease the situation, when Meyers slammed his briefcase shut and stormed out of the room. The "strategy session," which everyone had entered with a renewed sense of hope, was now over, leaving Zorn and his team more than a little upset.

"Who does he think he's talking to? If we were back home, he'd have a rifle under his snoot." shouted Clement, one of the main programmers, in a deep Southern drawl.

Zorn glanced around the room and listened as his oppressed little group of fellow client-server NetSlaves went back and forth, venting their frustrations. Truth be told, they had worked their asses off to get the job done, pushing themselves to the limit for the past several months. But this didn't change the fact that they were young enough to be Zorn's sons and were so inexperienced as technologists that they didn't belong within 50 paces of anything mission-critical. In all fairness to them, however, Zorn realized that this multi-million-dollar storm really wasn't their fault. They should never have been assigned such a large project in the first place—a top-to-bottom mainframe replacement for an entire investment banking division was too much for an army of seasoned information technology (IT) professionals, much less this gang of Texas code cowboys.

"Remember the Alamo," Zorn sighed deeply under his breath and reached for the crab-shaped speakerphone in the center of the table. Picking up on Zorn's silent intensity, the team suddenly grew quiet.

"What're you doing?" asked Clement.

"We don't have the bodies or the bullets—I'm calling in air support."

## *Rightsized*

Zorn's unlikely career as a high-tech consultant began one morning in 1993 when Data Magic, the giant company that had employed him for 15 years as a mainframe applications programmer and project manager, "rightsized" him out of his $75,000 a year job. At 43, Zorn was just entering his peak earning years, but Data Magic was already in an alarming state of decline: its mainframe business had plateaued, and Zorn, despite his methodical mind, even disposition, and total dedication to Total Quality Management, was considered dead wood. Data Magic was nice enough to offer him a replacement job at Synergy, the company's ill-fated online service, but it paid much less: $45,000 a year and life as a "conversation manager" (a.k.a. Cyber-Cop) was so obnoxiously sordid that Zorn threw in the towel after three months.

By the time he left Synergy, Zorn felt burned out and betrayed. He smoldered with an angry sense that he'd been screwed out of his stake in the American Dream. His only joy was in noting how his once-great employer had become an industry joke—a pitiful, helpless giant who seemed incapable of making a correct move. Of course, Zorn felt like a joke himself—a fool for believing that, in this frantic age, careers (like marriages or anything else smacking of permanence) went on forever.

While rightsizing often drives people to drink, Zorn was too much of a family man to drown his betrayed illusions with alcohol. Instead of crying in his beer, Zorn wasted no time trying to tackle the immediate problem: he needed $75,000 a year to keep his quiet suburban life together. Between his daughters' orthodontic bills, the mortgage on the house in Sayreville, and the need to keep two minivans fueled, Zorn was already pretty tapped out. His wife made a few dollars here and there doing legal transcripts, but Zorn was the real breadwinner, and without his support, his family would collapse within a matter of months.

Zorn thought of going solo as a consultant, but was so broke that digging into his 401(k) to finance such a career move was out of the question. He briefly tried getting work as a programmer, but when no one returned his calls, he realized that his chances of getting this kind of work were limited. In an industry that got weak at the knees over 23-year-old codeboy geniuses, Zorn was a dinosaur—a middle-aged JCL/COBOL guy who wound up on the losing side of the client-server revolution.

Zorn knew his only chance of not ending up flipping burgers at Motor Chef was to upgrade his rusty skill set. Hitting up a friend for a loan, Zorn enrolled in an AppWiz certification course and, after passing his final exam with flying colors, received referrals for several prospective employers. AppWiz was a very popular and, hence, very marketable tool used to create Windows-compliant front ends that, like a streamlined shroud placed over a dirty old steam locomotive, made people believe the train could go faster. In computer terms, AppWiz put a graphical front end on the text-based mainframe, and integrated functions that ran on separate machines into one big, user-friendly interface.

Zorn looked over the referrals, and the one that really caught his eye was BDS (Best Data Systematics), a Houston-based consultancy that had recently opened a New York office to extend its reach into the reengineering market that was sweeping Corporate America. The company, like many things in Houston, had its origins in the oil business. Formed in 1989 by young bucks eager to break the reign of the IT department of OXON, BDS had grown to become one of the biggest outsourcing specialists in Texas. According to various trade stories Zorn found on the Web, BDS was growing at a gusher-like velocity, enjoying a significant lead in the client-server field, and seemed ready to tap into the fat budgets of New York's financial industry, whose ancient mainframes were in desperate need of replacement.

Zorn sent his résumé in, and after receiving a callback from a human resources person who reminded him of Hoss on *Bonanza,* he booked a seat on the next flight to Houston. Zorn hated flying but was so jazzed about his new career opportunity that he didn't mind making the trip.

## Ropin' Cattle

Zorn landed at Houston's George Bush Intercontinental Airport and took a cab to BDS's offices, which were located on the top floor of a 40-story skyscraper whose green-tinted, mirrored windows reflected Texas's big, flat sky. As he waited in the glass-enclosed reception area, Zorn felt like he was on another planet. And in a lot of ways he was–he had boarded the plane in filthy, smog-ridden Newark and in a space of a few hours was in the heart of this strange western land, where everything (especially the people) seemed larger than life.

Zorn's first interview was with Happer Harnitz, the person who managed all the project managers in addition to overseeing BDS's Applications Boot Camp. Harnitz was a 27-year-old, crew-cut-sporting former AWACs officer with a slight Virginia accent. Standing about 6'4" and walking slowly but purposefully, he greeted Zorn with a friendly, "How y'all doing today?" and proceeded to show Zorn around the Boot Camp, which consisted of two large conference rooms, a focus-group room with video camera, two classrooms with about 20 PCs in each, and the Video Suite, where weekly videoconferencing sessions were held.

"When it's all wired together, it's the best damned application simulation environment in the world," Harnitz boasted out of the side of his mouth, as if he were chewing on a cigar. "You should see what we do in there–you've got a client modifying a screen with a facilitator, and a VB guy in the next room coding it up, doing a quick compile, and 10 minutes later, the whole group can see the prototype on the big screen. Now, that's impressive. Sure, it's static data, but it really kicks the hell out of the client. They walk away saying, 'If that's what these cowboys can whip up in 10 minutes, *imagine what they could do in a few hours.*' "

Zorn himself was impressed by Harnitz's facility as well as the production area, which was immaculately clean and filled with young men buzzing back and forth between cubes armed with Solaris workstations and other cutting-edge hardware. But what kicked the hell out of Zorn more than anything was Maynard LeMay, BDS's CEO. With a wild huckster glint in his eyes that was very Foghorn Leghorn, LeMay did a quick two-step out of his vast corner office and greeted Zorn as if they were old friends.

"Well, hey there. I heard you were coming down. I sure do hope you like what you see so far."

LeMay's giant-sized hand swallowed Zorn's in a friendly grip, and Zorn stared up at his long, thin frame with a mixture of awe and total confusion. If LeMay was Foghorn Leghorn, Zorn was the Henery Hawk character, a small, roundish creature who, after spending his entire career in the gray, humorless world of Data Magic, wasn't used to such boisterousness in the workplace.

Zorn looked deep into LeMay's steel-blue eyes, trying his best to rise to the occasion. "Mr. LeMay, I am quite impressed by your operation. Your associate has been more than informative about your design methodology."

"I'm really glad to hear that. You know, I was just heading off to lunch—why don't you join me for a little heart-to-heart discussion?"

Zorn agreed with alacrity and soon found himself in the last place he'd ever imagine for a business meeting—Houston's legendary Hog Wild lap-dancing bar. An erotic oasis cooled by a 30,000-BTU air conditioner, it was LeMay's favorite hangout, or so Zorn surmised from the fact that he knew all the dancers by name. "Hey, Daisy! Hey, Emmy Sue!"

LeMay and Zorn took seats at the end of the bar. A second later a pair of beers and a large plate of ribs arrived, even though they hadn't placed their order. "Jesus," Zorn thought. "This guy must live here."

The "interview" officially began when LeMay clicked the neck of his beer against Zorn's and leaned toward him with a smile. "So, I hear you're an ol' Data Magic man," LeMay yelled over the thumping of the amplifed music.

"That's right."

"Too damned bad about what happened to that company. But you know, Zorn, we're delivering a form of justice back to them."

"Justice, sir?"

"Well, you got outsourced. So did I, once upon a time. Outsourcing's an evil thing—I've seen it destroy men, make them give up the fight. But it made you stronger, because you retooled, and evolved yourself. Now you want to be a consultant—well, now it's all a little different. Outsourcing is your friend now—your chance to get even."

The music had softened and a tall, blonde woman wearing a bolo tie and little else started dancing near them. LeMay lowered his voice, conspiratorily. "You know, Zorn, this business isn't about the enterprise as much as it is about people—people you can trust. Data Magic has a lot of brand equity, and it's as important for us to inspire trust in our customers as it is to build great technology. Do you know what 'BDS' stands for?"

"Best Data Systematics?"

"Well, that's what it says on the door, but let me tell you what it really means—'Bodacious Systems!' BODACIOUS SYSTEMS!" LeMay suddenly screamed over the music. Zorn knew that this was all some sort of come-on, but couldn't help laughing out loud.

LeMay was laughing, too, and reached across the table to grab Zorn's wrist. "You're a good man, Zorn—I sincerely hope you decide to come on board with us."

The woman who had been dancing near them was now up in Zorn's face, her bolo tie brushing his hair.

## *Boot Camp*

Neglecting to tell his wife, or anyone else for that matter, about the recruitment procedure, Zorn joined up with BDS in April. His salary was $80,000 a year, plus the chance to make a bonus if the jobs he worked on met all client expectations. Zorn spent a week at the Boot Camp under the watchful eye of Harnitz, who grilled BDS's new recruits on every last detail of AppWiz. Sessions were held from 7 a.m. to 7 p.m., when everybody went out to Hog Wild to "unwind." Despite being locked up with up 19 sweaty Texans, a maniacal drill instructor, and cryptic object-oriented programming (OOP) tools for a solid week, Zorn managed to enjoy himself. He stopped wearing his grim Data Magic–style two-piece suit and bought a golf shirt.

When Boot Camp was over, Zorn was thoroughly up to speed on how the tools worked and felt confident about tackling the corporate reengineering projects that lay ahead. But he did have a few nagging doubts about the programming skills of his fellow graduates. They were young and smart, and loved to party, but they didn't seem to care too much about planning applications in advance or about neatness—sacred virtues to a Data Magic man. These cowboys could code rings around Zorn, but they made a lot of mistakes, and Zorn shuddered at the thought that they'd soon be let loose on corporate back-ends across the U.S.A.

## *Malpractice*

At the end of April, Zorn was back in New York and had picked up his first consulting assignment through the New York office. It was a long-term implementation project for Kotler-Imbos, a New Jersey drug company that was desperately trying to convert 19 semitrailer trucks' worth of documents into a single, integrated digital records management system—or, as the sales guys called it, a "search engine." Millions of dollars hung in the balance—Kotler-Imbos was hoping to speed up the Food and Drug Administration (FDA) application cycle for a new generation of space-age antidepressants and needed to replace its slow, paper-based system pronto, or lose ground to other purveyors of space-age antidepressants.

The terms of BDS's contract called for consultants to bill by the hour, not by the job. This arrangement meant that BDS would build whatever the client wanted, even if it was unnecessary, misguided, or completely stupid. Because payment had nothing to do with application quality, it was in Zorn's interest to add a lot of silly frills into the software.

The application bloat that Zorn's team was creating was the lesser evil at Kotler-Imbos. What was really dragging the project down was the fact that one of KI's main IT people was a complete moron. He specified that each document had to contain more than 20 fields of information, *all* of which had to be filled in before the user could submit it to the database. As a result, it took users more than 20 minutes to complete each new entry, and worse, the user had to be an expert in FDA regulation codes to fill out the form. It was an absurd situation—especially so because the whole idea was to reach a point where the drug company could hire $5-an-hour temps to manage the system using a PC-based interface.

Zorn argued that embedding this kind of highly granular information into each document was a prescription for disaster. He did some calculations and determined that, at the current rate, it would take Kotler-Imbos more than nine years to enter all of its data. From a programming standpoint, it was far better to license a third-party search engine to work against one or two record identifiers, instead of building all the intelligence into the record level.

Nobody listened to Zorn, but on a time-and-materials contract, it didn't matter—BDS would still get paid for all of the hours his team worked. If the client wanted to shoot himself in the foot, Zorn wasn't about to stop him.

Zorn worked for almost a year at the Kotler-Imbos project, and rolled off before the shit hit the fan. The system as delivered was slow, unusable, and totally misconceived, but it did work, according to the contractual definition. The clueless client may have been to blame for turning the project into a monster, but would nonetheless have to pay BDS $2 million for building it.

## *Ghost Town*

By the time Zorn had finished his portion of the disastrous drug search engine project, BDS's New York business had all but dried up. BDS had burned a couple of clients, and checks weren't being paid. A disaster recovery project had gone badly, a data warehousing effort had crashed and burned, and a work group automation project had also tanked. The Texans' mistakes were adding up, and BDS was gaining a reputation as a ball dropper. With LeMay's down-home charm no longer working on the "uptight Yankees," Zorn had nothing to do and was forced to go on half salary, picking up small, one-person projects here and there.

Zorn's situation started looking up again a few months later when he was summoned to BDS's Boston office, which apparently had more work than it could handle. Zorn hated to be away from his family, but with no other prospects and a seriously depleted bank account, he agreed, on the condition that he could go home on weekends—provided, of course, that there wasn't an emergency.

From the second he entered the place, Zorn could tell that the climate at the Boston office was chillier than the backslapping, lap-dancing culture of Houston and the disorganized pit that was the New York office. Run by two highly intelligent, highly aggressive preppies from Harvard, the office made Zorn feel like he was back at Data Magic—it was all gray, from the walls to the carpets to the furniture.

Since there was no receptionist to greet him, Zorn wandered back to the massive production area, which was a beehive of activity—young men were running back and forth and there was nary a smiling face to be found. Zorn stopped one of these young men, introduced himself, and asked for Stuart Williams, the production head. Without missing a step, the young man, clad in tan Dockers, pointed to the corner office and kept on going, too busy to even stop and exchange the usual pleasantries.

Stuart Williams, a blonde-haired man of 25, also wearing tan Dockers, was equally hurried and mechanical. He nodded when he heard Zorn's name and within 15 minutes had one of his minions set Zorn up at his workstation and give him a quick rundown of what he'd be doing. As it turned out, Zorn would be the official AppWiz guy, providing the front end for all the applications they were currently building. The minion, who identified himself only as "Applebee," then handed him a piece of paper, which listed the projects, where they were located on the network, and the dates they were due.

Zorn got down to business immediately, beginning on the user interface for a large insurance company's intranet. Zorn didn't exactly get hot and bothered over actuarial statistics, but after months of doing absolutely nothing, he was glad to be busy. In the brief moments he looked away from his monitor to rest his eyes, he took note of yet another difference between the Boston office and the rest of BDS: aside from the WASP-y management, he was the only American citizen in the place and certainly the only American doing production. The cubicles around him and as far as his eyes could see were all occupied by immigrants from Russia, Taiwan, and India. Zorn later found out that they were all H1B workers who had been brought over and sponsored by BDS. To Zorn's ears, the arrangement sounded a lot like indentured servitude. They were paid less than market rate for their services and couldn't do a thing about it for the three years it took to gain residency.

Zorn tried on numerous occasions to strike up conversations with the immigrant consultants only to discover, like everyone else at the Boston office, that they were pretty cold fish. If they spoke at all, it was to each other, in their native tongue. Zorn nonetheless enjoyed working with them. In contrast to the loud and unruly Texans, Zorn found them to be methodical, hardworking coders, although their silent compliance with the unfair employment situation nagged at him. At his more cynical moments, Zorn concluded that they put up with such bull because they feared any complaints they made would be forwarded to the Immigration and Naturalization Service, resulting in immediate deportation.

In the weeks that followed, Zorn also learned other things. The preppies who ran the place didn't like the Texans and did their utmost to distance themselves and their business from them. In fact, they had even implemented a different revenue model: all contracts were "fixed-time, fixed-delivery," meaning that they never upsold. They delivered only what the clients agreed to beforehand and punished anyone guilty of scope creep and application bloat with a severity usually reserved for capital crimes.

For as much as they hated the Texas cowboys as a whole, the preppies did respect Harnitz, whose high-tech "enterprise battle simulator" via a fiber-optic linkup to his war room in Houston, allowed potential clients in Boston to virtually visualize what their applications would be like, without having to endure the Texas heat. Buggy at first, it became a very successful way to land new projects and proved to be the only friendly collaboration between the offices, which otherwise treated each other like competitors.

Zorn kept his head down and did his best to steer clear of such politics. It wasn't hard to do really because Zorn was busy beyond belief. He'd been in Boston for over two months and in that time had completed the insurance company intranet, in addition to two more similar applications for a large law firm. He'd come to enjoy the work, although it was taking its toll on Zorn's relationship with his wife and teenage daughters. The promise to let him go home on weekends had been quickly broken, as everything he was doing was considered an emergency.

Zorn's luck improved a few months later when he learned he was needed for a big new project in New York. Amid rumors of being closed down, they had apparently scored with a major financial institution that needed a top-to-bottom mainframe conversion. The news couldn't have come at a better time—between the six-day weeks and the need to compete with a roomful of highly motivated coders and please the dictatorial preppies that drove them, Zorn was so tired and homesick that he had been on the verge of quitting.

## *Robbing the Bank*

Like virtually every project that BDS Consulting ever took on, the contract with Global Pacific Securities started out like a marvelous love affair. After spending a week in Harnitz's battle simulator and working with BDS's application facilitators to design the perfect set of enterprise resource planning (ERP) screens, Chip Meyers, the CTO, was in heaven. He'd finally figured out a way to scrap his clunky old mainframe, reduce his in-house budget for programmers, save his own salary from outsourcing, and maybe even get a promotion.

Meyers knew all about the dangers of scope creep, so the deal called for a fixed-price, fixed-time agreement to cover the whole job for

$2 million. With check in hand, Zorn's team took on the task of turning the prototype front end that the client had designed into real executable code.

Zorn would have preferred to choose his own team for the job. He liked the work done by the Taiwanese, Indians, and Russians, but BDS had other ideas. Instead of shipping down some of the green-card programmers from Boston, they sent up six Texans from Houston who were cooling their heels in "a temporary Houston slowdown." Zorn had a hard time liking them—they were half his age, and they seemed to resent the fact that the only lap-dancing parlor was way uptown and that the bank had a general policy forbidding beer drinking while coding a 32-bit graphical user interface.

Zorn knew his team was being received poorly in Global Pacific Securities' stuffed-shirt culture, but he was more concerned with the other, more serious threats facing his project. It turned out that Meyers had more than a few enemies scattered through the bank's besieged and soon-to-be-outsourced IT department. These internal saboteurs put up a smoke screen that made it almost impossible for Zorn's team to work—for weeks, Zorn was denied permission to unlock data repositories, obtain write-access to needed directories, or get much-needed documentation for his job. Some sort of stonewalling was going on here, and, although Zorn repeatedly complained about it to the CTO, his team started to fall seriously behind.

Zorn teleconferenced with the Houston office at least twice a week, usually with Harnitz, who monitored all of BDS's projects using a 3-D project management package called WorkView, which let him view the status of each project at a glance. Harnitz used a color-coding system to identify trouble zones: green meant an application was on time, yellow meant late (but salvageable), and red meant trouble.

Harnitz agreed that Zorn's project was in jeopardy and had already moved it to yellow status.

"It says here we've already got a $1 million check from these people," Harnitz said.

"Yes. Half down, half on completion."

"You've got to complete. The New York office is depending on you."

"We're going to complete. But we're falling behind."

"File your report. We'll need it if and when this goes to litigation. Just keep your head low, and hope for better weather. That is all."

Zorn continued his bitter complaints to Meyers, who issued a threatening series of memos designed to coerce the saboteurs into submission. Slowly, Zorn started to get better cooperation and started to get back on track. But client-consultant relations continued to fray, because things weren't working right. The software was behaving fitfully—almost as if it had been drinking.

Zorn knew the Cowboy coders working under him were wild, but he didn't fully realize how bad their code was until he looked at a sample and was shocked by its poor commenting, cryptic structure, and messy syntax. He began to experience "disaster creep": the sickening sensation that whatever fancy enterprise-wide gizmo one is working on at the moment will never survive the transition from fancy prototype to stable system in one's own lifetime.

As the one-year project approached its 11th month, Zorn's mindset grew increasingly apocalyptic. Everything the Texans did seemed to be working against them. The more things they tried to build, the more things needed fixing. But when they fixed something, they inevitably broke something else. They'd been trained quickly—and badly. Try as they might, the team barely made any headway—every step forward took them two steps back, and they were all running out of time.

Now, with two weeks to go, the shit was an inch away from the fan.

## *Command and Control*

Zorn dialed the speakerphone, and after a few seconds, Harnitz came on the line.

"What the hell is going on up there?" Harnitz barked. "Your application was in yellow. Why's it suddenly in red?"

"We think it's the scheduler," said Zorn. "The application runs fine, but when we add the scheduler, the whole thing crashes. It's something with the back-end."

"Can you fix it?"

"Not with everything else that needs fixing."

"Can you crash the time?"

"Won't work. Only 330 hours left."

There was a long pause at the other end of the phone, as Harnitz analyzed all the contingencies.

"Well, just freeze it," he barked.

"You mean stop development?"

"Just patch it up, tie up the loose ends, and bug out."

"I've never walked off a job before it's finished," Zorn said.

"Zorn, do you believe in your mind that the software is done?" Harnitz asked.

"Well, it's partially functional."

"What percent?"

"I'd say 75, maybe 80 percent," Zorn said.

"So just freeze the damned thing and move on," Harnitz said. "Think damage control, boy—call it finished, patch up the gaps, and exfiltrate the team. Can you do that?"

"Yes, sir," Zorn said.

"That is all," Harnitz said, and hung up.

"Gentlemen," Zorn said to the weary Texans. "Let's get out of here."

## *Virtual Bugout*

Zorn's team never actually walked off the job, but they did stop working. They all agreed to speak of the application as "finished," and didn't change a single line of code during their final two weeks onsite at Global Pacific. Zorn put in a few patches and removed as many misspellings as possible from the documentation, but it was just busywork—painting the shutters on a house that was about to collapse. The deep flaws within the system—the gremlins that caused it to crash, reboot, and freeze—were going to be there forever.

To celebrate the "successful" launch of the software, smooth over any bad feelings, and cover up the truth, Harnitz rented a 200-foot dinner boat to take GPS's jubilant technology infrastructure executives around Manhattan in a two-hour tour of the harbor. Harnitz even had 200 T-shirts printed up that said: "GPS AND BDS: THE ENTERPRISE A-TEAM."

Even Meyers was happy: his program had been delivered on time after all—the best little piece of 32-bit client-server system ever coded by the human hand. He strolled around the upper deck with a glass of champagne in his hand and backslapped with LeMay, who had flown up for the festivities and strutted around wearing a black cowboy hat.

At the rear of the ship, Zorn drank a beer and talked with Clement, who, like Zorn, had rolled off of the successfully completed project.

"I wonder how long it will take them to find out that it's a lemon."

"Two days is plenty of time to get out of town," said Clement. "C'mon, have another beer. Hell, you ain't paying for it."

## *Epilogue*

Global Pacific Securities' widely hyped Enterprise-Wide Executive Information Service never met expectations, even after the bank paid another consultant $2 million of its depositors' money to undo the mess that Zorn and his team had made. In a fury, GPS held back payment on the final $1 million it owed to BDS, and BDS countersued, claiming that the project failed because of GPS's "stonewalling." Long before the whole mess was resolved in court, Meyers was fired and became a consultant for BTT (Bean Town Technology), BDS's former Boston office and currently its main competitor.

Unfortunately for Zorn, the scandal caused New York to finally wake up to the fact that BDS was a company whose elaborate "application simulations" and "rapid prototyping environments" were really just a smoke screen for a bunch of Texans who didn't write very good code. When the New York office finally closed, Zorn was forced to give up on the hotshot company (whose last-known project was an e-commerce portal for cattle ranchers), and downscale his career aspirations once again.

Zorn now works at home, and consults on small jobs for retailers. It nets him only $50,000 a year, but there's no lap dancing and he's never had to bug out of a situation or call in air support.

# LEVEL 6.0

# Fry Cooks

**Confessions of Real-Life "Dilberts"**

## 6.1 Who Are They?

Steve and I tried postponing it, but we had reached the point in our journey when we couldn't put it off any longer. It was now time for us to face the Fry Cooks–the most stressed out, and for that reason, the most dangerous of all NetSlaves.

If the Internet were an all-you-can-eat restaurant, open 24/7 and one which prided itself on lightning-fast service and customized meals, Fry Cooks would be the overheated culinary engineers handling the flaming-hot grills. Sounds like fun, right? Well, Fry Cooks must get some enjoyment out of it, or else they are the biggest masochists in the world, considering the aggravation they must endure just to put food on their own tables.

A spatula in one hand, a Gantt chart in the other, Fry Cooks are the "get it done at all costs" project people of the New Media Caste System. As such, Fry Cooks lead a strange, hybrid existence–they have all the pressures of management and none of the perks, a fact which makes them amount to nothing more than glorified grunts. Fry Cooks divide their time between fighting grease fires and responding to the insane, often inane, orders of customers, barked at them by the Waitstaff, better known as the sales force:

"Give me an HTML Lite–hold the pickles, traveling, easy on the personalization."
"I'll take a Portal–extra commerce, Solaris back-end, Java on the side."
"We need a pre-alpha, alpha beta, beta beta alpha, Streaming Media Surpreme."

The heat of the kitchen was almost unbearable, and Steve and I got tired just watching the Fry Cooks in action, slicing, dicing, prioritizing. We asked the few who could pause long enough to speak to us about how they kept it together. The response of one Fry Cook named Terry was particularly interesting:

"You know, people talk about 'facilitating' and 'managing expectations'–but that's all bull. You work as hard as you can, while knowing in the back of your head that you're only as good as your last project, maybe not even that good."

The other Fry Cooks were not so friendly or articulate. They growled at every one of our questions and one in particular chased us out of the kitchen, swinging a large carving knife. Steve and I escaped unscathed and bear no ill will toward this caste. If we had a hundred projects due at once and had the last bit of strength wrung out of us like an old slop rag, we'd be pretty dangerous, too.

## 6.2 General Characteristics

*Where they can be found:* Fry Cooks are most often found sweating profusely over a legion of projects that are behind schedule ("I need the copy, the graphics, the database—basically, everything by tomorrow, or I'm dead!") or else taking the brunt of managerial tirades over projects that are already late ("What do you mean the site's not up yet?! We told the client we could get it done in three days!"). Note: The fact that no one involved, including the client, answered e-mail or returned phone calls from the get-go is no excuse.

*Average age:* 92.3 (in Internet Time; for details, see Cab Drivers).

*Average income:* $60K per year (which amounts to $20K per year, after factoring out exorbitant bar tabs and/or weekly trips to a shrink).

*Favorite at-home activities:* Trying to coax the administrative assistant over for a "romantic evening"; watching *On the Waterfront* for the 200th time and mouthing the words to Brando's "I coulda been a contenda" speech.

*Last book read:* *Post Office,* by Charles Bukowski. Also partial to anything by Hemingway, Celine, Hamsun, Baudelaire. Main criterion for enjoying a work of literature: it has to be written by an angry loner on the verge of cracking up.

*Average number of jobs they've had:* 7. Like Cab Drivers, Fry Cooks tend to work on a per-project basis, even though upper management gives them every impression that they are an integral part of the team when they are hired. Having been burned several times before, most Fry Cooks have stopped believing this come-on and never keep more in their desks than they can pack into a small bag. (Can you say, "lean and mean"?)

*How they view the Internet:* Fry Cooks view the Internet as a way to earn more money than they would be making had they pursued the more traditional paths offered them by their educational backgrounds. Note: Given their tastes in literature and movies, many Fry Cooks are often English majors in disguise, who got into the Web biz completely by accident and have remained in it due to a bone-chilling fear of ending up back in graduate school, writing books on the role of mustaches in Dickens.

*Psychological profile:* Fry Cooks are in many ways the most existential members of the New Media Caste System. If a project is late, it's their fault. If it's on time, it's also their fault because "key features" no one ever mentioned to them have been left out. Their universe is cold and absurd. Fry Cooks are the whipping boys (and girls) of the Waitstaff (salespeople) and the Head Cook (chief developer), who, rather than blaming themselves for glitches and miscommunications, find it much easier to palm it off on them.

*Why Fry Cooks are more dangerous than Cab Drivers:* Cab Drivers can at least roam free, from company to company. Fry Cooks, by contrast, are bound to the success or failure of one company. "Dilberts" in the truest sense (of being potential homicidal maniacs, that is), Fry Cooks should not be messed with—unless of course being boiled in oil is your idea of fun.

## 6.3 The Story of Boyd

*When Boyd was hired as a writer at CPU Central he thought he had left the sleaziness of his porn store job behind. Little did he know that he was about to get wrapped up in 14-hour days and a level of human depravity lower than anything he had experienced to date. The perverts and junkies of Market Street had nothing on these people.*

Boyd worked as the overnight cashier in a porn shop on Market Street. It was a tight little place with three narrow aisles full of videotapes, and Boyd worked near the door in a plexiglass cage. When the store was busy, Boyd would pass a stream of crinkled twenty-dollar bills and fifty-dollar bills to the register, make the change, and snap off the magnetized tags in a smooth rhythm, before bagging the tapes and shoving them through a slot sawed through the plexiglass. When business was slow, Boyd would take off his glasses and stare nearsightedly at the videotapes, and all the colors would merge together into an orange-tinted collage of blurry, writhing flesh.

Boyd was 26 and had been in San Francisco for less than a year. He'd come from Arizona with a degree in journalism from a second-tier college, some computer experience, a strong desire to become the next Bukowski (his favorite writer), and an even stronger desire never to return to Phoenix, which he called "the armpit of the Southwest." Boyd had reason enough to hate Phoenix. By 1994, its once-thriving tech business had evaporated, leaving few options for Boyd's ilk—young men with degrees who lacked a very clear idea of what they should be doing with themselves.

Boyd's first job in San Francisco was as a junior assistant buyer at Macy's, but he lasted less than three months—his job was eliminated when the store went into Chapter 11 and reorganized. One of Boyd's roommates worked at the porn shop and was so sick of spending his nights "facing the scum of society" that Boyd offered to take over for him. Going from Macy's corporate offices in the high-rent district to the trashy sidewalks of Market Street was a shock, but Boyd put his nose to the grindstone and within a month he was bumped up to assistant manager.

Within three months he had convinced the owner to install an automated point-of-sale system, linking up the five other stores in the chain. As a reward, Boyd was made manager of the stores, and manager of an X-rated nightclub that the owner had opened in the Castro.

## Out of the Frying Pan

Money was pouring into Boyd's life, he had written several hard-edged, Bukowski-esque stories about his experience in the porn business, but he still wasn't happy. Spending long hours with the "scum of the earth" started to dig at his mind. "If they're scum," Boyd thought, "what does that make me?" One night, after the strippers had all gone home, Boyd approached the owner and tried to make his thoughts clear.

"Give the kid a beer," Saperstein called to the bartender, as Boyd sat down next to him.

"You know, Mr. Saperstein, it's not that I don't like doing this. The money is very good, and you've been good to me."

Saperstein looked at him hard, and Boyd knew that this older man had seen many young men in similar struggles.

"The grass is always greener," Saperstein said.

"I know what you're saying."

"You're a young man, Boyd, with a lot to offer the world. But if you want to move on, that's your privilege."

"Thanks," said Boyd.

"Just remember one thing," the older man added. "There are only two kinds of businesses in this world—those that sell things that people really need, and those that don't. Make sure you sign on with a business that's real."

"Thanks, Mr. Saperstein."

Boyd bummed around for a few months, eating through his "blue money" cash savings, but soon found another job a little closer to the greener side of his aspirations. It was a tech support position for a San Francisco ISP. For eight hours each day, Boyd was point man in the ISP's daily war against clueless users who couldn't connect, didn't know what a port was, and were too dumb to find the Windows "Dial-Up Networking" folder on their desktops.

Boyd knew very little about networking when the ISP hired him, but he took armfuls of manuals home to read on weekends and soon came up to speed. Moreover, he was patient; his marketing background had taught him the value of always keeping a smile in his voice, especially when under stress, and this quality calmed down even the most annoyed customers.

Despite the grueling hours and the endless complaints, Boyd didn't mind much—he was educating himself in all the things that could go wrong with systems. Although he was making a fraction of the money he'd made in the porn shop, he felt better about his life because he was learning new things and because his small, clean cubical was a million miles away from the condom- and whisky bottle–strewn sidewalks of Market Street.

## *Into the Fire*

Late one night, Boyd was flipping across the cable channels and saw something he had never seen before. It was *CPU Central,* a one-hour program on personal computing produced in San Francisco by a company of the same name. At the end of the show, its Web site address flashed across the screen, and Boyd logged onto the site and scanned its Jobs section.

Several positions were listed, among them a job in e-mail user support. Boyd faxed off his résumé, grabbed a beer from the fridge, and went to sleep.

Months went by, and Boyd labored on in the ISP's support cube, oblivious to the revolutionary forces that were swirling around San Francisco. He knew that something was happening, that learning about this networking stuff was going to stand him in good stead, but there were still pieces missing from the puzzle—a gap existed that separated Boyd from where he needed to be.

One morning, CPU Central's support manager called Boyd and asked him to come in for an interview. Boyd went the next day. The offices were down by Fisherman's Wharf, in a dingy building that had seen better days. Boyd walked across a big room filled with folding tables, where computers had been set up in an obvious rush. He was hired on the spot and spent the rest of the day in a kind of reverie.

The missing piece had appeared. The gap was filling in, and as Boyd stepped out into the sunshine, the thought occurred to him that he was a million miles from Market Street *now.*

By the time Boyd was hired in the summer of 1996, the senior managers of CPU Central had a very clear idea of how to seize control of the computer-oriented info-space. The company, much of whose brain trust consisted of disgruntled defectors from old-line PC trade publications, craved revenge against the Establishment, and a recent magazine industry shakeout had hardened the managers' hatred of print—a dead-tree relic of the stuffy, largely East Coast cartel that "didn't get it."

CPU Central's hard-eyed CEO, Hilton White, *did* get it. Wealthy, smooth-talking, and well-connected, White had no stomach for the incrementalist pabulum being served up at CD-ROM-oriented desktop publishing panels. Computer trade publishing was moving far too slowly, and White wanted to taste blood in a real, infra-capitalist revolution.

White knew that the old-line trade publishers had been stung by their pitiful experiments in CD-ROM and proprietary online publishing, and were vulnerable to a lightning-bolt offensive from the west. He firmly believed that a cable station catering to computer nerds, based in the world's most highly wired city, could divert a lot of advertising cash that Intel, Oracle, and other deep-pocketed companies in Silicon Valley wanted to spend in print, a rapidly fossilizing medium.

In late 1995, by sheer accident, White stumbled into a stunning, awesome truth: the Web was going to be big–much bigger than cable, a closed system controlled by the old-line media. This revelation was partly the result of what had happened to the *CPU Central* cable show: it had been relegated to a second-rate slot on the Sci-Fi Channel. This infuriated White, but the Web would change all that–it was completely open territory, and a perfect environment for content to easily be "repurposed" into its own independent franchise.

White's revelation was also based on the incredible response to a small Web site feature on virus scanning software, which had been launched to promote a segment on the *CPU Central* cable show. Although the few people on the CPU staff who knew about the site laughed off its paltry content (just a handful of product reviews), it ended up generating more orders in the space of a week than the show had in the entire history of its existence.

"What the hell's going on?" White screamed joyfully to the small roomful of his most trusted lieutenants, who sat there unable to come up with an explanation.

But White didn't need an explanation, and in a matter of days, CPU Central had a completely different strategy. All of its resources were to be focused on expanding the Web sites–the first great push that CPU Central would make into the Net space. And to expand quickly enough to gain the high ground before the East Coast guys could wake up, White needed bodies, lots of them–support people especially.

## *To Serve Humanity*

For Boyd, plunging into CPU Central's support infrastructure felt like sweeping up behind Hannibal's elephants. In July of 1996, CPU Central used a single, common e-mail address for its small cluster of sites, which included cpucentral.com and yournews.com. All user mail went to webmaster@cpucentral.com, which meant that Boyd and his small team would have to field a massive, undifferentiated, unparsed flow of mail, whose volume grew daily as White's offensive expanded.

Like all support desks within New Media companies, Boyd's crew was considered the lowliest of CPU Central's departments—uncreative, reactive, and droneworthy. They sat in battered chairs around rickety folding tables, used burned-out-looking old Quadras, and shared an ISDN line with everyone else in the massive production room.

Despite their low station on *CPU Central*'s masthead, Boyd knew that his humble team performed a vital public relations service. Timely message turnaround was key to impressing the growing throng of users with the fact that CPU Central was no ordinary computer e-zine—it was the future itself: informative, interactive, dynamic. White may have been crazy, but his strategy seemed to be working. The good word got around quickly and by July of 1996, the e-mail flow was roughly 1,500 messages a day. It soon grew to 5,000 messages a day after CPU Central bought yourfiles.com, yourmodem.com, and myscanner.com and ramped up content on these new domains.

Boyd's mail was 80 percent technical—messages from guys who had questions about a product mentioned on the show, or guys who tried to follow the upgrade instructions on a show and had blown up their systems. Boyd and the other help-desk drones used a library of canned responses invoked by special Eudora keystroke combinations. Boyd could average about 180 responses an hour, just by reading the message headers, and he got faster as time passed. The rest of the e-mail consisted of miscellaneous rantings, sales pitches, 900-number scams, and other dross that Boyd could safely delete without reading further.

Boyd didn't have an exact quota of messages he was required to answer each day, but he and the two other people who worked on his team were expected to keep the queue backlog to the bare minimum.

Boyd fought hard to keep the queue free, but it was a furious, exhausting battle. Each Wednesday, CPU Central updated its Web site, spurring a huge wave of user mail. Boyd and his team would churn through the messages for the next two days, right into Friday night. If they performed well, they could nearly unclog the queue. The next week, they'd tackle the backed-up weekend mail, which took them until Tuesday night to finish. On Wednesday, the whole cycle would begin again.

The team often worked late into the night, and sometimes Boyd would come in on Saturday to save himself from a hellish Monday. He got a key to the building and would spend many hours alone at his Quadra. The extra time didn't bother him much. If working unpaid hours meant his $22,000 yearly salary was safe, that was OK. If it meant abandoning any notions of a social life, that was OK, too. When Boyd got bored on the weekend shifts, he'd eschew the canned responses and reach out to a few of *CPU Central*'s irate or technically inept with a personal message about a modem, or an ATAPI CD-ROM drive. Support e-mail wasn't much of a serious literary vehicle, but at least Boyd was writing, and people were paying attention to what he wrote.

The two people whom Boyd worked with had little or no computer experience, nor much apparent interest in moving out of E-mail Hell. One was a burnout from academe–U.C. Davis or Berkeley, Boyd was never sure. Boyd learned not to talk to her, because she had a habit of breaking into tears and running into the bathroom when spoken to. She evidently had some sort of personal problem that Boyd wasn't eager to learn too much about.

The other one, Boyd's boss, was a laid-back hipster from Oakland, who liked to organize extracurricular parties for CPU Central–late-night drinking bouts where she could hobnob with people who worked at *Wired*. She might have been glib, but at least she knew the limitations of her team and didn't push them as hard as she could have. She knew that her chance of escape wasn't upward through CPU Central's hierarchy, but outward, through some New Media guy she was likely to meet in a bar.

Weeks turned into months, and CPU Central continued to gobble up computer-related domains such as yourshareware.com, yourpc.com, and fastmodem.com. With every new site launch, the volume of mail increased, but Boyd's help-desk staff wasn't beefed up (they were, after all, keeping the queues clear). Every possible dollar was being pushed into Web production–armies of content coders, clerks, and hack freelance writers. And everything these new content generators did created more of a demand for support–a rising outcry from hundreds of thousands of aggrieved, needy, time-sensitive CPU Central subscribers who were eating Boyd's life up, lock, stock, and barrel.

## *Over Easy*

Boyd began to undergo a subtle shift in attitude that many NetSlaves experience when they've read more than 250,000 support e-mail headers under intense deadline pressure. The shift manifested itself in a dawning realization that it was CPU Central's users, not its management or the dead-end job he was trapped in, that were the real enemy.

So to stay on top of things, keep his sanity, and have a few hours of leisure time each night to watch television, Boyd began to cheat a bit. He'd randomly swoop into the e-mail queue, highlight a few messages, and delete them. When he saw that his coworkers didn't notice what he had done, he'd do it again.

It soon got to a point where Boyd would think nothing of zapping 1,000 e-mails in an instant. He knew this was dangerous, because sometimes important questions from CPU Central's freelancers were intermixed into the flow of mail. If one of CPU Central's fact checkers or writers was looking for a response and it happened to be cut, there might be consequences, but Boyd never got a phone call from an angry fact checker or writer asking where his or her message was.

One day, however, Boyd's block-deleting habits got him into more trouble than he bargained for. It began innocently enough. A user in Minnesota with a Windows Registry problem wrote a message to CPU Central once and never received a reply. She sent another message a week later, with the same result.

She would try a third time, but before sending in her final request for help, this woman made a solemn vow: "If those bastards don't dignify my problem with an answer, I'll bomb their sorry asses all to hell." And when a sleepy Boyd deleted this woman's final help request on a late Friday night, he had no idea that on Monday, his team would be greeted by a massive mail bomb—65,000 messages which jammed CPU Central's support queue as effectively as a gallon of bacon grease dumped in a toilet.

There was only one thing to do to get the queue moving again—delete the entire smoldering pile of 65,000 e-mails, plus any messages that happened to be intermixed in the queue. This meant that users unlucky enough to send mail during the attack would have their messages deleted as well.

"There are a lot of crazy people out there," Boyd's manager observed.

"Everybody's angry about something," Boyd responded coolly.

Boyd survived nine grueling months at CPU Central's help desk. In his few moments of free time, he pursued the malevolent mail bomber, wreaking vengeance on her every chance he got. He knew enough about her (she was a CPU Central subscriber) to get her signed up for every perverted mailing list in Webdom.

Bayoneting an enemy user brought some color back to Boyd's pallid cheeks, but he knew that life in the support queue was killing him. Its grinding routine was making him small-minded, evil, vengeful—in short, a mess. It wasn't long before revenge got old and Boyd set his sights on something better, something less evil. "If I'm going to be a writer, I've got to get closer to the content," he thought to himself.

When a job opened in Software Services, he pounced at the chance. SS was a new department thrown together to produce reviews to adorn CPU Central's recently acquired software library. It offered Boyd the chance to start his real life as a geek writer, authoring reviews of personal information managers (PIMs), HTML editors, and utility programs. After reading more than 200,000 complaints about software, Boyd figured that he'd have an edge on less qualified candidates whom CPU Central was hiring from outside. He also reasoned that writing about software would be less of a killing, monotonous treadmill to waste his life on.

Boyd was wrong on both counts. If he could have seen the future that lay ahead of him, he would have hunkered down behind his old Quadra 650 and stayed in the support queue. But Boyd, like many young NetSlaves who foolishly attempt to cross the steel-reinforced barriers of the caste system, didn't see the Silicon Ceiling until he smashed straight into it.

And so Boyd bravely printed out his résumé, marched into CPU Central's human resources department (which the company called "The People Network"), and applied for the Software Services job.

It was a mistake that Boyd would regret for the rest of his life.

## *The Grill Is Hot!*

Three years before the wretched term "portal" was coined, Hilton White knew that downloads—not content, community, or other crap— could deliver a limitless supply of hungry users to his growing network of computer-oriented Web sites. For years, the East Coast computer publishers had quietly been making a fortune on connect-time charges associated with shareware downloads on CompuTime and CyberAmerica. White wanted in on the action—it was the only way to keep CPU Central going.

Two obstacles lay in White's way: first, the fact that the online services would greedily demand a huge share of his connect-time charges, and second, that his old-line publishing enemies commanded an arsenal of PC-oriented magazines with unbeatable promotional punch. White, who didn't own a single techie magazine, faced the grim specter of having his nascent download service being overwhelmed by a blizzard of house ads that would button down his electronic blitzkrieg in a matter of weeks.

In September of 1996, White held a marathon session with his senior editors, and after 11 hours of sequestered debate, all agreed that a frontal assault was useless—they didn't have the deep pockets of their East Coast rivals. Their only chance at success was a daring act of sabotage. The editors' plan was simple: CPU Central would simply duplicate the old-line publishers' software libraries and give away the files on the Web without charge.

"The bastards don't own the shareware," White observed. "All they do is package it—what idiot user is going to pay them a nickel extra when we're giving the same stuff away for free?"

In October, CPU Central bought up a 10,000-title shareware archive based in Eastern Europe, and activated CPU Central's download department, a new entity formerly known as Software Services, but informally known as "Triple D," an acronym that CPU Central's insiders knew stood for "Doomsday Download Device."

Boyd and his fellow help-desk scum completely understood the importance of downloads to CPU Central's users, who were often whipped into a state of wild, stampeding hysteria when they learned of a new file appearing on an FTP site. DOOM was big, and so were its imitators, Dark Forces, Descent, Rise of the Triad, and other 3-D shoot-em-ups.

Boyd was eager to join up with Software Services—reviewing games sounded like fun, and the mystique surrounding Triple D made it sound like an elite team. Boyd also figured that at least half of his time would be spent twiddling a joystick through some dark 3-D environment and writing up his impressions for all the Web to see. If he was good, he might even become the Faulkner of DOOM WADs.

To get the job he coveted, Boyd knew he'd have to run a gauntlet of interviews, because CPU Central's "People Network" subjected employees seeking promotion from within to a rigorous vetting process.

Unlike people hired off the street, who rarely had to endure more than one perfunctory interview before being assigned a job, Boyd was interrogated by a gaggle of supervisors, sub-supervisors, and assistant sub-supervisors. Each of them carefully recorded notes on a clipboard whose contents were kept hidden from Boyd at all times.

Despite feeling like a protozoan under a microscope, Boyd tried to keep an earnest smile on his face during his repeated grillings. Most of the managers Boyd faced were marketing people, who attempted to conceal their ignorance about computers with bland argot about "colonizable niches" and "defensible franchises." Boyd was able to conceal the fact that he actually did know something about PCs, so he avoided rubbing these well-meaning cretins the wrong way.

Boyd's faux-happy demeanor seemed to work, although he found his meeting with Triple D's Mac shareware director, Heisler, a little frightening. Heisler eschewed the unofficial uniform of CPU Central's management: tan Dockers, blue shirt, and black loafers. About 23, hairless, and lean, Heisler favored Ninja-style clothing and spoke in a low, toneless voice, while avoiding all eye contact with Boyd throughout the interview.

Beyond these Gen-X affectations, it was Heisler's hands that really scared Boyd. They were smooth but strangely clawlike, and Heisler kept them clutched in a fixed position around something—a controller of some kind. Every 30 seconds or so, Heisler's index finger would twitch, as if he were squeezing a trigger. Heisler gave Boyd the creeps, but Boyd reasoned that Heisler might just be having a bad morning—perhaps an Ecstasy hangover induced from an all-night rave.

## *Slow Service*

Boyd would have to wait several weeks before learning whether his application had been accepted by "The People Network." The delay was exacerbated by the fact that CPU Central was thrown into chaos by a company-wide move from its dingy facility to a large, converted warehouse near Fisherman's Wharf. It took almost a week to get settled, but Boyd's support team was finally set up in a corner of the raw, open space.

The new production hall was what acoustical designers call a "highly ambient field," and Boyd was impressed by how effectively the walls of the space reinforced sounds, especially those emanating from Hilton White's office, situated at the opposite corner of the massive room.

Each morning at 10:30 sharp, all conversations in the hall would cease when White, glowering across his desk, would dress down his senior site managers, who weren't getting CPU Central's work done fast enough, or were getting it wrong. White's 100-decibel, profanity-laced tirades would last for exactly 20 minutes and then shut off, like a faucet. The last 10 minutes of these "dynamic interactions" were filled with the pitiful, whimpering excuses of White's lieutenants, who'd emerge, red-faced and sometimes in tears, to filter back into the front section of the hall.

Everyone was so terrified of White that CPU Central's staffers would often run the other way if they saw his grim visage appear in the distance. One morning, while Boyd was returning to his workstation from a trip to the soda machine, he found himself trapped at the end of a corridor, with White rapidly approaching from the other end. His only possible means of escape was to hurl himself backward through a nearby doorway, which Boyd believed to be an unlocked server closet.

Boyd was greeted by a scream from a female content clerk who was washing her hands—he had mistakenly plunged into the ladies' room.

"Sssh!" Boyd said, paralyzed with fear that White would bang on the door, demanding to know what manner of perversion was transpiring within. But White passed by—either he hadn't heard the scream or he didn't think it out of the ordinary—and Boyd, safe for the moment, apologized to the content clerk and beat a hasty retreat back to his Quadra.

Just before Christmas, Boyd received e-mail from "The People Network." His promotion had come through, and he was assigned the title "Senior Producer: PC Games," with a raise that boosted his pretax compensation to $45,000 a year.

With such a prestigious new job to get ready for, Boyd went shopping and bought some new clothes (a sky-blue shirt and some khakis) and got his hair cut. To celebrate the occasion, his roommates chipped in and got Boyd a registered copy of DOOM—all 29 levels—and Boyd happily spent most of Christmas morning blasting mutants to hell with a double-barreled shotgun.

When Boyd reported for his new job, he was surprised to learn that his job description had radically changed. Management had decided that because he had done so much time with a Quadra 650 at the help desk, he would oversee all operations functions related to Mac games shareware in addition to product management for the release of all new games.

"But what about writing? I thought I'd be doing reviews."

"Oh, don't worry," Heisler responded with a slightly sadistic smile. "You'll be doing those, too."

"Me? What about a team?"

"You're the team," Heisler responded, this time without a trace of a smile.

Boyd didn't know what to make of his job responsibilities, which more or less had him doing everything. But he accepted the position with grace—shareware was shareware, after all, and if he couldn't be the Faulkner of DOOM, he still had a chance at becoming the Hemingway of Mac PIMs and PhotoShop plug-ins. And of course, the $20K raise wasn't bad either.

It didn't take Boyd long to realize that he had really put himself in a pressure-cooker. He went from having one nearly impossible job to now having at least three. Or, in the parlance of the Internet business, he was "wearing many hats"–he was by turns a Garbageman, a Cab Driver, and a Fry Cook, whatever the moment demanded. Boyd knew damn well he wouldn't be doing any writing, but he bit the bullet and soldiered on. "It'll lead to something better," he thought to himself.

Boyd spent most of his time in Garbageman mode. All day long, he'd troll through the Macintosh software archives, meticulously sift through description files sent in by shareware authors, and process this information into CPU Central's content entry system, which used a staging server to preview content before writing it to CPU Central's public site.

To keep himself amused amid the mind-numbingly boring work, Boyd held "approval sessions" with "his team"–an imaginary group of producers he'd invented to assist him and who came to him for sign-off on completed projects.

"How's this look, boss-man?" said "Joe," a perpetually unshaved fellow with a baseball cap turned backward on his head.

"Fine with me, send it up!"

"What about this?" asked "Suzie," an ex–philosophy major, who wanted to become an actress.

"I think you missed a link at the bottom of page three."

"Oh, sorry," said the young woman, blushing slightly.

Boyd laughed to himself throughout such "interactions," which included his speaking in different voices and adopting various character traits for each of his virtual "minions." It was all in good fun, and helped keep Boyd's spirits up for the most part, although at bottom, Boyd was miserable with the workload and, in the rush to process hundreds of shareware titles each day, he began making a few small mistakes.

Given the volume of files processed and the content entry system's formal copy flow procedure, which caught errors before they were published, Boyd's editorial slips were no big deal. But Heisler, like any good micromanager, had altered the system to serve his predatory need to hassle and control his underlings. He had told the copy editors not to inform Boyd of any mistakes he'd made; instead, reports of all of Boyd's mistakes were routed directly to Heisler, who gleefully compiled a list of them. Once or twice a week, Heisler would print out a list of these mistakes and confront Boyd in a public dressing-down that would echo through the huge hall.

"YOU THINK I'M PAYING YOU ALL THIS MONEY TO PRODUCE THIS KIND OF RESULT?!" Heisler would scream to Boyd and the surrounding multitudes. "What are you, some kind of incompetent moron? Do you have any idea of what the public is going to think of us if errors like this get through the system? . . . DO YOU?"

## *Fried*

As the months passed, and winter turned to spring, Heisler's in-your-face malevolence wore terribly on Boyd, filling him with dread each morning and soaking his innards with adrenaline throughout the workday. Heisler had clearly based his persona on White's—a phenomenon that many NetSlaves encounter in personality-driven New Media startups, where character traits flow downward and become reinforced as they propagate throughout the organization.

In CPU Central's psychological environment, emotional fascism was a mark that "you got it," or, as one of Boyd's coworkers put it, "You are who you eat for lunch." But Heisler on his own wasn't destroying Boyd—it was CPU Central's meeting schedule, on top of the workload, that was grinding him to a pulp. Now that Boyd was "management," he was required to attend a nearly endless series of meetings and still meet his informal quota of 60 software titles per day. Formally scheduled meetings included a Monday morning production meeting, a Wednesday update meeting, and a Friday content meeting, plus the inevitable ad hoc meetings required to tackle unexpected crises that sprang up during the week.

Because the shareware database was constantly being reorganized, reclassified, and reindexed and the content creation software was constantly being updated, Boyd soon was logging 25 hours a week in these meetings. He rarely left the building before 10 p.m.—sometimes as late as 1 a.m. One night on the cable car, Boyd figured out how much he was making, given all the unreimbursed time he was putting in, and it came out to less than $7.50 per hour, before taxes—about the same that he'd be making flipping burgers at Wendy's.

Like many Fry Cooks cursed with sadistic micromanagers, sentenced to endless meetings, and saddled with impossible-to-meet production quotas, Boyd began to fantasize about killing his boss. Too weary to go out at night and too poor to drink at one of San Francisco's trendy bars, Boyd would buy a six-pack of Schmidt's on the way home from work on Friday, fire up DOOM, and release tension by spraying indiscriminate gunfire across the game's subterranean expanses.

DOOM's ghoulish mutants already looked a little like Heisler, but Boyd went out of his way to make the game's ugly gang of evildoers even more realistic. He swiped a picture of Heisler from the lunchroom, scanned in the photo, and substituted it for one of the monster's faces, using some shareware utilities he found on a DOOM site. He even doctored up some of DOOM's levels, so that they more closely resembled CPU Central's warehouse space.

Some nights Boyd would decapitate Heisler with a chain saw, blow his head off with a shotgun, riddle his torso with a Gatling gun, and beat him to death with his bare fists. Other nights he would tease Heisler into standing near a radioactive barrel and explode the barrel with a single pistol blast, splashing Heisler's guts across the marble floor.

His favorite trick was to assign Heisler's face to every monster in the game and let them all charge at him in a fury. Boyd would race to the end of the production hall, charge up DOOM's BFG ("big fucking gun"), and kill everything in the room in one single blast. To a psychiatrist, all of this might have seemed a bit sick, but Boyd reasoned that as long as he could kill Heisler safely at home, he'd be less likely to choke him to death in CPU Central's real-life production hall.

People who knew Boyd could tell he was on the verge of losing it. His roommates, who rarely saw him anymore, tried to get him to slow down, but he didn't hear them. He was too caught up in work or thinking about work to see what he was doing to himself. The deep blue circles under his eyes and his more-pallid-than-usual complexion were his stigmata from a job well done. Heisler may have thought Boyd was an ass, but Boyd's achievements since entering Software Services were undeniable: he had kept the games shareware area running smoothly and had successfully launched 33 games—a figure which amounted to a game a week since he had ascended to the dubious position of product manager.

Boyd was too tired and too hazy to take pride in his achievements, nor did he know that, for all he had done, he was about to face his biggest challenge.

## *Last Supper*

One morning in early July, Triple D held an emergency meeting to prepare the group for its response to the biggest news in the gaming world: ID software's long-awaited release of Quake, the successor to DOOM.

Hilton White addressed the group in person and announced that CPU Central had arranged for an exclusive on ID's 9-MB file. Having a "shareware exclusive" meant that ID would embargo distribution of the file for 24 hours, having named CPU Central as the exclusive source of this highly desirable file. In exchange, the software vendor would receive an enormous amount of publicity, editorial coverage, and other promotion across all of CPU Central's sites.

For White, having an exclusive meant being able to rack up millions of hits—and thousands of dollars—within a few hours, as long as CPU Central's FTP servers could withstand the strain. In a hastily drawn-up plan, server space was "borrowed" from underutilized machines, extra bandwidth was leased from CPU Central's ISP, and a small team was assigned the role of being in place to respond as soon as ID finished coding its masterpiece, which, according to early reports, would be the most ultraviolent and most popular computer game in the history of humanity.

Boyd, much to his surprise, was picked to head up the team. He was handed a sealed packet containing instructions, a phone list, a beeper, and an envelope of remote access software diskettes. ID's download was supposed to be ready the evening of July 10, but might be released later—perhaps on Saturday the 11th, or even on Sunday the 12th.

Because ID's programmers (who were rumored never to sleep) were still actively coding and debugging Quake, it was impossible to predict exactly when the game would be released. But when it was, CPU Central had to have the download with the minimal possible delay, in order to reap the full benefit of the 24-hour exclusive.

Boyd was especially surprised that CPU Central had issued him a remote access software pack, given the company's long-standing hostility to telecommuting. White had apparently ordered that a temporary exception be made for the Quake team. He was paranoid about the download coming through at 6 a.m. on a Sunday, when even a workaholic maniac like himself was unlikely to be in the production hall.

All Friday night the Quake team waited, going about their mindless content processing, while at the same time they remained logged onto ID's FTP site to check its status. Boyd stayed until midnight, then raced home. He was caught in an unexpected thundershower at the cable car stop, but made it back by 1 a.m., and logged in using his home machine. There was no file.

On Saturday, Boyd didn't eat anything at all—he couldn't even call out for food, because he had to keep his Net connection open, constantly monitoring the site. All day he waited, and far into the night, but again, no file appeared.

Finally, at 4 a.m. on Sunday, a 9-MB file suddenly appeared in Boyd's FTP client window. Boyd brought it across to CPU Central staging servers, checked it for viruses, and pushed it out to the public area. He e-mailed everyone in the group, frantically coded up some prefab promotional copy, and coded in the links. Banner GIFs were pushed out, server-side includes were coded in, and CPU Central's subscriber list was spammed with the news: "QUAKE IS HERE: COME AND GET IT!"

By 9 a.m. Sunday, Boyd had finished his work and fell over from exhaustion on his mat, with his PC still on. He awoke 12 hours later, with a high fever and a terrible headache. "God," he said, "what's wrong with me now?" He crammed two aspirin tablets into his mouth, and washed them down with some lemonade from the fridge, but he felt so weak that he could hardly stand up.

Boyd fell back on his mat, but couldn't fall asleep. Instead, he entered a nightmarish swoon filled with grisly, 3-D images of monsters surrounding his bed, Heisler's face swirling around in a cloud, and shotgun blasts going off in all directions in CPU Central's conference room.

By 8 a.m. Monday, Boyd felt even worse, and knew he wouldn't be able to trudge into CPU Central. He could barely speak on the phone, and when he called Heisler at 9:30, every word from his mouth was laced with pain.

"I ... don't ... think ... I'm well enough to make it ..."

Heisler interrupted: "What the hell is the matter with you? Did you know that one of the links you coded—the one to Yournews's Quake editorial—is broken? I've just heard from White. Do you know what he said to me? Do you know what this means? Do you have a clue?"

With stammered, strained speech, Boyd spoke into the phone in a flat, toneless voice that surprised him with its clarity. "Heisler," Boyd uttered, "fuck you—I quit."

Boyd put the phone down in its cradle. He wanted to sleep again, to drift away from White, CPU Central, and Heisler's murderous micromanagement, which had reduced his life to a dark, sleazy, panic-ridden hell. But he slapped himself in the face, and with the last of his strength, turned his PC on again.

Realizing that he had precious few moments to do what he had to do, Boyd activated his remote access software and reached into his workstation across town. He could see Heisler in his mind—Heisler approaching, Heisler reaching to pull out the modem cord, Heisler trying to stop him from nuking everything on his hard drive—every piece of contact information, every software review he had written that hadn't yet staged, a year's worth of work, documentation, and other intelligence that Boyd had accumulated while slaving away at CPU.

Boyd worked quickly. He formatted C:\, and when he was finished, he stopped. He thought for a moment about formatting the hard drives of all of CPU Central's servers, but he stopped short of doing so. In that moment, he found out what it was that made him different from Heisler, White, and the others. He might have been a NetSlave, a loser, a man with no power or future in the Internet business. But he was no NetAsshole.

Boyd went down to CPU Central's offices on Friday—the first day he felt well enough to walk. They gave him a paycheck for two weeks' work: $867.56. He used part of the money to get drunk—and he stayed drunk for most of the weekend.

## *Epilogue*

Within a month, Boyd left San Francisco and headed back to Phoenix, where he took a room near the abandoned computer mail-order warehouses he had grown up staring at. Boyd didn't know exactly what he was going to do to keep a roof over his head, but he hoped that his computer expertise might land him a sane, sensible job that wouldn't drive him crazy. A few months passed; his savings dwindled to a dangerously low level.

Late one Saturday night, fearing destitution, while desperately going through the early edition of the Sunday paper, Boyd spotted something right up his alley: a listing for a clerk's position at an all-night porn store.

Ignoring the irony of taking the same job he had left for the promises of the Internet, Boyd sent his résumé, went in for a quick interview, and was hired on the spot. The job paid $18,000 a year, with benefits, and it was strictly midnight to 8. There was room for advancement—word was that the owner was going to be launching a Web site soon and needed some help setting it up. Best of all, Boyd would be able to do something which he hadn't done during his entire time at CPU Central—*write!* With the flexibility of his schedule, he could pursue the Muse on weekends, during the daytime, and maybe even on the job when business was slow.

It wasn't heaven, but it sure wasn't hell. Boyd might just catch up to Bukowski yet.

# LEVEL 7.0

# Gold Diggers and Gigolos

## Sex, Lies, and Hypertext

## 7.1 Who Are They?

Steve and I opened our closets and picked out our "hippest" clothes–a pair of black jeans and some OS/2 developer's T-shirts we had gotten free at Comdex a million years ago. We wanted to look our best because we were about to step out with the movers and shakers of the New Media Caste System's hard-partying, nightcrawling set.

We proceeded to a series of bars that a puffy NYC e-newsletter had ranked "Best Places to Meet Venture Capitalists." Perhaps we were expecting too much, but the bars turned out to be nothing more than a bunch of pseudo-gentrified East Village dives that sold cigars and strange, bluish drinks that looked like *Star Trek*-inspired martinis. Steve and I had already taken enough chances with the violence-prone Fry Cooks and Cab Drivers, so in greasing the conversational gears, we decided to stick with the tried-and-true–beer, the "official" NetSlaves elixir.

As the evening progressed, we weren't having much luck with the biz dev dealmakers, CPM salesmen, and miscellaneous schmoozers that constitute this caste. We didn't just get the cold shoulder, we got the no-shoulder. Our less-than-friendly reception was probably due to our shabby threads and our pallid complexions that had "these guys don't have time-shares in the Hamptons" written all over them.

But we weren't about to let these shallow, press-the-flesh types get us down. We jumped from bar to bar, drinking as much high-priced lager as we could stand ("What? No Schlitz?") and sometime around 3 a.m., when we were sure that the Gold Diggers and Gigolos were intoxicated enough to believe anything, we decided to pull a little trick that would hopefully get us an in. We began passing ourselves off as two easily exploited lower-caste NetSlaves with a killer idea–a concept that really wasn't too far from the truth.

In any case, our ruse worked big-time. We were soon drowning in a sea of slurred buzzwords like "brand equity" and "vertical strategy." It was all gibberish to us, but it got the Gold Diggers and Gigolos talking and allowed us to reveal our true purpose to the incredibly drunk and/or desperate. What follows is but a small excerpt of the reams of material we gathered–material which would have been enough for a separate tell-all tome that would probably read like the Web equivalent of the *Red Shoe Diaries*.

*Warning:* If you have children, please ask them to leave the room. You are about to read some steamy stuff, which, in addition to having inherent prurient entertainment value, should hopefully give you an idea of the depths to which many people sink in prospecting for IPO gold.

## 7.2 General Characteristics

*Where they can be found:* Not a night goes by that these cyber-social butterflies aren't off at some tony industry event, launch party, or awards ceremony, having a good ol' time on their expense accounts. While it might seem downright unfair that Gold Diggers and Gigolos are able to have so much fun while their grunt-level colleagues (Garbagemen, Fry Cooks) are back at the office logging their 32nd consecutive hour, the truth of the matter is that it's not what you do that counts, it's what your manager thinks you do.

*Other habitats:* The CEO's bed, the COO's bed, the CFO's bed, and so on.

*Average hours worked per week:* 25. Because of their busy nightlife, Gold Diggers and Gigolos put in the bare minimum during normal business hours. They usually arrive at 10:30 or 11, shoot off a few quick e-mails to the more influential people they met the previous evening before heading out the door to a power lunch. Come 5:30, you will be sure to find them pressing the "down" button on the elevator.

*Gender:* Female *and* male. Unlike more traditional, male-dominated industries, the Web biz has a good share of companies where estrogen is the ruling hormone, from the CEO on down, and the young, good-looking, outgoing Gigolo can advance very quickly, provided, of course, that he has the "bandwidth" to satisfy the "right" customers.

*Average age:* 15 (in Buffy-the-Vampire Time).

*Average salary:* $90K (plus "performance" bonus).

*Number of jobs held in the past three years:* 50.3. Gold Diggers and Gigolos are wherever the party is, literally and figuratively. Shifting companies is as natural to them as changing sexual partners or shoes. The first sign that their sexually induced promotion or sales commission isn't coming through will find them calling their contact over at "thenextbigthing.com."

*Mode of dress:* *Friends* hair-dos (Gold Diggers); tan Dockers, Macanudos (Gigolos).

*Current technical fetishes:* None. Gold Diggers and Gigolos can barely work their scheduling software, much less distinguish a line of C++ from a vermicelli noodle.

*Favorite at-home activities:* None. Gold Diggers and Gigolos are only home long enough to perform image maintenance: showering, changing, sleeping a few hours before heading out again.

*Romantic attachments:* None. This highly sexed caste of NetSlaves is spread too thin and is too busy to commit to anyone except themselves. (Translation: You're better off without them, even if they do have a point about your, like, need to go clothes shopping.)

*Psychological profile:* Freud would have a party of his own trying to unravel these people. But forgetting the fancy-pants stuff, fellow NetSlaves should remember that with their ties to the powers that be, Gold Diggers and Gigolos could send you to the unemployment office quicker than an IP packet hitting the proxy server.

*Career aspirations:* All the trappings of success (wealth, fame) without having to work too hard to obtain them. Some will soar to the highest heights; the meteoric career paths of the rest will fizzle out in the gutter of traditional advertising and PR agencies.

## 7.3 The Story of Kellner

*Kellner had an idea which would make him the King of the Web Revolution. And when he met a shapely ad exec named Mira, he thought he had found his Queen. But what Kellner didn't know is that, in addition to being smart and beautiful, Mira was also dangerous, very dangerous. A word to all would-be royalty out there: Sex and ambition don't mix.*

Kellner stared out the greasy window of the 7 Train in a daze. He was tired from a long day of pounding the pavement and was on the verge of falling asleep, when two teenagers approached him out of nowhere.

"Hey, mister, you got any change?" one of them asked.

Kellner tried making a joke of the situation. "No, but do you have any change for me? I'm out of work."

The teenager who asked the question nodded his head and the second reached into his pocket. Kellner, who was still a bit sleepy, was suddenly roused to a state of panic at the sight of a .22-caliber pistol pointed directly at his head. The teenager holding the gun said nothing, while the other continued.

"Yo, I'm not asking you for money—I'm telling you. This here is a robbery."

Kellner's face went completely white. He dug into his right pants pocket and quickly handed his wallet to the teenager doing the talking—there wasn't much money in it and the credit cards were all maxed out, but he didn't want to take any chances.

"This," he stammered, "this is all I've got."

The teenager eyed him for a long, frozen moment. Kellner closed his eyes, bracing himself for the worst. A full 30 seconds of pure terror passed before Kellner summoned up the courage to open one of his lids ever so slightly. To his relief, the teenagers had disappeared.

Kellner sat very still in his seat. He didn't know if the teenagers had gone to another car or had gotten off the train. Ten minutes later, with no sight of the pair, he assumed that they had beat it somewhere around Elmhurst Avenue. Kellner let out a deep sigh and began looking for a cop. Never around when you need one, he griped to himself.

When the train pulled into his stop in Flushing, Kellner was still a bit shaky, but his heart had stopped pounding and most of the color had returned to his face. Kellner walked slowly out of the train, lost in thought.

Kellner's indifference was understandable: parting with a few bucks at gunpoint was nothing compared to what he had already lost.

## Vamping

It all began three months ago at the Kewl Universe Awards, a glitzy Web site awards event held at Webster Hall, a nightclub that Kellner knew well from his days as a music video producer. Kellner, at 35, was sick and tired of scripting idiotic music videos for lip-synching no-talents from the Bronx. In truth, he was souring on the industry altogether. As a guitar player friend of his noted, "Music's just wallpaper today: the scene is dead." Kellner's friend was right–rock had died and had buried itself in L.A., and Seattle's gloomy grunge was just a rehash of the garage band sound, another dead form.

For months now, everyone in New York's show business scene had been talking about "interactivity" in the same hushed, reverential tones they'd once reserved for Patti Smith, and Kellner jumped on the bandwagon by buying a PowerBook, opening a Cyber-America account, and trying to get up to speed. He'd even launched a small site of his own, but it was pretty pathetic–just a résumé containing his video and record credentials, and a phone number that nobody ever called.

Nothing Kellner saw on the Web knocked him out. It was a freak show of wannabes–one big demo for people who lacked the talent to score a major deal. But Kellner also suspected that things were moving fast, and maybe jumping in deeper wasn't such a bad idea after all. So he read some *Dummies* books, got a subscription to *Interactive Week*, and began soaking up the buzzwords. By early 1996, he felt ready to take the plunge, but there was a missing piece in the puzzle, and Kellner needed to find it soon or he'd be left behind by the interactive tsunami.

Webster Hall's bar was dark and crowded. A few pinhole spotlights in the ceiling cast small circles of light across the crew-cut heads of men shouting drink orders across the bar. But then suddenly, there was something moving in one of those halos–the naked shoulder of a woman. Kellner's eyes fixed on it and followed the sinuous curve of the woman's spine down to the base of her backless dress. When a crew-cut moved away, Kellner saw her face reflected in the mirror. It was a face that needed no retouching. Kellner moved in, thinking of a good opening line.

"You from the West Coast?" he asked her casually.

"What makes you think that?" she shot back.

"It's just that there seem to be a lot of California people here," he said, nodding in the direction of the crowd. "I don't think I'd call this a New York event."

"What would you call it?" She smiled conspiratorially, lowering her voice.

"A bunch of nobodies looking for a big score."

She smiled again, which made Kellner think he was getting somewhere. He was.

Kellner and Mira could have taken a cab to his loft, but instead they walked together down Lafayette Street toward SoHo. Mira, as it turned out, was an account executive for an ad agency—one of the big ones, Dennis Burnham Lanker and Young. Kellner joked about recording jingles for DBLY years ago and how none of them ever made it onto the radio. Mira laughed and asked him what he thought of the Internet, about where it was all going. Kellner waxed poetic—he had pegged her as a word bird from the start.

"It's a medium that defies conventional programming because its users are the ones programming it. It's radically unlike radio, or TV, or text, or anything we've ever seen before. It's so new that nobody's going to be able to put it into a box—not yet. But the guy who figures out how to put it into a box will become the richest bastard in the world."

## *The Goddess of Interactivity*

They made love for an hour at Kellner's loft, but Mira didn't want to relax after he'd finally taken his pleasure with her. She was tense and told him that some coffee might calm her down, so he obliged by putting on a bathrobe, shuffling into the kitchen, and loading up the Melitta with Bustelo. As the coffee was brewing, he rolled a big joint out of the film can he kept in the freezer. When he carried the coffee tray into the main room she was standing at his CD collection, wearing one of his dress shirts.

"You smoke?"

"When I feel safe, yes."

They settled around the low coffee table that was in the center of the loft's vast living area. It was the only recognizable piece of furniture in the room, other than a battered couch and a couple of director's chairs. They sat Zen-style and talked, mostly about Kewl Universe— how it was a shame and a scandal that the best Web sites were little more than one-dimensional, cartoon-like caricatures of what Mira called "rich media." Kellner said that maybe New York deserved to lose the electronic culture wars to California because of its "hubristic ego." Mira disagreed—in her view, "New York hadn't even woken up yet." They talked about everything, it seemed, except each other, and that was fine with Kellner, because what Mira said was turning him on.

"I have this feeling about you—you're not like all the geeks stumbling around trying to find themselves, or each other, or this medium—you seem to know who you are," Mira said wistfully, taking a long drag from the joint.

"I'm a freelance music video producer."

"And you're doing nothing now?"

"I live on my royalties. I'm a man of modest tastes," Kellner lied.

"But you understand show business. You've made it already—you don't need to climb over bodies to get to the top. You're an idea man, and you can see how small all this bullshit interactive dorm-room Web shit really is—it's a pitiful little wasteland."

"It's growing."

"I'd like to really do something," she said, finally passing the joint to Kellner.

"Something like what?"

"Real entertainment—what the masses really want."

"You're a real goddess of interactivity, aren't you?" he joked, and then realized he might have offended her. "I'm sorry. I just don't know what you're talking about. How do you know that the masses on the Internet aren't perfectly happy with what they have now?"

"I don't," she said, but Kellner knew she was lying—she'd cut him off after his crude remark. Mira got up, walked into the bedroom, and gathered up her clothes from the various places they'd been tossed. He followed her in, helped her find a missing shoe, and watched her dress.

"Where can I reach you?"

"Call DBLY's main desk and ask for Mira Racinek," she said, making her way toward the door.

Kellner went down the stairs with her and even walked her to the corner, where she got a cab uptown. Kellner stood waving at her as the cab pulled away. It had been a very good night. He had gotten laid—and made progress on his Web career. Not bad for a music guy down on his luck.

## *Planning the Score*

Kellner called Mira on Monday morning. She spoke rapid-fire into the receiver, as if she was juggling a lot of priorities. Kellner sensed this and let her go, but not before Mira insisted on another meeting, the next night, sometime after work. She buzzed the front door around 8:30, and Kellner flicked the Melitta to "brew" before he hit the electrically controlled downstairs lock that let her in.

"It's all about 18-to-35 males," she said, gulping at the cup.

"Careful, that's hot!"

"They're disappearing. Defecting. Out-of-network. Gone!" she said.

"Yeah, well, they're online now. You've got to program for that, I guess."

"But it's not television—you said so yourself. The users program it."

"Maybe I was wrong—maybe it's TV. You know, WebTV is going to be coming in very soon—I read it in *Billboard*. This early-adopter stuff—the pointers and clickers—they'll be history by 1999. The whole thing is going high-bandwidth—it'll be just like TV with more channels. You'll just have an 'interact' button on your remote, so you can talk back to Oprah, or L.L. Cool J, or whoever."

Mira grinned, "You know, I wish I could get you into the agency, so you could talk to my boss. I can't tell you how many of our clients are asking us about this Web stuff."

"What the hell do I know about it?" he asked, with feigned modesty.

"More than they do. The only one who has a computer in the office is Julian. And you've done jingles, Kellner—you know what grabs people, what motivates them."

This really put him on his high horse. "I only know that every medium that comes along absorbs all media that came before," he began. "Radio absorbed newspapers and the telegraph, television absorbed radio, and now the Web, which is sucking everything in. The irony is that the actual programming doesn't change much. You remember *Dragnet*? It started out as a radio show. The same thing with Westerns, soap operas, and quiz shows—they all began on radio. If Dickens were alive today, he'd be..."

"Hold it!" Mira said, excitedly. "Hit 'pause' on that!"

"On what, *Dragnet*?"

"No, on soap operas!"

Kellner now knew what she was driving at. "If you're thinking of a Web-based soap opera, you're out of your mind," he said.

"Why not?"

"I can think of a million reasons why not. I mean, soap operas were designed for bored women stuck at home with ironing boards. Why would men—your 18-to-35s—want to watch a soap opera?"

"Because I could sell that idea," Mira said.
"You could sell it to who?"
"Nike, Stolichnaya, Bayer, Listerine—any one of them. You're a genius, Kellner. My clients don't know beans about the Internet, but they do know about soap operas."
"Maybe you could sell it, but I'd do it way different—this isn't a medium for housewives—not yet, anyway. The Net is full of risqué stuff—porn and all. For a soap to work online, you'd have to play up the sex and skin, big-time, maybe put it in some ultracool place. Lots of women—kind of like *Baywatch*—but with more drugs and intrigue, betrayal, a few murders."
"Can you write me a pilot?"
"I'm a good conceptualizer, but I'm not much of a writer," Kellner said, before sealing a new joint with his lips.
"I know a good writer—Julian, at the office. The agency has the poor guy writing travel brochures, but he's itching to do something more creative. He wants to be a screenwriter."
"All right," Kellner said. "Fire that thing up, and I'll tell you what I think this thing needs to fly."

## *SoHo Nights*

Kellner's first concept for an episodic Web site was loosely based on *Saturday Night Fever*, the last movie he'd seen that had really made an impression on him. But instead of basing it on a blue-collar hardware store worker in Bay Ridge, *SoHo Nights'* lead character was a 20-something graffiti artist who was a cross between Keith Haring and Jean-Michel Basquiat. The artist's quest to conquer Manhattan's elite art world was continually being thwarted by indifferent gallery owners, transit cops, greedy landlords, and constant drop-ins from groupies seeking a moment of his time.

Mira didn't like it—it was "too '80s."

To be more '90s, Kellner came up with a second treatment, which was to base *SoHo Nights* around the mythical misadventures of a small startup Web company whose quest to conquer Manhattan's elite design community was constantly being thwarted by flaky Javascript, erratic servers, and slow-loading pages.

"It doesn't have the ring of truth," Mira said. "Besides, the characters never seem to leave their computers."

Kellner's third and final treatment called for the soap to be based on a greedy bunch of predators working in a chic downtown Manhattan advertising agency, who waste millions of dollars of their clients' money diddling around with silly interactive experiments.

"It's very '50s," Mira said, "but I like it—very biting. The '50s are in now. I can probably sell this, if you tone it down a bit."

"Can we have sex now?" Kellner asked impatiently.

"That's all I think about," Mira lied.

## *The Bait*

Kellner didn't hear from Mira for a week, but when she did call, she gave him some good news.

"They're interested, Kellner—I can tell they are."

"Oh come on, Mira. Don't jerk me around."

"I mean it. My boss thinks an episodic Web drama is a wonderful idea."

"It's so damn self-referential—the whole ad agency thing—it's like a song about the music business."

"That's what they like—it's very $8\frac{1}{2}$. But they need a treatment—a sample episode—before they'll commit any development money."

"I told you—I'm not a writer."

"Don't worry about a thing. I've got Julian all geared up about this. You've got to meet him—can I bring him by tonight? He's dying to meet you."

"Bring him over," Kellner said. He didn't like the idea of bringing an outsider into something which by rights belonged to himself and Mira, but if that's how the game was played, he'd play it.

Julian was a few years younger than Kellner—his face was pink, which led Kellner to believe he suffered from hypertension, a skin allergy, or a drinking problem. He spoke with a slight Connecticut accent that Kellner believed was probably an affectation.

"I still don't get a strong interactive feel," Julian said, unfolding his ThinkPad on the low coffee table. "You've got all of these people working to undercut each other—but where does the user come in?"

"Well, maybe the user can warn, say, Janice, that Rachel is trying to steal her account from her. If enough users send her enough e-mail, maybe she'll realize she's being set up, and lash back at Rachel. We could set up a CGI form so that users could vote. You know: (1) Attack Rachel in the ladies room, or (2) Spread lies about her to client A through Z—that kind of thing."

"It seems really silly," Julian said. "I'm not sure I can write that silly."

"I don't think we need to get too elaborate for the pilot," Mira interrupted. "Can't we just start out with some diary entries to get a sense of who these people are?"

"I've already done one," Julian said. "This one's for Janice–the account exec: 'August 15, 1996: Saturday morning–feeling bad–hungover from the gin I was drinking with Steve, from Metro Motors.' We can hyperlink both 'Steve', who's a bad guy, and 'Metro Motors', that's a fake company," said Julian.

"It could also be a link to a real company, if the guy happened to be a good guy," Mira added.

"You're thinking of adding a lot of product placement to this?" asked Kellner.

"Yes. 'Jane got into her Lexus with a bottle of Cutty Sark in her hand'–that kind of thing."

"Go on," Kellner said.

" 'Why did God sentence me to pay $2,000 a month to live underneath a performance artist who uses a trampoline as his oeuvre, instead of a nice quiet minimalist painter? Am I wrong to be pissed when tourists gawk at me–what am I, a freak for living here? Sometimes I fantasize that I'm a Palestinian terrorist, so that I could blow up the Holland Tunnel, and keep those damned Long Island tour buses away from West Broadway forever.' "

"I guess that's witty enough," said Kellner.

"It's not supposed to be witty. It's supposed to be stupid," Julian shot back defensively. "See, she wants to blow up the wrong tunnel."

"We can always change it later," Kellner observed.

Julian's treatment was, in Kellner's estimation, pretty lousy literature. But it captured the flavor of *SoHo Nights'* pea-brained clique of 20-somethings clearly enough, and its product placement angle gave it what Julian called "embedded sponsorship potential." Only one of the characters–Rachel–was at all likable, but that was the whole idea–to play on the voyeurism, and also the sadism, of the Net's audience. *SoHo Nights* was predicated on the idea that New Media people would like nothing better than to see "Old Media" people suffer in their $300,000 lofts, develop terrible chemical addictions, and tear each other to shreds whenever they went to work.

Kellner spent the next day setting up a Web site for *SoHo Nights*, using the services of a small ISP on Broadway. He paid them an extra $500 to slap together a basic design–just a home page, individual character pages with space for diary entries, and an "about" page. He made sure the site was built to accommodate banner ads, and sprang for the ISP's extra-fare group e-mail program, which let him specify individual e-mail addresses for all the characters. It took about a week to get done, but Kellner was happy with the ISP's design: it was a very simple layout with few graphical flourishes that would serve as a good proof-of-concept for Mira to show to her masters.

"Well, they really really like it," Mira said on Friday, "but they want to see more. Not more content—just a better sense of what the final site will be. I took down some notes. First off, there's too much text—it's hard to read, and it would be nice if people could see what the characters actually look like."

"What did they think of Julian's shitty writing?"

"They were OK with that—they just want something with more visuals that's more TV-like. So when Rachel goes into the file room and finds Jeff lying there drunk, they'd like to see at least a few shots suggesting what she's looking at."

"This is getting expensive," Kellner complained. "Figure 4, maybe 5 photos per story, times 6: that's 24 shots an episode. I figure that's at least a grand a week just for photography."

"We can probably do it cheap with a couple of Apple Quicktakes."

"Yeah, but how about the actors?"

"Get them off the street."

"Sure, but we still have to pay them something. Even nonunion people will run us, say, a thousand dollars a week."

"Look," Mira said, "why don't you go figure out what this is going to cost us to do and mark it up by 100 percent. I'll submit that as our budget."

"Fine, but am I still producing the demo out of pocket?"

"Can you take a risk?"

"I don't like doing deals on spec."

"Just this once?"

"For you baby, sure."

"For us, baby," Mira cooed, kissing him gently on the neck. "Oh, and one more thing. Nobody at the agency is to know that Julian and I are doing this for you. It might look like a conflict of interest."

"My lips are sealed."

## Casting Call

Kellner spent $3,500 on the first full-blown episode of *SoHo Nights*. His biggest hassle was actors. Finding the males wasn't a big problem—

frankly, it didn't matter what they looked like. Kellner hired the first three men who responded to his *Village Voice* ad. But the females were more problematic–Julian's character sketches called for two to be "beautiful, thin, and drop-dead evil." Mira looked the part, but didn't want to appear in the show for obvious reasons and Kellner wasn't happy with the women who responded to the ad.

"They're beautiful *or* they're evil–but not both," he explained to Mira. "But I'm not through looking yet."

Kellner put up posters at the New School, the HB Acting School, and the American Academy of Dramatic Arts. He came up with two hawk-faced brunettes whose barely repressed hostility qualified them to play Janice and Christine, the evil account execs.

But he still had a problem casting Rachel–"the beautiful, slightly neurotic 20-something whose hometown morality is constantly at odds with the demands of the big city workplace." Kellner figured that he needed a blonde to play the part, but wasn't satisfied with the blondes he'd seen; they seemed to him to be either totally neurotic or completely amoral.

"I'm hung up. Stuck. Ready to slit my wrists," Kellner complained to Mira. "I need a blonde."

"I've got one for you."

"Who? Where?"

"Her name is Dale. She works right here–I can bring her down tonight. She's just off the boat–Iowa, I think. Completely innocent creature. She'd be great as Rachel."

Kellner met Dale that night, but wasn't impressed. She was young and pretty, and seemed innocent enough. But she also seemed to Kellner to be holding back something–a cipher who wasn't very good at expressing her true feelings.

"But that's exactly what we need," Mira said. "The lead character is supposed to be an outsider–someone new in New York–innocent enough to be hurt, but grounded enough to hurt back when it's necessary."

"Yeah, I guess," Kellner said.

## *Shooting*

With the cast in place, Kellner mocked up the storyboards from Julian's notes and scheduled the first cast meeting for a Saturday morning in his loft. Julian and Mira were on hand to answer questions the actors had about motivation, and Kellner wasted an hour trying to videotape them interacting in a simulated storyboard meeting. It was a chaotic, frustrating scene, because the actors were preoccupied with finding their characters, even though the script just called for them to pose and shut up. Kellner vowed never again to bring this talky, egotistic bunch of losers together in one room again—he'd much rather PhotoShop them in one by one, even if the end results didn't quite look right.

On Monday, using one of two Apple Quicktakes he'd bought, Kellner began shooting the first storyboard, which illustrated Janice's grim, bar-hopping life in SoHo. He did a few shots of her in an art gallery and outside a clothing boutique, and posed her at the Spring Street subway station, where they were both accosted by a homeless man. Kellner snapped a photo of the man—it was just the kind of lucky break that lent atmosphere to the drama, but when the man angrily demanded payment for the shot, they were forced to beat a hasty retreat to street level.

By Friday, after shooting four other characters, Kellner was frazzled and exhausted from filming scenes in alleys, offices, galleries, and his own loft, and from the pressure of doing all the work himself. And since it was also ridiculous trying to do everything on his PowerBook, he bit the bullet and bought a $5,000, fully loaded Quadra 800. It was a lot of money, but at least PhotoShop would run acceptably.

Kellner spent most of the afternoon setting the machine up and prepared for the afternoon's work. He had only one last storyboard to shoot: the one that depicted Rachel's lonely, tortured existence. Like the asshole writer that he was, Julian had scripted it as a montage: Rachel painting a picture, Rachel at a tobacco bar, Rachel at a nightclub, and Rachel on a rooftop, staring out at the beckoning lights of the uptown world.

"There's no way any of that's going to come out on the Quicktake," Kellner groused in a voice mail to Julian. "It's just too grainy."

Kellner rewrote the script so that he could shoot Rachel under a few spot lamps in his loft when she came by after work. He caught Dale washing dishes in his sink, reading *Details* on his couch, and putting a CD into his hi-fi system. Then he did a few shots of her clicking away at his PowerBook. Finally, he shot her pretending to sleep in his bed for Julian's obligatory "waking up with a hangover" shot.

"That will probably do it," Kellner said, when he'd transferred the last images across to his Quadra at 2 a.m. "You can go home now."

But Dale didn't seem to be in much of a hurry to leave. She had wandered over to the window and was looking down at the street. With her back turned, she looked beautiful, and when she turned around to face him, Kellner suddenly realized that he had to have this woman.

"So what do you want to be in real life?" Kellner asked her flirtatiously.

"I've been thinking about getting into Web design," she responded, picking up on his vibe immediately.

"Do you know PhotoShop?"

"Yes," she said. "I've got a site up."

"Show me," he said, beckoning her over to the Quadra.

She was his before they had seen half the JPEGs on her site.

Kellner woke Dale up around 9 a.m.—he hated to kick her out, but couldn't bear the distraction of having her around, because he had too much work to do. He needed to finalize the graphics and FTP all the files to the server.

"Why don't you let me do some of the work for you," she offered.

"I'll give you $20 an hour, but don't mess it up," Kellner said.

By Sunday night, the full-blown demo was online. Dale was pretty adept at handling graphics, the most time-consuming chore in the production process. He asked her if she couldn't stop in two nights a week, to keep the files moving. She agreed, so he made copies of his loft keys for her and gave her his boot password. They kissed, and she went home.

On Monday, Mira reran her pitch. This time, the agency bought it, and Mira called with the fabulous news that DBLY was drafting a letter of intent to Kellner for eight weekly shows. At a fee of $7,000 per episode, it was right in line with Mira's 100 percent markup estimate—a grand total of $56,000 for two months' work.

"When do I see some money?" Kellner asked.

"When we execute. You get half down, the rest on completion."

"When do they need the next installment?"

"By launch time: three weeks."

"Does that mean we have to throw a launch party?"

"Leave that to me," Mira said gleefully. "Don't worry—I'll keep it under $2,000."

## Let's Do Launch

It now occurred to Kellner that he was moving into dangerous territory—both Mira and Julian were doing an end run around the agency's ethical guidelines, and not one of them had a contract with the other. Kellner knew all too well from the music business that today's handshake deal could easily become tomorrow's knife in the back, but he'd never done a Web development deal like this before, where things moved so quickly, with so much cash looming over the horizon.

Kellner was working around the clock producing *SoHo Nights*, but he'd already hatched plans for a follow-up show that he called *The Webmaster*. It was based around the idea that Mira had rejected—a Silicon Alley startup run by a diabolical system administrator who monitored all the voice mail, e-mail, and ugly office politics through a network of hidden WebCams. Each week, users would be treated to a fly-on-the-wall view of truly outrageous office romance, corporate espionage, and other shenanigans. It was a killer idea that Kellner hoped to sell directly to Hollywood. He buried his detailed notes deep within his PowerBook and kept his idea secret—even from Dale.

He was stunned at the end of the second week of shooting to find a check for $7,000 issued from DBLY sitting in his mailbox. He called Mira immediately.

"Why am I getting a check? I still haven't gotten the letter of intent, much less the contract."

"Just put it in the bank. Accounting-wise, things sometimes don't move in synch up here."

"When do I execute?"

"I just saw the contract—it's still in Legal."

It was lucky that the check came in, because Kellner had already payed the six actors $2,400, was due to pay them another $1,200, and owed $6,500 to American Express from his recent hardware spree. He'd also verbally agreed to kick back $750 a week to Mira and Julian for "consultative services," a fact which would remain a deep, dark secret among the three of them. After paying all the bills and depositing the DBLY check, Kellner realized he was just about breaking even. But more costs were on the way: he'd still have to fund the party, and any other costs that came up, out of pocket—about $5,000 in the next two weeks. But with $56,000 coming his way in the next two months, Kellner didn't mind footing the bill.

*SoHo Nights* launched on Friday, July 11, 1996, with three complete episodes online. On each of its 32 pages of content was a banner ad from DBLY that functioned as a "this space for rent" announcement for prospective advertisers. Kellner was depressed that Mira hadn't actually sold spots to Nike or Sony, but his spirits were lifted by Mira's fabulously orchestrated launch party, which packed Kellner's loft with a constantly circulating crowd of 300 media people, who partied all night.

It was a true SoHo party in the best sense—lots of cigar smoke and jostling shoulders, smoked salmon from Dean & DeLuca, and plenty of hard liquor to wash it all down. But the real brilliance came from Mira, who had hired two Robert Mitchum lookalikes to man the bar. They dressed like country preachers and had the words "SOHO NIGHTS" tattooed on their knuckles, just like the psychopathic killer in *Night of the Hunter*. People would, of course, say, "Hey, isn't that supposed to say 'LOVE' and 'HATE'?" whereupon they'd answer "That's what *SoHo Nights* is all about!"

## *The Setup*

Thanks to the party, an aggressive PR campaign that DBLY was running, and the fact that *SoHo Nights* was new in the "convergence entertainment" category, it started getting some publicity. *Fame* magazine ran a largely favorable review in its Multimedia section, Yoohah made *SoHo Nights* a "cool pick," and *Silicon Weekly* hailed the project as "cutting edge." Within weeks, *SoHo Nights* was racking up 30,000 page views a day—enough to land a booking from a major rollerblade manufacturer who bought a four-week sponsorship for a grand total of $6,000. Kellner was glad but also disappointed: DBLY was spending $28,000 for a month's production and certainly expected to be making money—not losing $22,000 a month.

Kellner did the math. The monthly break-even point, at a penny a page view, was 1,400,000 page views—about 93,000 page views a day. He could count on some page view growth in the future, but could he triple the views?

"You've got to build more pages," Mira said. "More characters, more stuff going on."

"I'm already running myself ragged producing six characters," Kellner said. "Can't the client pay more than a penny a page? This is a highly targeted demographic—young, rollerblading males."

"We tried, Kellner, but this whole thing is experimental for them. If we can deliver the hits, they promise to revisit the issue in a month."

"I don't know if I can do that."

"Well, you've got Dale working for you now—I'm sure you two can find the time to get more content up," Mira said.

"I need another $7,000 to keep going," Kellner said.

"I just saw the check—it's in accounting."

"But I still haven't executed . . ." Kellner said, but Mira had already rung off.

## The Heist

Kellner ran himself ragged again the following week and withdrew the last $4,000 from his bank account to pay his rapidly mounting costs. He desperately needed another check from DBLY and was growing panicky over the fact that Mira wasn't answering his calls. Dale came by on Thursday and Friday to process the graphics and load them online. Kellner, for the first time in his life, was too tired for sex. Instead, he slept, and woke up long after she had left.

He spent Saturday going over his expense reports and the server logs. He was flat broke, but *SoHo Nights'* page views had doubled: 60,000 page views a day. With four episodes now online, he was halfway there, but DBLY still hadn't sent him what Mira told them they'd promised–another $21,000. He added up all his expenses so far: about $16,000 in the hole, instead of $5,000 in the clear.

On Monday, he called all the actors and suspended that week's shootings. This way, he could save $1,200, by using outtakes from the previous shoots. Dale came over again to help process the graphics, and he got the fourth issue online by the end of the week. He still hadn't received a check, a contract, or any official communications from DBLY.

On Sunday night, Kellner felt restless and needed to get out, so he took a long walk to clear his head–up West Broadway, across Houston, and up Sixth Avenue to the all-night newsstand near Waverly Place.

He looked down at *Billboard* and was shocked to see an astounding headline:

> "WEBMASTER" OPTIONED TO FOX FOR $3M
> Premiere Online Webisodic Drama from DBLY Interactive
> Makes Use of Technology To Offer Compelling Consumer Experience

He read on, past the description of *The Webmaster*, a word-for-word copy of his secret idea.

> "We are privileged to promote Julian Garrett and Mira Racinek to Senior Vice Presidents of DBLY's newest division, and realize that their abilities have already proven themselves," said Chairman Duke Lambert. "Their pioneering vision in this new category of convergence entertainment speaks for itself."

"You bastards!" Kellner shouted, and ran down Sixth Avenue.

"You bastards!" he yelled into Mira's voice mail, and Julian's, and Dale's.

Somebody—probably Dale—had delivered his idea directly to Julian, who had passed it on to Fox. But there was nothing he could do. Even if he could prove that Dale had carefully copied all his files from his PowerBook while he was sleeping, or that Mira had lied to him from the beginning, or that Julian had put them all up to it, Kellner was powerless. He'd been hung out to dry, cut to shreds, left twisting in the wind. But there was nothing he could do; he was too tired and too broke to fight.

## *Epilogue*

Kellner never received another check from DBLY and was thrown out of his loft at the end of September. His American Express account terminated, Kellner's debt was referred to a collection agent. *SoHo Nights* survived as a ghost site until December of 1996, when Kellner's ISP took it down for nonpayment. Kellner now lives in Flushing, Queens, with his parents, who constantly nag him to "get a decent job and get married." Kellner has given up on becoming a Web entrepreneur, although he still gets the itch occasionally when he's not trying to get back into the video production business. As for Kellner's former partners, they all lost their jobs in late 1997 when DBLY Interactive canceled *The Webmaster*. Despite the fanfare and more than $300K in development money from Fox, the site failed to attract more than 30,000 page views a day. This was a turn of events which thrilled Kellner to no end, although the whole experience of having his ideas stolen still left him with a queasy feeling, like he had been ambushed by a gang of mental succubae.

LEVEL 8.0

# Priests and Madmen

**Infinity in a Grain of Sand**

## 8.1 Who Are They?

To gain access to the next level of the New Media Caste System, Steve and I enrolled in an "Internet Guru" correspondence course. According to the ad in the back of *Fibre Magazine*, it would set us back only 50 bucks, so we figured, what the heck?

From an address in Pueblo, Colorado, the packet we received in the mail a week later was so heavy that it took three sweating, straining postal workers to lug it up our front steps.

"Your lead shipment's here!" griped the biggest, who was probably the leader.

"Sorry, guys," Steve responded, handing him a twenty.

"That's it?" he sniffed.

"Hey, man," I added. "We're NetSlaves."

An unintelligible curse followed, whereupon the postal workers let go of the packet, causing it to drop with a loud *thud* against the stoop, almost pulverizing our toes in the process. "How are we supposed to get this thing inside?" Steve called to them as they were getting into their truck.

"You're computer geniuses—you'll figure it out!" the leader shouted back with a grin.

Some 3.5 hernias later, we did succeed in our task, and then the real fun began. We cut open the packet and were caught in a landslide of papers, disks, and miscellaneous textbooks the size of the *Oxford English Dictionary*. "Jesus," I screamed, "what have we gotten ourselves into?!"

Over the next several weeks we read and studied like mad for courses ranging from "Advanced Buzzwords" and "Voodoo Economics" to "Seducing the Future" and "The Principles of Networked Asininity." Our hard work apparently paid off because a month after sending in our final exams, which we had scribbled on the back of shirt cardboards, we received two laminated, wallet-size diplomas stating that we were now "Certified Technology Gurus," entitled to not only a free breakfast at Denny's but passes to the "E-Commerce B2B A-Z Conference," which was being held this year in (you guessed it!) Pueblo, Colorado.

Despite a four-hour layover in Omaha, Steve and I arrived at the conference just in time to witness a noted Wall Street analyst, or "Priest," get heckled by a rowdy horde of influential trade journalists and modem-waving futurists ("Madmen"). A minor riot ensued, but it wasn't nearly as much fun to watch as the faces of the people we cornered at the evening's cocktail party, as we asked the question, "So, what's it like to lend intellectual depth to an otherwise shallow medium?"

Steve and I aren't expecting to be invited back to next year's conference, but we could care less. We ate enough smoked salmon to last us a lifetime and gathered sufficiently insane material for the following profile and story. Now that's what we call a return on investment.

## 8.2 General Characteristics

*Where they can be found:* When not squirreled away writing their latest white paper, how-to book, or "Buy NOW! Buy It ALL!" stock recommendation, Priests and Madmen are out evangelizing at industry conferences. But don't let their fiery rhetoric fool you—like their brethren Gold Diggers and Gigolos, they are only in it for the photo op and to collect their hefty speaking fees.

*Average age:* 72 (in Esther Dyson Time).

*Average salary:* Unknown (at least until the offshore banks disclose all foreign holdings).

*What they did before getting involved in the Internet:* Covered the salty treats market for *Snack Foods Weekly* (Priests); smoked pot and wrote their dissertation on Hegelian feminism (Madmen).

*Where they work:* Investment firms (Priests), independent consultancies (Madmen).

*Percentage of NetSlaves population:* 2 percent. (Simple theorem: The higher you go up the New Media Chain of Being, the fewer people you find.)

*Number of jobs held in the past three years:* 0. The genius of Priests and Madmen is that they can get by doing next to nothing at all and make the nonsense they cranked out in a haze seem believable.

*Mode of dress:* Navy pinstriped suits (Priests); Birkenstocks, fanny packs (Madmen).

*Education:* Too much. The greatest liability of Priests and Madmen is that they spent too much time in the hallowed halls of academia and too little (if any) in the industry in which they are supposedly "experts." (Advice to people out there with money to burn: Do your own homework and go with your gut. Or if that fails, try the "Dogs of the Dow" approach, in which investors manage their portfolios based on the bark patterns of their favorite canine companions.)

***Psychological profile:*** Like most people too intelligent for their own good, Priests and Madmen took a lot of abuse in the Great American Schoolyard–a trauma which has left them seeking attention and approval wherever and whenever possible (something to think about the next time you're watching their gums flap on CNBC).

***Career aspirations:*** To be kissed by Oprah, after their new book sells more than 50 copies.

## 8.3 The Story of Barstow

*Talking about the Glorious Future of Technology was beside the point. Barstow's real job, as he saw it, was to amuse and abuse Internet CEOs. If his legendary, lucrative, and always-packed speaking engagements were any indication, Barstow was very good at what he did. His orange juice trick alone was enough to keep them coming back for more.*

Barstow piloted his neon-blue Harley up the twisting road that curved around the mountain and led to the cloud-obscured summit. He made this journey once a year, to lecture New Media executives on how to think about the future, and as long as he could make $5,000 for a few hours' work, he would continue to do so.

Barstow didn't think of himself as an Internet Guru, but somehow it had happened. He was approaching 50 and had come of age in the 1960s, when revolutions were fought on street corners against helmeted police, not behind computer screens. But his path to the summit of cultural influence had been short and fast. In the early 1990s he'd been recruited to write for an underground San Francisco publication called *High Frontier* that specialized in designer drug paraphernalia and within a few years had moved upstream to become one of *Fibre Magazine*'s leading columnists.

In San Francisco's tightly knit intellectual circles, moving from psychedelics to cybernetics was as easy as crossing the street. Barstow keenly remembered when high-tech acquisition deals involved Acapulco Gold, and the only technology that really mattered was being able to reprogram one's own brain, not some inanimate lump of silicon in a beige case—*the Internet in one's own mind*. But now it seemed as if the only thing Barstow did was talk about the Internet, and his habit of speaking off the cuff had propelled him from Haight-Ashbury obscurity to world renown as a "deep thinker."

Barstow parked his Harley in the shade of a juniper tree and turned off the engine. Road dirt caked his face, so he pulled off his helmet, got a bottle of Perrier out of his travel bag, and poured it over his head. He shook his long gray hair and mopped his face down with a red bandanna. He put on his trademark Stetson hat and checked his reflection in the handlebar mirrors. He felt strong and formidable—intentionality itself.

He cast a long shadow as he strode across the parking lot toward the chrome entrance to the conference hall. It was the only aboveground feature of the Big Sur Space, a massive complex of meeting halls built into a berm that was designed to survive the impact of a neutron bomb. Once each year, the BSS housed the Digital CEO's Working Group, an exclusive get-together in which wired executives networked, schmoozed, and plotted strategies to harness "the great whirlwind sweeping over the land like a Bengal typhoon."

A small crowd of CEOs hung about the entrance smoking, but they parted like the Red Sea to let Barstow by. He checked in at the speaker's desk and received a pass from a young woman whose hands shook slightly when she checked his identification. Even the sunglasses couldn't disguise Barstow's craggy, weather-beaten face—as memorable a feature in the digital mindspace as George Washington's visage carved into Mount Rushmore.

"Hello, Jane," Barstow said, showing her his driver's license.

"Welcome back," she said. "I can't believe it's been a whole year. Are you going to do the thing with the . . ."

"Sshh," Barstow said. "That's a trade secret."

It was almost 8:40, so Barstow checked the stage in the main conference room to make sure that it had a working microphone, and wandered back toward the refreshment table. He poured himself a glass of grapefruit juice from one of the carafes and winced at its bitterness. When the CEOs started filing into the room at five of nine, Barstow was still there, hovering over the juice carafes.

As the last executive took his seat, Barstow strode to the stage. After a short, respectful round of applause, he launched into his speech.

"I'm Jason Barstow, and I think you all know enough about me, and what I do, to dispense with a lengthy introduction. I'm a former chicken farmer from Alameda County, and I used to play guitar with the Strawberry Messenger Service. People tell me I know a thing or two about this medium, but I'm always stunned by my own ignorance about things—to me, the Internet is all about waking up and being shocked by the world that, little by little, changes every day. That's the way fundamental change occurs—it seems to move like a glacier sometimes. You really can't see it until you open your eyes one morning and realize that you're living in a world that's been radically transformed.

"Now the organization I do most of my work for is called the Earth Business Network—the sponsor of this two-day conference—and we don't do things the way most seminar groups do. Has anyone been to one of my lectures before? A few—OK. So you know what's going to happen. The rest of you can settle back.

"Some of what you're about to experience—and especially the way you're going to feel—might make you a little uncomfortable, but I'd ask all of you to stick with me. From time to time, what I say might not make much sense to you, but it's all part of a larger process that's designed to let you work through things that might not be possible in a more, ah, formal way. All right, now—are we all ready? Good. First of all, I'd like you all to get up out of your chairs. C'mon now, let's all stand up."

Slowly, awkwardly, the 100 CEOs rose.

"Now I'd like you to reach over and shake the hand of your neighbor—come on, shake his hand."

Each tensely shook the hand of his adjacent competitor.

"OK. You can sit down now. All right. Now the topic of today's presentation is e-commerce. How many of you are in the e-commerce business?

About 60 CEOs raised their hands.

"All right, who is *not* in the e-commerce business?"

About 30 CEOs raised their hands.

"Put your hands down. We're all in the e-commerce business. You want to know what the truth is? The whole damned world is for sale. I don't care what you make—or don't make. We're all selling stuff—even if it has no value. Even if it's a piece of junk. You're all salesmen—I'm a salesman, too. Got it? All right, then. Now how many of you had orange juice just now? Grapefruit juice? OK, that's just about everybody. Anybody not have something to drink?"

Royster G. Pfeiffer put up his hand.

"Get Mr. Pfeiffer something to drink."

"I'll just take a glass of water."

"No. You can't drink water. It's against the rules. Get him an orange juice. Now, we're all going to wait around until Mr. Pfeiffer drinks his orange juice. Good—drink it all down. We don't want to waste a single drop—orange juice is scarce, even in California."

"All right. Now let's come back to e-commerce. I suppose you want me to tell you what it all means. Now let me tell you a little story—it's about something I did today—last night actually. Do you know what I did? Well, I'll tell you—I bought about five milligrams of acid."

A wave of nervous laughter moved through the room.

"The reason I like acid is that long before anybody began talking about global networks, or technospheres, or the wired economy, it was a pretty high-tech way to directly reprogram the ultimate computer—the one that runs the whole damned show."

"You know, when people think about us old graybeards—the '60s people who actually invented the Internet, they talk like we were a bunch of lazy, spoiled antiwar wimps. But it was pretty ballsy. I mean, think about it–doing acid was like trying to reprogram the operating system of your PC while it was running Excel, Word, and a bunch of things at once."

"Now I know I'm supposed to be talking about e-commerce here, and I will in a minute. But first, I want to ask you: does anybody in this room know what five milligrams of acid can do?"

No hands rose.

"No? Well, I'll tell you–it takes only about fifty micrograms of acid to turn a person on–to really light them up, so that the veil of misperception is lifted forever from their eyes. Fifty micrograms of acid takes about 15 minutes to start working, and it's like a great bull eradicator–you can still shoot the bull, if you like, but you don't have to, it's not necessary, it's not essential. It's just–bull, you know?"

"OK. Now let me ask you something to kick things off. This is how I usually begin these things, as a kind of confrontation exercise. So let me ask you this: what is your greatest fear? Go ahead–you don't have to raise your hands. Just shout it out–what is your greatest fear?"

"Royster G. Pfeiffer!" one CEO shouted out.

"Hah hah hah," Barstow laughed. "Seriously, though–what are you guys really afraid of–what really does it to you–keeps you awake at night? Anybody!"

The crowd of CEOs shifted slightly in their seats.

"Well let me suggest something here. I might be right, and I might be wrong, but I've generally found this to be true among elevated captains-of-industry types. All right–I'll just come out and say it. You're afraid of the future."

Barstow knew he was facing 100 incredulous stares from this thoroughly future-oriented crowd, but he kept at it.

"Hear me out here. I know that all of you think you're embracing the future–what we used to call 'progress.' Now it's called 'change,' but it's the same thing. Progress implies change plus growth–that's what you guys do, isn't it?"

A few heads in the audience nodded.

"Now I know you all *think* you know what the future is going to bring. And your knowledge informs your actions–it conditions your responses. But what I'm asking you about is different. I'm asking you to confront a future that you *can't* know about. What would you do then? What would your reaction be? How would you feel about it?"

"Let me put it to you this way. The future is in your mind, right–it doesn't exist. You think that by controlling your mind, you can control the future, but it doesn't work that way. Nor does its corollary—the idea that if you lost control of your mind, you'd lose control of the future. For all we know, the opposite might be true—that by losing your mind, you'd actually be *finding* the future."

The audience looked confused, but most were still attentive. Barstow knew he had only a few moments before boredom set in. He looked down at Royster G. Pfeiffer, who sat in the third row.

"Royster, have you finished your orange juice yet?"

Pfeiffer looked up at him blankly, and then nodded.

"All right—now five milligrams of acid is about 100 times the normal dose. But distributed among, say 100 people, it's a perfectly safe dose. It fact, it's actually quite a light dose."

The audience didn't react, but now it was completely still—frozen. Nobody moved.

"Does anybody see what I'm driving at here?" Barstow asked.

"You've spiked all of our drinks," said Royster G. Pfeiffer.

"Aha. We have a smart man in our midst," said Barstow. "Now why would I want to spike all your drinks with acid?"

"Because you think it would be a great joke," said Pfeiffer.

"Well, I do think it would be pretty funny. But I wouldn't do it as a joke. You see, you'd probably put me in jail, and then I couldn't do things like this—big conferences in front of people like you who pay me $5,000 for a weekend appearance. I couldn't do that from jail. But let's get back on track here. I'm here to talk about e-commerce."

There were a few nervous whispers in the room.

"You see, the way I see it, you people have it all wrong. None of this is about disintermediation, or about efficiency, or about friction-free selling, or about empowering the consumer. How are you going to empower the consumer when the endpoint of what you're all trying to do is wipe out every business that's on the face of the planet? What's going to happen when every stockbroker, travel agent, real estate office, bookstore, and clothing retailer is run out of business? I mean, think about it: where are all your customers going to get the money to buy anything? Do you think they're going to spend their food stamps on a faster modem?"

"I want to know if my drink was spiked," said Pfeiffer.

"All right, I'll get to that," said Barstow. "But let me finish what I'm saying about e-commerce. Now the Texas Rangers recently found a bunch of Mexicans lying dead in the Arizona desert. See, they'd been abandoned by the smugglers that had brought them across the border, and they'd run out of water. Now these people had nothing—absolutely nothing. They'd come into this country to work as migrant laborers–absolutely impoverished people. But do you know what the Rangers found on these poor people? Do you what they had with them?

"LSD?" asked a voice from the crowd.

"No. Videotapes. Do you get it? These people didn't want to load themselves down by carrying enough extra water to survive, but they did have enough room to carry their damned videotapes. Do you know what that means?"

"People don't know what's good for them?"

"Wrong. People have a very good idea of what's good for them, but they'd rather have something that they'd paid money for than something that's free. Videotapes have more value than water because you pay for them. That's what gives anything–bits or atoms–value. In the old days, in the world of atoms, people had a pretty good idea of what value was–it was the food on the table, or the refrigerator you kept the food in, or the gas you put in the tank. But in the world of the bitstream, it's only the context that gives anything value–in the particular arrangement of the bits into pictures, or numbers in a bank account. This is an attention economy; you don't get paid for an object, but for how much you can get people to think about it. If you can get them to pay you for thinking about it, it's even better."

"Mr. Barstow, I want you to tell us the truth about your little prank," said Slim Clarkston, of NetScathe.

"What do you think, Mr. Clarkston? Are you tripping now? Do you feel a little out of sorts, a bit unsteady? Is my hand making trails in front of you?"

Barstow moved his hands back and forth quickly, mocking Clarkston.

"All right, Slim, let's talk about drugs for a minute. This whole business is on drugs–but the wrong ones. It's like crack cocaine–your IPOs and your acquisitions and your endless growth cycle–you're a bunch of speed freaks sucking on a high-bandwidth crack pipe. Cocaine is fine–but all the time, people? All the time, Slim? It stops you from thinking. How can you think about anything but your next hit and where you're going to find the money to fund it?"

"I think this has gone far enough," said the head of Edler-Watson. "As a journalist, I see your points, but if you're going to go on a political rant, you should save it . . ."

"SAVE IT?" Barstow asked theatrically. "Save it from what? Look around you, Don. Do you see any security here that's going to come and take me off this stage and save you from what I'm going to tell you? I've been up here for maybe 10 minutes. Do you know what's going to be happening to your brain in the next few minutes—how many little neurons are in that great brain of yours, and how they're all going to be exploding in in a hundred million gazillion points of light?"

Barstow leapt up and, without benefit of microphone, began preaching directly to the crowd.

"You all pay lip service to the whirlwind of change that's ripping through your industries, and transforming the economy, and making multi-billion-dollar industries worth nothing, and taking zero-worth industries and putting stratospheric market caps on them. You all want to control this thing—to put it in a box, so that you can understand it. But you're not going to be able to control your minds in another two minutes—none of you."

"What are you going to do, when your flowcharts and carefully crafted business plans and five-year plans all melt into the air? Who are you going to blame when the whole house of cards comes down—when the Internet in your mind comes to the surface and you see yourself for what you are: a bunch of interchangeable packets in a great swirling matrix of nonmeaning?"

Barstow was on a roll now. His audience had broken into a cold sweat, riveted with the terror of imminent insanity.

"You're all one minute away from seeing it, from being part of the grand cosmic convergence that's going to rip away all your precious paradigms and render your best-laid plans as obsolete as a clipper ship. Are you ready for the revolution? Do you really want to see the future? Don't you know that it's a dream—a consensual hallucination—reason's sallow ghost? You want to sell the ghost in your mind to America—this bit-happy dream? Well, go mental—feed your head—get overwhelmed—BREAK DOWN!"

"You have 15 seconds left before the future really begins—but get this, THERE IS NO FUTURE! THERE IS NO INTERNET! It's just a partialized, sanitized, corporatized fragment of the eternal now that's unrepresentable—chaos without end—a nameless object that's a placeholder for the PURE CONSCIOUSNESS that you're about to feel, when your mind breaks up on the rocks of acid and you can only fall, over and over, into the yawning abyss that is your fate. IT'S OVER!"

Barstow stood still as Gibraltar, as the last echoes of his voice died in the room. Fixed on stage, with eyes that were cold, brilliant beads calling for the immediate destruction of all reality in 100 heads, Barstow slowly, methodically, reached into the pocket of his suede vest and retrieved a small packet. He unwrapped it and held up a small sugar cube for everyone to see. A palpable sense of relief swept the room, as it became apparent that he hadn't spiked the grapefruit juice at all.

"Why should I waste this valuable technology on you?" Barstow asked. "After all, you're tripping all the time."

He walked off stage and out of the room. He turned in his pass to the young woman at the security desk and signed out.

"How did it go, Mr. Barstow?" she asked.

"Same bull," Barstow responded, "but they never seem to get tired of it."

## *Epilogue*

Jason Barstow's phenomenal success on the lecture circuit was cut short when he suffered a serious motorcycle accident in early 1999 while attempting to handle a left turn, a paradigm shift, and a blinding revelation, all at the same time. He's expected to make a full recovery and should return to abuse and confuse well-heeled New Media executives early in 2000.

# LEVEL 9.0

# Robots

### Kill, Crush, Deploy!

## 9.1 Who/What Are They?

And so we had made it this far—almost to the top of the New Media Chain of Being. We were proud of ourselves—we had a right to be—but we were also disgusted. In any industry supposedly rife with technical geniuses, we had found only bull artists and bottom-feeders. Had we missed something? Were we the lousy anthropologists we feared we were deep down?

We walked into the 7-Eleven and bought two large coffees to raise our spirits. As we sat on the curb drinking them, we complained back and forth about our situation.

"Jesus," Steve began, "how are we going to do justice to NetSlaves everywhere without a story about supergeeks—the people who are really responsible for creating this stuff?"

I usually had a response for Steve, but at this point in our journey, I was too tired and frustrated to do anything except echo his sentiments.

"Dude, I hear you. We've gotten Garbagemen, Cab Drivers, Cowboys, and Gold Diggers to talk to us, but Robots—the closest we came to one was a former lead engineer from NetScathe who blew us off after a few e-mails."

Steve sat there silently drinking his coffee. He had nothing to say; in truth, there was nothing he could say. Our journey was turning out to be a bust; there would be no NetSlaves book. We'd have to go back to coding HTML, if someone would actually hire us. In short, we were in serious trouble.

That night we were sitting in our respective dive apartments, when out of the blue, an e-mail arrived in the official NetSlaves inbox. It was from a gentleman named Ken Hussein, spokesperson for a group called FACEChipTek (Former and Current Employees of ChipTek). The e-mail was brief, stating that he'd love to talk to us. I think I saw it first and dismissed it as one of the many nuts we'd attracted. But Steve, ever the newshound, followed the link Hussein had provided and quickly forwarded his impressions to me at my private address. Steve's e-mail read simply, "We've found our Robot. This guy's got a story you won't believe."

The next night I was on the phone with Hussein. I too was shocked by what his Web site had to say and had called him just to see if it wasn't all some sort of put-on.

It wasn't. In fact, Hussein's story was deadly serious, which made everything else we'd written and experienced ourselves pale in comparison. Hussein and I spoke for about three hours, and when we were about to hang up, I thanked this man for being so open—for sharing an account of things that shouldn't happen to a dog, much less a person who had worked so hard to do something with his life, only to have it all taken away from him so violently. We've included our usual jokes, but if you choose to skip over them to get to the meat, we won't be offended.

## 9.2 General Characteristics

*Where they can be found:*   Robots, thanks to the gizmos that serve them, can exist in many places at once and none in particular. In terms of physical location, Robots are most often found in server rooms, wire closets, switching stations—basically, anywhere that offers maximum exposure to technology and minimum interaction with human beings.

*How to spot Robots in a crowd:*   If their antennae aren't a dead giveaway, watch for at least six alphanumeric pagers lining their belts and a 3,000-page SNMP manual suspended from their gleaming domes by a repurposed phone cord.

*Average salary:*   $200K.

*Percentage of NetSlaves population:*   1.5 percent.

*Fueling patterns:*   Robots feast solely on high-octane, low-nutrition treats, including Philly cheesesteaks, curly fries, doughnuts, and two-liter Cokes by the score.

*Marital status/emotional status:*   None. (Reason: genitalia are strange interfaces.)

*Favorite offline activities:*   None. (Robots are always networked in some shape or fashion.)

*How to tell a good Robot from a bad Robot:*   Good Robots find your comparative lack of technological knowledge amusing and seek to help out whenever possible; bad Robots use it as an opportunity to make you look bad in front of other people ("Gee, now, if I were running SuSE Linux v6.1 featuring 2.2.7 and started having problems with my ISDN adapter, which is pcbit-d by Octal, I wonder what I'd do! Bill, do you have any suggestions?")

*How to tell a Robot is annoyed with you:*   Not only do you have no connectivity whatsoever, but your bank account is empty, your credit cards no longer work, and when you frantically show someone your ID, they tell you you don't exist.

***How Robots view the NetSlaves they employ:*** Garbage in/Garbage-men out.

***Psychological profile:*** 11111000000001111100000011.

***Career aspirations:*** To beta the next-generation Intel chip, which, when inserted beneath the skin of the forehead, allows the user to perform point-and-click tasks upon mental command.

## 9.3 The Story of Hussein

*Ken Hussein had a dream, an American Dream, which delivered him from a bloody revolution in the Middle East to a new life in California. But just as he was about to achieve the success he'd worked so long for, something happened which would land Hussein back in a desperate fight for freedom.*

Ken Hussein fidgeted nervously in his seat at the back of the plush auditorium. He knew that if he went through with his crazy, kamikaze plan, his life would never be the same. But if he lost his nerve and backed down, he'd betray the people who were counting on him the most—the legions of oppressed NetSlaves working at ChipTek, the world's largest manufacturer of computer CPUs.

The auditorium was filling up with $1,500 suits: high net-worth investors, analysts, and stockholders who'd made their annual pilgrimage to ChipTek's shareholders' meeting to worship at the shrine of double-digit growth. In the row ahead of Hussein, an exquisitely coiffed institutional investor spoke a few final words into his cell phone and checked his Rolex. It was 10:58—two minutes before the big show would begin. Hussein fingered the lapels of his cheap suit jacket and felt the weight of the oddly shaped metallic object he'd concealed within his clothing. With help from a friend—someone deep inside ChipTek, he'd been able to smuggle the device past the guards' metal detectors.

At exactly 11 a.m., ChipTek's senior executives—the chairman, CEO, and COO—took their seats on stage beneath an 80-foot banner that read simply: INNOVATION. Two thousand well-manicured hands came together to applaud these indomitable men, who directed technology's trajectory toward the trillion-dollar apogee of e-commerce.

The auditorium lights dimmed, and deep-toned, Wagnerian music began to rise from the 12-foot-high speakers framing the stage. A huge still-frame image of an Olympic javelin thrower appeared below the INNOVATION banner, and the camera began a slow zoom until the athlete's face completely filled the screen.

Invisible now to all who could have stopped him, Hussein put his left hand inside his jacket and slowly pulled out the device. He ran his thumb over it and felt for the activation switch. He waited for the music to rise to its inspirational crescendo, and then, setting his mind again to the fact that there was no turning back, he took a deep breath and pushed the switch from "off" to "on."

In a split second, all hell had broken loose in the hall.

## *Asylum*

Ken Hussein's long, inevitable descent toward the nadir of self-destructive rage began when he came to the United States in 1978, fleeing the Islamic revolution which installed the Ayatollah Khomeini as the effective CEO of Iran.

He, his wife, and their two-year-old daughter narrowly escaped persecution and were granted political asylum in the United States. They took up residence in Sacramento, California, renting a small room near the bus station. With barely $3,000 to his name—most of his assets, including his home, had been frozen—Hussein had to rebuild his life from scratch in a new and strange land.

Although he was 33 years old, he immediately enrolled in night classes to improve his English. After passing his GED, Hussein headed straight for his local community college. By day, he worked as a Mercedes-Benz auto mechanic, a trade he'd learned while serving in the prerevolutionary Iranian army.

Like many immigrants seeking asylum from the bloody purges of offshore dictators, Hussein felt lucky to be alive and free. He never complained about the long hours and lousy pay he got working as a mechanic, but when the hostage crisis ignited a wave of anti-Arab sentiment, he again found himself facing a rising tide of intolerance. No amount of hard work could stem the waves of hatred radiating from his fellow mechanics, who'd delight in insulting his parentage, his race, and his family name. His boss, who was Jordanian, tried to protect Hussein from the worst excesses of his coworkers, but could do very little to stop them. Four weeks into the crisis, an incensed mechanic broke into Hussein's locker, doused his textbooks with motor oil, and urinated on his street clothes.

The hostage crisis ground on for many months, but Hussein never let his hopes for betterment fade. Although he saw America from the bottom of a grease pit, he had faith that by turning the other cheek, keeping his cool, and dutifully fixing the cars that rolled in and out of the shop, he'd someday make it to higher ground. He was living for the future—for the time when he, his wife, and their daughter could live in a world where brutish stupidity had been abolished, and a hardworking, modest man with a dream could rise up to claim what was rightfully his.

## Up from the Grease Pit

Night school took five years to complete, and then Hussein entered college, where he studied electrical engineering. With each rung of the educational ladder that Hussein climbed, his employer let him rise out of the pit a notch. Soon he was dividing his time between auto repair and administrative tasks: ordering parts, keeping the books in order, and dealing with finicky customers. Juggling schoolwork and a full-time job was a challenge, but Hussein never dropped the ball. For the first time, he could see that he was getting somewhere—his pay was better, and so were his working conditions and his prospects for the future. By 1983, after he'd finally gotten his EE degree, Hussein sought out a real engineer's job and sent out upward of 100 résumés to employers in the Sacramento area.

Hussein landed a job at Centauri, the maker of Tank Attack and other second-generation video console games. The company was based in Florin, a short distance from Sacramento, but, because of the traffic that was already beginning to clog the area that would later be known as Silicon Valley, it entailed a lengthy, two-hour commute.

He began his new life in July, excited to be trading the low-tech, analog world of automechanics for the high-tech world of interactive gaming. He was hired as a quality assurance (QA) engineer in Centauri's manufacturing division—a job with a lot of responsibility. Hussein did everything from making sure that the explosions in Tank Attack were appropriately loud to double-checking that the voltage range of Chomp Chomp (a PacMan arcade machine knockoff) didn't diminish the gaming experience by frying players to a crisp.

## Go-Getter

In the go-getting, winner-take-all cultural climate of the mid-'80s, Ken Hussein blossomed. At Centauri, he found that the same "perfection is not enough" work ethic that worked so well for him in the garage directly translated to success in the gray hallways of Corporate America. Unlike his fellow engineers, who'd often complain about overtime or having to come in over the weekend, Hussein took every extra assignment with a smile. His "just say no to defects" attitude endeared himself to Centauri's management. Whenever something blew up, their immediate response would be, "Get Hussein on it!"

On top of his weighty QA duties, he'd gone ahead and enrolled in the college's MBA program because he knew that a degree in business, coupled with his growing technical background, was a sure ticket to the top. Hussein never fell behind in his work and was well rewarded for his performance and can-do attitude. After 26 months at Centauri, he'd already been promoted twice and was closing in on a third—a VP slot—when the gaming market went bust.

Hussein knew that Centauri was living on borrowed time and, four credits away from completing his MBA, he quietly began circulating his résumé again.

The gods must have truly been watching over Ken Hussein because two weeks before Centauri laid him off, he had already received a firm offer from ChipTek, the largest microprocessor company in the world. Unlike Centauri, a small company in a shaky, volatile market, ChipTek's position was valued in the billions, and the company enjoyed an unassailable market position. The chance to work at such a large company thrilled Hussein to no end. "I've finally made it!" he said over and over again to himself. "I've finally made it!"

## *The Big Time*

Hussein wasted no time getting started. ChipTek gave him a mere two weeks to relocate to Santa Clara, but as with every project he ever worked on, he told the human resources person he'd be ready in one. While this undoubtedly impressed his future bosses, it didn't sit so well with his wife. "I have an entire house to pack up! Have you lost your mind? Where will Lisa go to school?"

Her protests fell on deaf ears—Ken Hussein was a man possessed with success. And with good reason. Out of nowhere, he had blazed a trail into a middle-management slot at ChipTek and was looking at a 30 percent pay increase, which would boost his annual earnings to just below $100K. It was a remarkable achievement for someone who had come to the United States only eight years before.

The year was 1986. While the rest of the nation was beginning to suffer from the fiscal exhaustion of the go-go '80s and corporate behemoths like Data Magic were laying off people in droves, Hussein walked into a plush position at ChipTek as one of three lead QA engineers in the North American Automotive Group. It was his responsibility to ensure that the electronic fuel injection systems and other embedded components built for the major U.S. automakers were not only up to spec, but were compliant with everything else the company was producing. He advanced quickly: in six months he was promoted to lead QA engineer and a year after that, he became the main technical liaison between ChipTek and the U.S. automakers.

There was a heavy price to pay for such advancement, and Hussein paid it. His shortest working day was 10 hours, and most weekends would find him in the office catching up on unfinished business and preparing for the week ahead. Also, because his job now involved fewer hands-on duties and more client interaction, he would be on the road frequently, visiting clients in Michigan and other plants in the Midwest. Hussein found it all very exciting, despite the fact that he was quickly becoming a stranger to his family. His wife told him as much on several occasions, to which he invariably responded, "I can't do everything! I can't be a great husband and father and give you all this!"

Hussein's hands reached out to embrace the $500,000 ten-room home he had bought them in one of Santa Clara's most exclusive zip codes—a veritable palace situated on 5.6 acres of land that shared part of a lake with its closest neighbor.

Hussein's wife knew better than to argue with him when he was in such a state. She was very proud of him for everything he had achieved, but she did wish that he would come to his senses and realize that there was more to life than work and money.

In her heart, though, she knew that he was doing so well that any major spiritual breakthroughs were unlikely, if not impossible.

## *Going Global*

In early 1989, Ken Hussein's fortunes improved yet again when he was promoted to Global Liaison for ChipTek's Automotive Group—a position which meant that his roster of clients would now reach to the other side of the planet, from the major industrial nations of Europe to the fierce up-and-comers in Asia and the Philippines. What it also meant was that his workload and responsibilities doubled again, along with the amount of time he'd be spending on the road. In fact, Jeff Hearns, the head of the group, anticipated that Hussein would spend so much time overseas that he arranged to rent him a corporate apartment in London to use as a home base whenever he was traveling in Europe.

Hussein's career at ChipTek continued to gather steam. He was earning well into the six figures and had over 100 engineers in various time zones reporting to him. Ever the modest man, however, Hussein attributed his success as much to ChipTek's corporate culture as to his own Herculean efforts. Unlike the repressive stereotype of corporate culture he'd seen depicted in American movies, ChipTek was actually quite friendly and laid back. Employees dressed casually at all times and had authentic smiles on their faces, and management really didn't care what time you showed up or when you left as long as the work got done and you made it to all your meetings.

But what pleased Hussein the most about ChipTek was its managers or, as they preferred to call themselves, "cultural representatives." Hussein was particularly taken by Norm Wallace, his boss in the Automotive Group. Wallace was a man in his late forties who lived by the "ChipTek Code" that was posted on every bulletin board throughout the company: "Empowering Our Employees with Solutions." Whenever Hussein had a problem with a client or had to deal with an unruly engineer, Wallace would always step in to help–smoothing things over or, if necessary, playing the bad guy.

Hussein appreciated Wallace's support and regretted never having the opportunity to thank Wallace for nurturing his career. But Wallace had disappeared suddenly without a trace. The rumor was that he had been transferred to a secret, high-level project. And Hussein could only assume this was true because everything at ChipTek seemed to flow upward.

## *Crack-Up*

Ken Hussein's life started flowing in an entirely different direction on a hot July night in 1990. He had just returned from three weeks in Europe and was on his way back from Chandler, Arizona, where he'd stopped off for a two-day engineering conference. It had been an informative session and a very productive trip, but after being on the road for so long, he was eager to get home to Santa Clara to see his family for a few precious hours. He was so eager, in fact, that instead of pulling off and finding a motel, he decided to drive on through.

Night was falling and he was tooling along Route 10, just outside Phoenix, when a van in the left lane cut him off. Swerving to avoid getting hit in the front, Hussein's rented Ford Taurus took a terrible shot in the back, which sent him flying through the windshield.

Hussein was immediately rushed to a nearby hospital where he was treated for head and neck trauma and severe facial lacerations. The hospital called his wife, who traveled to Phoenix on the next available plane.

He slept for a long time, but around midnight, he suddenly woke up. "I've got to get out of here," he said. "I've got things to do."

"You can't go anywhere right now—the doctor said you've got the worst case of whiplash he's ever seen and thinks that you might have serious neurological damage as well."

"I've got to get out of here. When can I leave? Can you get me a phone? I have to push back the meetings I've scheduled!"

Hussein remained in the hospital—very reluctantly—for about a week and was discharged only after the hospital forced him to sign a pile of release forms stating that it was indemnified for the medical consequences of his decision. Hussein's wife and the doctor who treated him tried to talk him out of it, but as usual, he couldn't be reasoned with—work came before everything else, including his health.

## *Fit as a Fiddle*

Hussein returned to the office and downplayed the incident in typical fashion to both his superiors and his colleagues.

"I'm fine. It was just a minor fender bender. The doctor gave me some pills and said I should be completely back to normal in no time."

In the months that followed it became apparent to everyone who knew him just how messed up he was. His mind would wander off in midsentence. People asking him questions would have to repeat themselves several times before getting a straight answer. And even when his head was clear, his face was permanently clenched into a fist, because he was in so much pain. When the pain became unbearable, he'd take a painkiller, sometimes two. Soon he was popping them like candy, just to keep going.

To compensate for his damaged abilities, Hussein worked harder than ever—he put in 24, 36 hours at a clip and oftentimes only came home long enough to take a shower and change into a fresh set of clothes.

Hussein's wife cried every night—she was angry at her husband for his incredible stubbornness and years of neglect, but she still loved him and felt much of his pain. Here was a man who knew no limits; a man who never took a day off, much less a vacation; a man who had beaten all the odds and who seemed on the verge of rising to the top of his field and now this, this terrible thing had to happen to him and he was so sick he couldn't even think straight.

On several occasions, his wife caught him slipping out the door at one o'clock in the morning.

"Ken, where the hell are you going?"

"The clients in London are just getting in—I have to talk to them about the new fueling system we're shipping."

"Why don't you call them from here?"

"I can think better in the office," he said, and drove away into the night.

## *Slipping Away*

Six months later, Hussein's unrelenting pace finally caught up with him. He had traveled to Frankfurt with ChipTek's sales force to land a luxury automaker as a new client. The meeting, which had taken months to arrange, was just getting started when Hussein fainted dead away right in front of the horrified Germans and the totally shocked salespeople, who had been warned not to take him.

"Mein Gott!" said the young administrative assistant who had been called in to take the minutes. "I will call ambulance."

The client barked something at her in German and walked to the other side of the long conference room table. He bent down and looked at Hussein, who had slipped beneath it. He shook his head and threw a cup of water in his face. Hussein came around immediately; in fact, he seemed rejuvenated by the incident, which had provided the longest period of uninterrupted "sleep" that he'd gotten in weeks.

"I'm fine, fine. Sorry about that," he said. "Must be jet lag—let's get on with the meeting!"

"Are you sure?" asked one of the sales guys.

Hussein nodded his head firmly, trying to avoid grimacing as the pain returned.

The rest of the meeting went off flawlessly. Hussein managed to stay conscious and when it came time for him to present, he spoke brilliantly about ChipTek's new embedded product line. In fact, he made a far stronger showing than the rest of his colleagues, who weren't suffering from chronic pain, narcosis, and extreme sleep deprivation.

All's well that ends well, Hussein thought as the meeting broke up before noon. He returned to his hotel room and tried to take a nap, but the pain kept him awake.

Later that afternoon, the Germans, who were sticklers for detail, called ChipTek's lead sales guy to let him know that the deal was off.

"But why?" asked the sales guy.

"Why?! Because if your engineers are losing consciousness, what is our product going to look like?" the German huffed.

It was a brutal response. But the sales guy didn't have a leg to stand on—Klatch Motors was known universally as the most technically advanced and risk-free automaker in the world, and they weren't about to do anything to put that reputation in jeopardy.

"But he's just had a serious accident—he's sick."

"The sickness is not with that poor man," the German said. "It's with the organization that allowed him to attend such an important meeting in his condition."

The salesman knew he was beaten and hung up the phone. Of course, he was burning inside—he had just been screwed out of a deal that would've netted him at least $100K in commissions.

The flight back to California was tense and uncomfortable. The sales staff sat in the row next to Hussein in a low dudgeon. Hussein was tempted on several occasions to try to talk to them but knew that something was very, very wrong and decided to put off all apologies and discussions until another time, after his colleagues had a chance to calm down.

For Ken Hussein, unfortunately, there would never be another time.

## *Impact*

Hussein arrived back in Santa Clara late Friday night and come Saturday morning was doing the unthinkable—he was sleeping peacefully. His wife was so astonished to find him next to her in the bed that when the alarm rang at 8 a.m., she got up quickly and turned it off. Nothing short of an act of God or a fire was going to disturb her long-suffering husband.

At 9 a.m., when she and her daughter were finishing breakfast, the phone rang. It was Jeff Hearns, the head of the Automotive Group, demanding to talk to Hussein.

"But Mr. Hearns, he's sleeping. I'm not going to wake him. He's a sick man."

"That's what I want to discuss with him."

Hussein's wife, against her better judgment, carried the cordless phone in to her husband. Hussein was groggy at first, but when his wife uttered Hearns's name, he sprang up in a panic. He grabbed the phone and listened to what Hearns had to say for about 20 minutes. When it was over, Hussein hit the "off" button and tears welled up in his eyes.

"What's wrong?" his wife asked.

"They're forcing me to go on a three-month sabbatical," he wailed.

"Why are you crying? That's great news! You're finally going to get the rest and the care you need!"

Hussein was inconsolable. Three months in the quick-moving world of technology was an eternity. As far as his career at ChipTek was concerned, it was a death sentence. "Don't you understand? They might as well have fired me. They're probably going to give my job to some 25-year-old!"

Hussein continued in the same hysterical fashion for the remainder of the weekend. But when a ChipTek HR person contacted him on Monday, he tried valiantly to be the old Ken Hussein, the Indestructible Man of Silicon. "I will have my physican send you over the treatment plan right away. But bear in mind, I will be returning in two months, not three!"

He hung up the phone confidently. He'd show them. He'd not only come back, but he'd come back better than he was before. And if they demoted him, he'd work hard and rise even higher. He had given ChipTek five years of his life—he was a model employee and had won countless awards. There was no way he was going to give up so easily.

## *Who?*

Hussein spent the rest of the week lazing around the house and reacquainting himself with his family. Being idle depressed him, but he reasoned that, after working so hard for so long, perhaps he deserved a break. Anyway, it was all just a prelude to a glorious comeback he'd make in just two months. On Friday afternoon he went food shopping with his wife, and on the way home, he stopped in at the pharmacy to refill his legion of prescriptions. To his shock, when the cashier tried to run his drug card, it was rejected.

"Try it again—there must be something wrong with the system."

The cashier had already done so, but complied with his request. The result, unfortunately, was the same.

"I'm sorry, sir. It's not taking your card."

Hussein grumbled and handed over his credit card. "As soon as I get home, I'm going to straighten this out," he said in a slightly raised tone. "There has to be some mistake."

This is exactly what Hussein did, but to no avail. After haggling with an HR woman, he learned that ChipTek's policy for "sabbaticals" didn't include medical coverage. After a few more attempts at convincing her that the policy was unjust, she stopped returning his calls.

Hussein didn't know where to turn. After exhausting his options with HR, he decided to go straight to the top, so he wrote a letter to Edward Meeker, the CEO, and included in the envelope photocopies of all the awards he had won during his tenure at ChipTek. While he tried to maintain a professional tone throughout, he couldn't help expressing his frustration and growing desperation at the end:

> Mr. Meeker, I appeal to you to bring this situation to a speedy resolution. My continued unemployment, combined with my medical bills, has put a great financial strain on my family, which if continued, will have very serious consequences. I know that you are a fair man and will do the right thing.

A week later the phone rang. It was Meeker himself calling. He apologized profusely for what had happened and told Hussein that he would personally take care of it. He even intimated that there might be new opportunities on the horizon for Hussein, once his recovery was complete—perhaps in the consumer division.

Hussein's conversation with Meeker lasted less than five minutes, but it was enough to give him a renewed sense of hope. He ran into the kitchen and told his wife and daughter the good news.

"ChipTek is the greatest company in the world!" he said proudly. "I knew they wouldn't let me down."

Two months passed. Hussein spent the entire time on pins and needles. Every time the phone rang he'd rush to answer it, only to be disappointed.

"There must be some mistake. He gave me his word," he said over and over again.

Hussein did eventually hear from ChipTek. But it wasn't by phone and it wasn't the news he was expecting.

A week before his sabbatical ended, his wife walked into the den, looking sullen, with a letter in her hand: a thick parchment-quality envelope, emblazoned with the ChipTek logo. It was a termination letter, filled with a lot of legal mumbo jumbo, along with a check for four weeks of vacation time that Hussein had never taken.

Hussein sat on the end of the couch, speechless. He dropped the letter, walked out of the room, and went straight to bed. He remained there, lying for a week in a silent twilight zone halfway between wakefulness and sleep. On several occasions his wife tried to speak to him, but he would say nothing. He wouldn't eat or even look at her. After her repeated efforts at breaking his spell failed, she called a psychiatrist, who arrived at the house, looked him over, and without successfully rousing him from his silent, empty-eyed stupor, advised her in a serious, hushed tone that Hussein might need hospitalization.

Hussein's mind might have taken a vacation, but his hearing was still on duty. Less than an hour after the doctor left the house, Hussein disappeared—from the looks of things, it seemed that he'd simply walked out of the house in his pajamas. Twelve hours later, the Sacramento police found him wandering along the side of the highway, covered from head to toe in mud. They asked him his name and his response was "Meeker Creeker Fleeker."

Ken Hussein, the great believer in the American Dream, was brought to Santa Clara General's psychiatric emergency room, where he was immediately put on suicide watch. The doctor who'd earlier visited him at home was soon at his side, trying his level best to get him to talk. Hussein remained sealed in his world of silence for another two weeks. The doctor was on the verge of filing a report recommending indefinite institutionalization when Hussein finally piped up.

"I threw myself off the overpass. But it wasn't high enough and I landed in this huge mud puddle."

## *Relapse*

Hussein left the hospital three months later, a profoundly different man. Once an optimistic, positive-thinking Boy Scout, he had now become an angry man possessed by one goal: revenge. He sold his house and used the money he received to pay his extensive medical bills and hire the best lawyer he could afford to sue ChipTek for wrongful termination. After months of preparation, the case went to trial in March of 1993. He was asking $10 million in damages and was confident that the judge would rule in his favor.

What he didn't count on, though, was that his case would be picked apart by ChipTek's legal team, who allowed their client to escape through a loophole. They argued that because he returned to work after his accident, it proved that he was physically capable of performing the responsibilities of his position. They also maintained that his termination was not based on any "physical debility," but on the "psychological irregularities," which later caused his suicide attempt. The lawyers then produced a pile of sworn affidavits from his former colleagues, stating in no uncertain terms that "Ken Hussein was a danger to himself and anyone around him."

The judge threw the case out and Hussein was back on suicide watch that very night. Once again, the Sacramento police picked him up on the side of the road, walking in a wild-eyed daze.

## Rebirth

Dr. Mailer, Hussein's psychiatrist, was at his wit's end. His efforts to return Hussein to the land of the living using hospitalization and space-age antidepressants had failed, so he tried a new tack. It wasn't orthodox medicine, but Hussein's condition, which Mailer dubbed "extreme termination-induced melancholy," required unorthodox measures. So he got on the phone, and although it was against the rules, called up some of his other patients and asked them for a favor.

A week later, Hussein was lying in his ward, staring up at the ceiling, reliving the final moments before his car crash, when Dr. Mailer loomed over his bed. "Ken, I've told you that you're not the only one who's been mistreated by ChipTek. You've refused to believe me, so here's proof."

A small group of people stood by Mailer. Slowly, agonizingly, Hussein moved his eyes to take them in. He recognized the face of Norm Wallace, his former boss. "Hello, Ken. Nice to see you."

Hussein's eyes grew wide and he fumbled over the first words he had spoken in months. "Mr. Wallace, what are you ... doing here? ... What happened to that secret project you were working on?"

Wallace laughed heartily. "The 'secret project' I was working on was having a complete nervous breakdown and ending up in the same mess you're in right now."

"And these people, who are they?"

"They're also ex-ChipTek people. This is Wong, who was in engineering, and Cahill, from the consumer side. You might remember Ferris and Scarlotti–they used to work in the Arizona Fab. We're forming a little support group to try to put our lives back together and maybe spread the word. And we'd like you to join us."

"Count me in," Hussein said.

## The Plan

Within a week of this strange visit, Hussein was discharged from the hospital. He had a few fitful moments when he imagined that Wallace and the others were just a hallucination, but Mailer assured him that his visitors weren't ghosts. Shortly after getting his walking papers, Hussein joined Wallace's support group.

The first meeting of the group that would later be known as FACEChipTek (Former and Current Employees of ChipTek) took place in a pizzeria in Santa Clara. Despite the informality of the surroundings, Hussein was brimming with the facts and figures he had culled from the week he had spent at the library.

"Between 1985 and 1992, 56 cases of sexual harassment, racial discrimination, age discrimination, and wrongful termination were filed against ChipTek."

"Any winners?" Wallace asked dryly.

"No, but that's not my point. My point is here are more people to join our group and people who will help us try this case—not in the courts, where we will lose—but in the media."

Hussein then sketched out a rough plan whose opening shot would be a lightning-bolt offensive to take place at ChipTek's annual shareholders' meeting. He'd been to enough of them to know that they were smoothly choreographed, multimedia-laden love fests that used the latest presentation technologies, the most basic being wireless microphones that sent FM signals to the auditorium's rented PA system.

With a little bit of research, and about $200, Hussein was able to buy a wireless microphone that precisely matched those used at the annual shareholders' meeting. With a few components picked up at Radio Shack, he modified its sending frequencies and boosted its wattage so that, when the time was right, he could simply turn it on, break into the sound system, and hijack the whole show.

## *Jihad*

Hussein switched the microphone from "off" to "on," and a tremendous squeal of feedback burst through the auditorium. In the shocked, dark silence, he began speaking, knowing that he had very little time to make his point. "Ladies and gentlemen—shareholders of ChipTek, friends, and former associates. I'm very sorry to be breaking in like this, but I have an important message for all of you. You see, I'm Ken Hussein and I represent FACEChipTek—an organization of employees who've been hurt by the cruel conduct of this company."

The shareholders sat in shocked, open-mouthed, unbelieving silence. Confused, frantic technicians had now brought up the lights to expose the intruder, and Hussein realized that he had only a few more seconds before the audio system was shut down. Farther down in the audience, three of Hussein's coconspirators were standing up–they'd stripped off their jackets to reveal FACEChipTek T-shirts that had been hastily pressed up the night before.

"Remember this, Ladies and Gentleman, as you are sitting here in this comfortable room, there is suffering going on, real suffering that no amount of flashy PR, no amount of multimedia . . ."

The sound system was turned off, and several plainclothes security men had already leapt from the wings to accost the standing men. The guards tugged at the men, who offered no resistance, and dragged them up the aisles, like prisoners. Soon a guard was tugging at Hussein, pulling him roughly toward the exit. He raised his voice to a shout.

"You can take us away–you can look the other way–but you can't avoid the truth. We're watching you, Meeker–you can't stop us. We'll be back!!!"

Hussein and the three others were pushed into the men's room and kept there, out of sight, until the police could be called. They sang "We Shall Overcome" at the top of their voices, but the shareholders never heard them because, by now, the inspirational music had been turned up to a deafening volume.

## *Epilogue*

The advent of the World Wide Web provided the FACEChipTek conspirators with an unparalleled medium for disseminating their continued critique of the way ChipTek treats its employees, and in early 1996, a Web site was launched that continues to serve as a forum for current and former ChipTek employees to vent their rage. ChipTek, with all its global power, is helpless to quash the site, but has repeatedly taken Hussein to court to stop him from sending critical e-mails to the company's 14,000 employees.

Although Hussein's online exploits have made him a hero not just to unhappy ChipTek employees, but to NetSlaves around the world, his family has given up any expectation that Ken's activities will gain them anything more than continued grief. Their sole consolation is that Ken spends more time at home, sending e-mail, updating the site, and working with his pro bono lawyer to prepare defenses against the latest cease-and-desist orders prepared by the corporate giant. So far, ChipTek has won every legal battle against Hussein, but, at least at the time of this writing, is powerless to shut him up permanently.

To make ends meet, Hussein's wife recently formed her own business, the Squeaky Clean Housekeeping Company, to provide housekeeping services to wealthy homeowners in the Santa Clara area. Ken, now age 53, has abandoned the technology business and makes about $500 a week working as a part-time paralegal, a position which gives him unlimited access to the firm's law library, copy machine, and, when needed, its supply of aspirin.

# LEVEL 10.0

# Robber Barons

**Who Needs Dynamite When We've Got IPOs?**

## 10.1 Who (We Think) They Are

CEOs are a lot like unicorns—everybody's seen pictures of them, would recognize one in a second, but when it comes to actually tracking them down and studying them in the flesh, they might as well be imaginary, mythical creatures.

Such was Steve's and my conclusion when we reached the misty summit of the New Media Caste System and found nothing up there except a pile of magazines filled with articles that quoted these Robber Barons just short of claiming that their gangbusters IPO was a predestined occurrence that had been announced to them years prior by the otherworldly voice inside a burning bush.

In our hearts, though, we knew the truth. These people were just a bunch of lucky so-and-so's. A second earlier, a second later, and their "revolutionary paradigms" would have shared the fate of most technology companies—oblivion.

In any case, after we had used the magazines to start a fire that we hoped would warm our cold and tired bodies, we sat down to plan our next move. Our conclusion was that we would retreat slightly to a level surface and, failing to find someone to talk to there as well, we would throw ourselves from the precipice. It wasn't the ending we had envisioned to our great quest to uncover the real people who work the Web, but it was something.

Our strategy soon proved successful. While we were unable to catch any Robber Barons in their natural habitat, we did come upon roaming herds of former associates who not only claimed to have seen these elusive creatures, but offered us firsthand accounts of the Robber Barons' most closely guarded secrets, including what foul beasts they were to their employees, what utter losers they were in high school, and what really happened on that hot, sweaty night of unbridled passion at PC Expo 1995.

It all sounded pretty good, but for the life of us, we couldn't tell you it was true. It was at least more convincing than the nonsense we'd left in a charred heap at the top of the mountain. Now, before any of you accuse us of copping out, we'd like to leave you with an observation/rationalization: even if we did find one of these people and get him/her to talk, we would never have gotten the straight story anyway—being masters of self-mythology (and delusion) they are the last people to turn to for the real deal.

Are we full of it? Perhaps. But that's nothing we haven't heard before.

## 10.2 General Characteristics

*Where they can be found:* Robber Barons can be found, by turns, on the covers of mainstream magazines, giving keynote addresses at high-profile industry conferences, or in the case of Bill Gates, taking the hot seat in Washington to defend his empire from the trust-busting efforts of the Department of Justice.

*Why we need Robber Barons:* With the traditional parent/child relationship between companies and employees as dead as the dodo, coupled with the probability that there will be no Social Security when they get old, people need to believe that the American Dream is still alive and well—that if they play their cards right they can reach the Shangri-la of getting rich from virtual companies with no tangible profits. Sad, but true.

*Average net worth:* $20 million (reaching all the way up to billions).

*Percentage of NetSlaves population:* 0.1 percent.

*Marital status:* Married, usually to a former/current employee. Examples: Steve Case, Bill Gates. Why? Well, Robber Barons, despite the risks they've taken in their professional lives, are quite conservative on the home front. They mate only within familiar social circles and, being geeks and pragmatists at heart, would never engage in the sexual antics of rock stars, movie stars, and other members of the entertainment elite. Too bad. These people could use a little Charlie Sheen style to show them what big fun they're missing.

*Things that piss Robber Barons off:* Negative earnings reports, dips in the stock market ("I'm only worth $1 billion today, goddammit!"), product delays, gains by the competition, not having things exactly the way they want them ("I asked for a 2.5-minute egg; this is a 2.7-minute egg!").

*Mode of dress:* Having beaucoup bucks hasn't improved their fashion sense one bit. Robber Barons sport wrinkled, uncomfortable-looking suits and the same hairstyles and eyeglass frames they've had since 1982.

*Pet phrases:* "I don't know what you're doing, but make it brilliant." ... "If you don't play ball with us, we'll crush you."

*How Robber Barons view the NetSlaves they employ:* With disdain. If they could outsource all their development/manufacturing to the Philippines like good ol' Phil Knight of Nike, they would. As it is, they've relegated most of their staff to perma-temp status and use inmates from local prisons to package software.

***How they view the Internet:*** As (a) the greatest scam ever, or (b) the second phase of their 1,000-year business plan.

***Psychological profile:*** Napoleonic complex, Hitler complex, always-picked-last-for-touch-football complex. In short, watch out!

***Career aspirations:*** Who knows? Enough is never enough with these people.

## 10.3 The Story of Welch

*Welch was a lucky so-and-so turned not so lucky so-and-so. But before you get out your handkerchiefs, remember the words of the great unknown philosopher who once said, "Suckers step up, just to get beat down"—something to think about the next time a NetSlave with delusions of grandeur utters those three horrible letters, "IPO."*

Walter Welch turned to the other side of his king-size bed and smiled. "Good morning, precious!"

Where there might have been a wife, a lover, or even a pet, there was instead the coveted Technology Innovation Award—the Net biz's equivalent of the Oscar—which Welch had won the night before at TechInno, Comdex's ritziest, most exclusive black-tie event.

Welch kissed the award's cold, metallic surface and cuddled up as best he could with the elongated pyramid. A second later Welch's alarm clock started buzzing, but he didn't move to turn it off. Welch's mind was too busy replaying his greatest moment of triumph—the lights, the applause, the horde of journalists stepping over one another to get an interview. It was too much to believe. And it was far beyond anything even the megalomaniacal Welch had ever dreamed of.

It had been a long road from the garage in Illinois to his current state of grace. Welch could rattle off the facts of his ascent down to the last detail, yet was still at a loss to explain it. One thing he did know was that he owed it all to WebMan—his simple, handheld device that the entire industry was hailing as the key to universal, pervasive e-commerce.

Visions of IPO glory danced in his head. His company was slated to go out in three months and if the market's insatiable lust for tech stocks continued, he'd be worth billions—enough for a hundred men to retire comfortably, but, for Welch, just enough to implement his plan to become the Henry Ford of the latter half of the twentieth century.

The more Welch thought about such a possibility, the more excited he became. His first impulse was to call Royster G. Pfeiffer and scream, "You and your desktop-centric paradigm are headed for the dustbin, so you can spare me the dirty looks!" Welch next considered phoning all the women who had spurned him back in high school for being a nerd. He wasn't sure what he'd say to them, but it would probably be something like, "Hey, do you still think I'm a 'loser'? I'm about to be a gazillionaire!"

Welch laughed out loud, giving the pyramid another kiss. "It doesn't get any better than this!" he shouted. "It just doesn't get any better than this!"

Welch's shouts echoed throughout his recently purchased $1.2-million home, complete with game room, marble hot tub, and 2,000-square-foot living room, which would be great for parties—if, of course, he had any friends and wasn't completely estranged from his family.

Such gaping holes in Welch's "perfect life" were the furthest things from his upside-crazed mind. Welch didn't know the meaning of "failure"—but he would soon learn it when he arrived at work an hour later and was greeted by two FBI agents.

"Are you Walter Welch?"

"Yes, I am. Are you gentlemen with the press?"

"Mr. Welch, you're under arrest."

## *Value-Added Child*

Born in 1966 and raised in a leafy Chicago suburb called Laurel Pond, Welch began his heroic sojourn on earth as a squalling baby with an enormous appetite for breast milk, branded baby food, and shiny, spinning crib toys. Like many kids of his generation, Welch grew up watching TV and was so immersed in it day and night that the Tin Tin and Babar books he'd been given to start him off on the right path remained in an unread pile in his bedroom.

Welch's middle-class, middle-aged, highbrow parents didn't know what to make of their only child's lack of intellectual pursuits. They were academics who enjoyed safe, tenured positions at a local university and saw his parroting of commercial jingles and growing "gimme, gimmie" attitude as the manifestation of their worst fears. They'd been hoping for a scientist or at least a painter, only to be cursed with this capitalist succubus, a situation they'd often attribute to a mutant strand of DNA from a long-lost businessman in the family—perhaps a failed gold prospector who'd somehow managed to pass his instructions on before being buried in the shifting desert sands of 1849.

By middle school, Welch's material lusts had manifested themselves in his industrious hoarding of baseball cards, Hot Wheels, and Star Wars toys. He'd buy them in bulk from children seeking to upgrade to another hobby, repackage them, and retail them out to kids who fell for his pitch that these items had "great collectible value."

While Welch was neither athletic nor particularly outgoing, and eschewed Little League, the Boy Scouts, and after-school sports programs, he was good with his hands. By age 11, he'd become a proficient model airplane builder and excelled at marketing his 1:87-scale, superdetailed F-4 Phantoms (complete with realistic battle damage) to other kids for a 200 percent "value-added" markup.

By age 15, Welch's model-building business was providing a revenue stream profitable enough to pay for his own phone line, which he glibly assured his parents he'd use "to talk up girls." But before his next birthday rolled around, Welch had already lost the line—his parents had discovered, much to their horror, that he was using the phone to run a $100-a-week, just-in-time marijuana delivery service for local dopers.

Fearful that their son, unless promptly straightened out, was headed right for juvenile hall, and possibly Leavenworth, his parents practiced tough love and sent the young man to a faraway prep school in Colorado. They chose the school because its glossy brochure showed earnest young men studying Latin and Greek at an idyllic mountain retreat, undistracted by the crass commercial concerns that were obviously polluting Welch's impressionable mind.

## *Feral Youth*

Welch's parents were well-meaning people, but they really couldn't have chosen a worse prep school for their son. After Welch arrived in Colorado Springs in the fall of 1980, it took him less than two days to determine that most of his fellow students were psychotics who'd been kicked out of exclusive Eastern prep schools, such as Exeter and Andover, for serious criminal offenses.

In Mesa Prep's Colorado-style version of *Lord of the Flies*, the toughest, most thuggish teenagers ruled the roost, and top-dog status was determined in bloody fistfights that took place each Friday in the shadow of the library. Welch's small size and lack of training in the martial arts worked to his disadvantage, and he tried desperately to keep a low profile. But he still couldn't escape being used as a punching bag by every big, pimpled thug who walked by his dorm door. Throughout Welch's two-year ordeal, not one grown-up lifted a finger to stop his torture. Mesa Prep's overcultivated masters preferred to "let the boys sort things out themselves," because, in truth, these wimps were more terrified of the thugs than Welch was.

The one bright note in Welch's painful two years at Mesa occurred when he and two other oppressed freshmen arranged to escape the campus one weekend by borrowing a pickup truck that the groundskeeper kept parked by the riding stables. Their plan was simple and remarkably stupid: to visit a whorehouse in Mexico, about 500 miles directly south, just across the border at Nogales. With the smallest of the bunch standing guard, they hot-wired the truck's ignition, drove past the sleeping compound, and headed south, driving all day and far into the night.

After abandoning the truck on rocky ground south of Tucson, they attempted to cross into Mexico, but were picked up almost immediately by the border patrol. After a brief and terrifying interrogation, the three were returned to school in handcuffs. Welch was nearly expelled for this exploit, but his neck was saved by a sympathetic master, who reasoned that the boys "deserved a break from all the fistfighting," and purged all entries of the offense from Welch's record.

Traumatized, but toughened, Welch returned to Laurel Pond in 1984 and prepared to enter college at nearby Illinois University. He had learned a powerful lesson about life, and vowed to himself that he'd never let himself be dominated, beat into submission, or ganged up on again.

Welch didn't have much fun at college and grad school. He endured the platitudes of his left-leaning, progressive professors, and passed all his exams, but he itched to get out in the "real world" to test his mettle against time, fate, and the market. His MBA was in industrial process, an arcane body of knowledge pertaining to the design and operation of production systems. With such a pragmatic-sounding degree, Welch figured he'd have no trouble finding a high-paying job, but he was more than a little disturbed to find that by the time he graduated in 1991, the aftershocks of the savings and loan scandal had so depressed the job market for MBAs that his degree was worthless.

For a year, Welch did work that he knew was beneath him—department store sales clerk, Motor Chef management trainee, and telemarketing cold-caller. In an attempt to step off the low-wage treadmill, Welch even tried to revive his pot-selling business, but his suppliers had vanished, and many of his former clients had long since moved away. His parents were chomping at the bit, hoping against hope that this young, energetic 23-year-old would soon be making enough money to leave the nest.

## My First Clone

Welch's luck changed one balmy April day in 1992 when he decided to buy a PC to help him spruce up his résumé. Welch went down to Laurel Pond's local computer store and priced several of Data Magic's newest line of PCs. They were 16-MHz 386s that were priced upward of $2,500–about $1,000 more than Welch could afford.

In search of a better deal, he picked up a copy of *PC Buyers' Guide* at the store's checkout counter, and pored over the ads during lunch. Welch had heard terrible things about mail-order computer companies from people who'd made the mistake of buying a computer through one. Although these computers were hundreds of dollars cheaper than a Data Magic machine, they were often shoddily built pieces of junk peddled by fly-by-night shysters whose front companies evaporated and re-formed under different names every two months or so.

After two hours spent sorting through the ads, one mail-order vendor caught his eye because it was located right in Laurel Pond. It was an outfit called A-Pro Computers Ltd., and its grainy, monochrome ad was buried in the low-rent back pages of the magazine. A-Pro was obviously a small-scale operation–it didn't even have an 800 number–but it sure sold computers cheap: for just $1,995, you could get a PC that was 20 MHz faster, came with a whopping 4 MB of RAM, a VGA monitor, and a huge 107-MB hard drive.

Feeling emboldened by his research and confident that any company doing business in Laurel Pond was unlikely to be a complete rogue, Welch called A-Pro's number and ordered a system. But when the machine showed up a week later, it didn't work–it just beeped desperately and made an awful clacking sound. Welch called A-Pro's tech support line, waited for 45 minutes on hold, and gave up. He called throughout the next day and left five increasingly angry messages on the company's answering machine, but never got through to a human being.

On the morning of the third day, Welch got tough. He called A-Pro's sales line and threatened to call the Illinois attorney general's office unless he got some help. He was bluffing, but his ploy got results–in an unprecedented bow to customer service, A-Pro's tech support rep agreed to examine his failed machine that same afternoon, if he'd just drive it across town to their facility. So Welch loaded the PC into the back of his Pinto and drove over to the industrial side of Laurel Pond.

## Welcome to A-Pro

Welch didn't expect A-Pro's headquarters to be very fancy–but even a rusty Quonset hut would have been a big improvement over what he found at 1101 Pond Lane. There, in a beat-up garage next to a small private house with a weed-infested lawn were the manufacturing, distribution, testing, assembly, and shipment facilities of A-Pro Computers.

He rang the buzzer of the house, but there was no answer, so he banged on the garage door. A few moments later, it clanked open, and Welch was greeted by a blinking, mole-like man in his forties wearing a T-shirt and oil-stained khakis. His name was Max Vollman, and he was A-Pro's chief assembler, tester, purchasing agent, tech support rep, and CEO.

Vollman grunted a resigned "hello," and pulled Welch's defective machine out of its box, showering the floor with Styrofoam peanuts. Welch hung around while Vollman set up the PC on a metal table and attempted to boot it up from an emergency floppy disk. It sputtered to life, but its screen quickly blanked out again.

"Looks like a BIOS thing," Vollman said, holding down the Alt-F10 key. He looked quizzically at the settings, changed a few of them, and rebooted the machine. After a few tries, it sputtered to life, accessed the hard drive, and displayed Aggro Software's familiar PANE 3.1 welcome screen.

"What went wrong?" Welch asked, as Vollman was repacking his machine in its box.

"Who knows? A cosmic ray maybe, or a static charge. I've disabled Shadow RAM—sometimes that helps. In truth, you never know how some of these components are going to work together."

"Well, thanks," Welch said, somewhat surprised by Vollman's candor. He glanced around the place, and saw about 20 PCs in various states of assembly. "Say, it looks kind of quiet around here. Where are all of your other employees?"

"There are no other employees—I'm it," Vollman snorted proudly.

"You mean you build these machines, do all the sales, and do the shipment *yourself*?"

"It's not as hard as it looks," Vollman chuckled.

And with that, he told Welch how setting up a mail-order computer business was about the damned neatest idea that anyone could imagine.

## *Garage Startup*

Back in 1992, before the Web was born, "starting up" meant launching a direct-mail computer company. All across America, but especially in California, Minnesota, South Dakota, and Arizona, the mail-order PC craze created the largest gold rush yet seen in the technology industry's march toward true greatness. The mail-order industry, despite its "get out of town before your angry customers hang you" mentality, had a 15 percent growth rate and a low barrier to entry, and was such a hot market that anyone who knew even a little bit about computers seemed to be getting in on it.

Vollman was one such individual. After being fired from Data Magic in 1988 for unspecified reasons, he started A-Pro with a $5,000 charge to his credit card. Half of this money had gone into the coffers of *PC Buyers' Guide* to pay for three months of cut-rate advertising in the back pages of the magazine. The other $2,500 went into buying the cheapest cases, motherboards, power supplies, and monitors that Vollman could acquire from equipment liquidators, odd lots, and his shadowy contacts in the "gray market."

The gray market, as Welch quickly learned, was an underground flea market of PC components, where components were dumped at a discount. What kept it going was the fact that the original manufacturers of these components "allocated" their goods, and preferred to sell to large accounts, such as Data Magic, which bought 100,000 CPU chips in one batch. True bottom-feeders like A-Pro would then wait for the surplus to hit the streets and gobble them up at a vast discount. As a result of this practice, buyers never knew what they'd find inside one of A-Pro's "Sizzling 386s." And for the most part they didn't seem to care, as long as the price was right.

Welch took his repaired PC home, along with some "free" software that Vollman had dealt him to compensate for his trouble. His bedroom door closed tightly behind him, he began working on his résumé again. But no matter how hard he tried, he couldn't seem to focus on the task at hand–his exposure to Vollman's enterprise had gotten him thinking about the career potential of working in the mail-order industry. Welch was no computer whiz, but he'd read enough articles in *Forbes* and *Fortune* to know that hundreds of thousands of aging, first-generation Data Magic PCs were due for replacement in a few years, creating the conditions for a boom market. There was also something about Vollman's sneaky, no-frills operation that appealed to him–it was almost like the marijuana business, except that the goods were shoddier.

A week later, he returned to Vollman's garage and asked for a job. Vollman was a lone wolf by nature, but it didn't take long for Welch to convince him that A-Pro could benefit from hiring a chief cook and bottle washer. Welch's proposal was simple: if he could grow A-Pro's orders 100 percent–to 10 per month–he'd take a one-third share of A-Pro's 15 percent margin–about $300 a week. To sweeten the deal, he also agreed to handle the phones, assemble PCs, pack them, and do whatever else was required to process the extra orders. Vollman mumbled something about "growing too quickly," but let himself be persuaded, and thus Welch's career in the computer industry was born.

## The Mail-Order King

Welch's first day began with a lesson from Vollman on how to build PCs "the A-Pro way": stick a motherboard and a power supply in a case, plug in an IDE controller card and a video board, mount the drives in place, and connect it all together. If smoke didn't immediately pour out of the machine, chances were good that it was A-OK; if not, a fire extinguisher would hose the whole mess down so you could start over from scratch.

During his first month, Welch was far too busy building PCs and boxing them up for shipment to focus much on expanding A-Pro's business to meet his pledge of an additional five sales per month. He worked fast and conscientiously, but Vollman obviously believed the young man was wasting far too much time fiddling with the machines before sealing them up.

"For God's sake, boy, you don't have to twist-tie every last wire in the case before you seal it up. Most people don't ever open the case. Who are you trying to impress?"

Welch obeyed Vollman's instructions, even though the result was that every one of A-Pro's machines was stuffed with a veritable rats' nest of cables. But he found it harder to give up his habit of "fire testing" A-Pro's systems by turning them on for at least an hour to make sure that the cheap components wouldn't set their customers' homes ablaze.

"Let 'em burn it in," Vollman told him. "They're getting the machine for practically nothing—just turn it on and if the monitor lights up, ship it. What do you think we are around here, the Underwriters Laboratories?"

Welch sped up production and gave up his futile QA habits. But he had one final blowup with Vollman over the issue of FCC licensing. By law, all computers sold in the U.S.A. had to meet baseline FCC emissions standards, to ensure that they weren't generating so much wattage that they'd knock out the sensitive navigational systems of overflying aircraft.

"I have never, repeat never, heard of a mail-order PC bringing down an airliner," Vollman raged among the assembly racks. "That's goddamned science fiction!"

"Well, it is the law," Welch said calmly. "Mr. Vollman, if you're ever going to really make this company legitimate, you have to play by the rules."

"Just get me my five additional orders per month," Vollman barked. "Then we'll talk about rules."

## Value Touchdown

Once he'd mastered Vollman's ultrafast, ultracheap assembly methods, it didn't take long for Welch to expand A-Pro's PC sales to 10, then 12, then 20 systems a month. Some of A-Pro's growth was doubtless due to the fact that hundreds of thousands of alienated Data Magic customers were now shopping the mail-order PC market. Outraged at Data Magic's unconscionable PC prices, they dug deep into this bargain bin in droves, putting millions of dollars into the pockets of fly-by-night clone vendors.

But most of the credit for A-Pro's sales boom belonged to Welch. In a stroke of pure genius, he arranged to have A-Pro's amateurish magazine ads redone to distinguish the company from its sleazy mail-order competitors. Using $2,000 taken from a discretionary fund, Welch arranged a photo shoot to produce an ad that showed himself and three busty Laurel Pond cheerleaders standing in a football field, dressed in Big Ten football regalia and surrounded by a stack of A-Pro's tower systems. The ad read: "Score a Value Touchdown with A-Pro!"

Vollman was furious when he learned that Welch had spent the $2,000 without his approval. He threatened to fire Welch, but apologized once the orders began to pour in. The ads worked, not because they so expertly combined sports, sex, and technology, but because Welch instinctively understood the first commandment of the technology business: *buyers always believe that big, expensive-looking magazine ads mean there's a big, expensive company behind the ad.*

Nothing, of course, could have been further from the truth.

## Quality Control

Two months after launching the "Value Touchdown" campaign, A-Pro was selling five systems a day—about $50,000 a week in gross revenue—and Welch, recently named president and COO, was supervising a small staff of NetSlaves hastily hired to handle the increased business. To keep costs low, he classified these workers as temps and paid them between $5 and $15 an hour to work on A-Pro's assembly line, which had recently relocated from Vollman's garage to a 10,000-square-foot space on Laurel Pond's Distribution Boulevard. It was a hot, dusty, non-air-conditioned hellhole that bustled with activity: salespeople taking orders, frantic box assembly, packing, and shipping. Welch's only concession to OSHA regulations was to make sure there were plenty of fire extinguishers within reach to handle any spontaneous motherboard combustions that might shut down A-Pro's assembly line for more than a few minutes.

Ten months of slaving in the mail-order channel had reversed Welch's once fastidious attitude toward tech support, quality assurance, and other frills. With margins so thin and competition so thick, he had little patience for whining, inefficiency, or nay-saying from his staff. When his tech support crew rudely demanded overtime for post-midnight shifts, he fired them all and outsourced the operation to a third-party company that didn't know a thing about what was inside A-Pro's boxes.

When ChipTek, his supplier of CPU chips, refused to allocate the latest and fastest chips to A-Pro, he bought engineering samples from Vollman's gray-market suppliers and used them instead.

Dealing with Vollman's gray-market contacts initially gave Welch the willies. These shadowy CPU brokers conducted business by night, packed 9mm pistols, and insisted that all meetings be held in an abandoned Illinois Central railroad yard on the outskirts of Chicago. There, in the shadow of a crumbling coal elevator, Welch would trade a Haliburton case full of cash for a Haliburton packed with CPUs.

A-Pro's 25 percent return rate was the highest in the clone industry, but it didn't bother Welch. A high defect rate just represented the cost of doing business using poorly manufactured, unwarrantied Pacific Rim components, with little or no quality control in place to weed out the lemons. Most of the components in the returned machines were stripped out and recycled directly into new machines on the assembly line, so A-Pro's bottom line wasn't seriously affected anyway.

Financially, Welch was in good shape. Vollman had no immediate plans to make him a partner, but he was pulling down $125,000 yearly running the plant, and sending $5,000 a month to an account that Vollman's accountant had told him he should open in Switzerland. Being a president was tough work: a lot of endless, browbeating meetings with A-Pro's staff of engineers, marketing dweebs, and headstrong sales force. But Welch loved driving his staff to the breaking point in the war for market share. He wasn't top dog yet, but he was learning to bite like one.

## The Power of the Press

To advance A-Pro to the next level, Welch realized that the company's PCs needed some serious press attention, because volume buyers, like horseflies, were highly influenced by the honey-sweet PC product reviews appearing in computer magazines. He ceaselessly badgered *PC Buyers' Guide's* editors for coverage, and sent several evaluation systems to the magazine's New York offices, but no review appeared. Unfortunately, the magazine's editor in chief, a part-time pilot, had a general policy against reviewing non-FCC approved PCs because he feared they'd bring down his Cessna if he flew over the wrong house.

It took a personal phone call from Welch to *PC Buyers' Guide's* publisher to grease the review process. He gave the publisher two options: either publish a favorable review of an A-Pro system or have A-Pro's $10,000 a month account move to a competitor across the street. The publisher balked and chewed out the editor in chief, who chewed out the review editor, who threw up his hands and reluctantly ordered a review of an A-Pro "Scorching 386."

A-Pro's first magazine review provided a lukewarm appraisal of the company's newest machine, a 40-MHz 386, and criticized its component selection, lack of documentation, unresponsive support lines, and middling performance. But it didn't mention anything about its lack of FCC certification or the fact that it blew up halfway through the benchmark tests, so A-Pro's orders ballooned skyward. Welch convinced Vollman to approve an increase in the ad budget, and a new series of six-page, four-color spreads began running in three of Hedge-Downs's most popular magazines: *PC Buyers' Guide, PC Byte,* and *Desktop Computing World.* At first, they used A-Pro's popular "Touchdown" motif, but later referred to other sports, such as hockey ("Check out an A-Pro!"), baseball ("386 Grand Slam"), and even auto racing ("A-Pro is No Drag").

## Danger Signs

Although A-Pro's business was booming, Welch could see clear danger signs ahead. A-Pro's once healthy 15 percent margin had dropped to 12 percent, and then as low as 9 percent, as defective PC returns, a vastly inflated ad budget, and swelling tech support outsourcing costs took their toll. By early 1994, competition in the mail-order industry was increasing by leaps and bounds, and a major shakeout had already occurred, causing a handful of vendors to flee to Mexico with unpaid creditors and angry customers snapping at their heels.

Welch realized that building mail-order clone machines wasn't going to make him much richer than he already was, so he lobbied Vollman to seek out some additional capital to help A-Pro make the next great leap forward. He enviously studied the success of Dole Computers and Gatewood 2000, both of which had managed to free themselves of the mail-order stigma by investing in advanced technologies and expensive (although sometimes less than Olympian) support infrastructures. Sooner or later, Welch reasoned, A-Pro would have to diversify its product line by attacking either the corporate market or the consumer market, where margins were generally better than the "onesie-twosie" clone market.

But Vollman was unconvinced that A-Pro needed a capital infusion, and Welch came to believe that Vollman, like a carrion-eating leopard, was incapable of changing his spots. So in early 1995, Welch, under the pretense of taking a vacation, set off for California, where he knew he could find some easy money to sink into A-Pro or perhaps another mail-order venture that Welch could head up on his own.

## *Hunting for Money*

Welch knew that the best way to find cash was to seek out a venture capitalist, but when he landed in San Francisco, he wasn't sure of where to find one. He holed up in his hotel room; polished up his business plan; read *Fibre Magazine,* the *San Jose Mercurial,* and a few other tech-oriented papers from cover to cover; and began to cook up a scheme.

One article in *Fibre* especially intrigued Welch. It concerned the fact that all of Silicon Valley's venture capitalists seemed to frequent the same restaurant, La Merdaise, in Woodside, where they'd nibble on ratatouille, schmooze with clients, smoke cigars without interference, and run up huge tabs. With this useful information, Welch immediately bought a pair of binoculars, rented a car, and staked out the place for two days.

Welch may have been inexperienced, but he realized instinctively that any venture capitalist worth his salt wouldn't wipe his nose with a business plan that didn't jump off the page with the crazed energy of a Hollywood blockbuster–the only difference being that instead of lots of car chases, a parade of scantily clad women, and a self-deprecating hero battling a likable villain, Welch needed a fairy tale of explosive capital growth to get them rolling in the aisles.

And so, in a move that would've made the great Charles A. Ponzi proud, Welch doctored up his projections for A-Pro's growth such that its revenue curve more closely resembled a hockey stick. The strategy he proposed to achieve such growth was to launch a new PC product category that would propel the company beyond its traditional low-end clone niche right into the fat part of the consumer market.

Welch's first product in this line would be called "the Genius Box": a portable wireless terminal that could plug into the Internet using radio waves. Unlike Nibble's failed Issac device, it would eschew fancy pen-based data entry by using a small but functional keyboard that folded out like a cell phone keypad. The Genius Box could send and receive e-mail, alerts, and other small morsels of content, and was aimed squarely at the consumer market—the 65 percent of Americans who didn't own computers because they didn't consider the beige boxes to be an indispensable part of their lives, but who craved "pervasive connectivity" to the Web's electronic Tower of Babel that drove their lives: stock quotes, horoscopes, breaks on airline tickets, and perhaps even messages from their marijuana dealers.

On the Friday of his first week in California, Welch finally summoned up the nerve to enter La Merdaise, with his A-Pro financial projections and his Genius Box specifications folded neatly into his suit jacket. He took up a position by the salad bar and buttonholed the first venture capitalist who came up, but was rudely spurned by the man. "Get out of my face," said the VC, blowing cigar smoke into Welch's face. "I don't talk to anybody who isn't personally referred to me by a client."

Welch tried to hold his position by the salad bar, but the second VC who came up to refill his plate of croutons was so outraged when he learned that Welch was with A-Pro that he talked to the restaurant's manager, who had Welch hauled out of the place by two burly bouncers, who rudely threw him into the parking lot.

"I'll sue you!" Welch yelled to the thugs. "Don't you know who I am?"

"Yeah?" said one bouncer. "You're the idiot who sold our friend a 486/50. It practically burned down his office!"

## *Mr. X10*

Welch was still on his haunches, dusting himself off, when he saw a large shadow looming over him.

"You're the second guy I've seen who's actually been thrown out of this place," said the man, extending a hand to help Welch pull himself up.

"Who was the first?" Welch asked, after he was back on his feet.

"Royster G. Pfeiffer," the man said. "But that was almost 20 years ago.... What's your name, young man?"

"Wally Welch."

The man smiled and gave Welch's hand a strong shake. "Elias Frauhaufer. But they call me 'Mr. X10' around here 'cause investments I make have a nasty habit of paying out early—at least tenfold—in a minimum of 10 months. What's your pitch?"

"Pervasive computing," Welch said.

"I like the sound of that," Frauhaufer said with a slight chuckle and gave him his card.

Welch walked away incredulously. He had just scored a sit-down with a VC. But was he for real? Between his chiseled frame, deep-bronze tan, and perfectly kept ponytail, Frauhaufer looked more like a well-preserved beach bum than someone who had millions of dollars at his disposal. Welch rushed back to his hotel room to see what he could find out about this guy in *Fibre Magazine*. To his amazement, he saw Frauhaufer LLP, listed as one of the Valley's top VC firms, having taken the likes of Yoohah, Aggro Software, and Cyber-America to the highest heights. But was this guy he'd met in the parking lot the same person? Or just some clever imposter?

A week later Welch found out how real Frauhaufer truly was. They met for lunch at Frauhaufer's posh office on California Street in San Francisco. With Welch nervously fumbling with one of the spring rolls that had been laid out for him on the credenza, they talked of many things. Frauhaufer was a keen mind whose investment interests ranged from South African diamond mines to Hollywood film scripts. He'd made his fortune as one of the founding members of Nibble Computers, but cashed out in 1987 in order to "diversify and grow."

Any lingering doubts Welch had about Frauhaufer's capabilities were quickly dispelled when Frauhaufer began giving his take on Welch's strategy. In a mix of financial jargon, tech buzzwords, and Zen argot, Frauhaufer affirmed that Welch's plan to reposition A-Pro as a "convergence company" was sound, but made no bones about "reengineering the current managerial system," which he believed "lacked the bandwidth to reach its full equity potential." When Welch asked him exactly how they would get rid of Vollman, Frauhaufer reclined in his high-backed, leather swivel chair, stared pensively at the Japanese silkscreen hanging on the wall, and responded dreamily, "Keiretsu: It's all about *now*."

Welch knew better than to ask this buddha capitalist what he meant, but when he returned to Illinois the following week holding a thick contract, it was more than clear. Vollman would be given an ultimatum: either take a check for $10 million to hand A-Pro over to Welch and Frauhaufer LLP or have Welch resign and face a hostile takeover, which would include a full audit of the company's finances.

Faced with the painful possibility of having his dirty laundry paraded about in front of the entire world, Vollman caved in immediately and cursed the day he hired Welch. It took less than two weeks to process the signed contract and Welch walked away from his former employer without a trace of guilt. After all, Welch reasoned, Vollman would get $10 million for a company that wasn't worth $10 when he started. Not a bad return on investment, is it?

## *California*

For the next 10 months, Welch shuttled back and forth between Laurel Pond and the office suite he'd rented in a slick, "samurai meets the space age"–style office park in San Jose. The San Jose presence was just a front, of course, but it was essential for wooing San Francisco's increasingly influential futurist press, including *Fibre Magazine*, which profiled Welch in its January 1997 issue devoted to the "Convergence Economy."

The picture *Fibre* ran of Welch showed him standing proudly in his office park's miniature Japanese rock garden holding a neon-blue cube toward the sky. It was a brilliant shot, worth its weight in PR gold, but what the gushy article accompanying it failed to mention was that the product didn't exist. The cube was just a design prototype. Filled with nothing more than the space between two clapping hands, it was an empty box—a yin without a yang.

Despite frequent screaming phone calls from Welch, A-Pro's Illinois facility was about five months behind in terms of delivering the components. Welch's original specs for the device, which called for 8 MB of RAM, a backlit color screen, a microphone, and a serial port, had to be massively scaled down to meet his targeted $99 price point. The resultant device had just 2 MB of RAM, no microphone, and no I/O except for its IR port, which would have to communicate with a transmitter connected to a nearby PC. Welch raised a hue and cry, and threatened to fire his engineers, but there was little that he could do.

Even Frauhaufer, with all his godlike power, couldn't wave his hands to magically reduce the price of Korean RAM or Japanese liquid crystal displays.

As the months wore on, the skin behind Welch's ear reddened and blistered as a result of his constant cell phone conversations. Thanks to the *Fibre* article, he had become enough of a celebrity to become attractive to the local women, who fawned over technology types the way women in other parts of the country, especially back home, would get weak in the knees over celebrities and superbuff firefighters. Welch had never been successful with the ladies and was quite surprised when he was frequently invited back to SoMa lofts, not even knowing the first name of his potential partner, much less the last.

While some of these "equity positions" did produce "liquidity," most of the time Welch found himself incapable of performing due to frequent interruptions from his cell phone and just plain exhaustion. As the Genius Box's features diminished, Welch felt reduced as well, and he soon gave up his nocturnal sojourns into San Francisco's New Media fleshpots, which he dismissed as a "poor time investment."

As Frauhaufer watched A-Pro's progress from his remote San Francisco skyscraper, it was plain to Welch that the VC was growing impatient. Almost 10 months had elapsed and there was still no sign of the product. But even worse, each of the Genius Box's features that were scaled back diminished its market reach, thus dampening its "explosive growth potential."

By February, Frauhaufer shocked Welch with a registered letter stating that he was abandoning their agreed-upon plan to take A-Pro public and had decided to sell A-Pro to a third party for $50 million—far less than he had hoped to make in an IPO offering, but enough to cover the $20 million he'd sunk into A-Pro, the $10 million paid to Vollman, and the cost of his own time investment.

Welch called Frauhaufer in a frenzy, asking him to explain the about-face, and his response was, "Keiretsu: It's all about *now*."

It was a big setback to Welch, but as long as the Genius Box was still the core of the deal and he was still the CEO, he'd bow to the whim of his new masters and stay the course.

## *HyperDynasty*

Frauhaufer's buyer for A-Pro was none other than HyperDynasty, a consortium of Pacific Rim component suppliers whose enigmatic CEO, Johnny Hu, was seeking entry into the lucrative U.S. market.

Welch's new masters made it clear that their acquisition of A-Pro was just a stepping stone in a path toward a much larger goal: total domination of the global PC market.

In a meeting held in March, Welch met Johnny Hu, a large man whose "300-Year Plan" had made him famous throughout the Pacific Rim as a far-seeing visionary and empire builder. So far, the U.S. assets he'd acquired had been carefully chosen: several radio frequencies that he'd bought cheap, thanks to the intervention of some "friends" in Washington, and a 50 percent share of Texas integrator BDS, which, as Hu joked, had become legendary for performing "cashectomies" within America's Fortune 500 IT departments.

While Hu's command of English was surprisingly good, he often interrupted Welch as they conversed to communicate instructions in Chinese to his quiet, Ray-Ban-wearing nephews, who made up the rest of HyperDynasty's executive staff. After a few introductory remarks, Welch briefed them on the Genius Box's production status—the first units would be ready by September, but many problems needed to be resolved before rollout. The biggest was Aggro Software, who had already told Welch that it would "reconsider" its license of the PANE 95 operating system to A-Pro unless Welch agreed to bundle its portable operating system, PANE Lite, inside the Genius Boxes—to the tune of $30 per unit.

"Don't worry about Aggro," said Hu. "Pfeiffer's a paper tiger."

Welch also let Hu know that he was still hunting for some compelling content to lure buyers to the Genius Box. He had prowled around for appropriate info-morsels to push through the Genius Box, but had only found a few third-tier players: a tennis news feed, a recipe feed, and a Russian currencies report. He'd have to provide sexier, more highly branded channels for his device, or the public would think the Genius Box was brain-dead. At the moment, he had high hopes for partnering with Edler-Watson, which was desperately trying to find a way to pay for its money-losing Challenger site. He was trying to con them into believing that if a million Genius Boxes were sold, they could have a share of the subscription revenues, which, at $19.95 for a "value-added alert channel," could add up to millions of dollars each month for the media conglomerate.

Hu was mightily pleased by Welch's aggressive plans for the Genius Box, which could shave 200 years off of his long-term plan to colonize the world. He did have a problem with the name "Genius Box" (which in Cantonese translated into "Fire Brain Coffin") and suggested the name be changed to "WebMan," a suggestion which Welch thought was brilliant and far-seeing.

Because he respected Welch's competence at running a cut-rate operation, Hu didn't force any significant changes on Welch, except to insist on installing his nephews to supervise A-Pro's production line. Welch was all for this, because having the Hus in Laurel Park would let him concentrate more fully on doing for WebMan what he had already done in the "Value Touchdown" campaign–create a "buzz." Hu cheered him on in this respect because the earlier effort was such a big hit in Hong Kong that thousands of local computer geeks paid the equivalent of $20 a pop to have themselves photographed standing next to American models, flown in especially for the occasion.

By early October, the first 500 production samples of WebMan were packed and stocked in the San Jose warehouse. Of these, 100 were set aside and promptly FedExed to computer magazine editors across America. Everything was now in place: Hu's radio frequency was active, Edler-Watson was pushing out daily content, and Welch had an army of over 200 NetSlaves from every caste–from Garbagemen to Cab Drivers–eagerly waiting to supply the demand.

The results of Welch's press blitz were immediate: a wave of glowing articles splashed across computer magazines, which hailed the product as "the next great leap forward in wireless computing" and proclaimed, "What the Walkman did for the '80s, WebMan will do for the '90s!" There were, of course, a few soreheads who groused that WebMan was essentially a one-way device which was less useful than an AM radio. Others cruelly pointed out that WebMan couldn't surf the Web at all–it was little more than a fancy pager with a cheap screen and a nearly unusable keyboard whose keys tended to stick.

But the sorehead who hated WebMan the most was none other than Royster G. Pfeiffer, who realized that the potential sale of a million WebMen represented a loss of at least $30 million in terms of software taxes he might have levied if the devices ran PANE Lite. The $30 million was chump change, but Pfeiffer didn't want any paradigms shifting that could endanger the desktop-centric model, which damned computer users everywhere to a life of carpal tunnel hell.

Pfeiffer's normal reaction would have been simply to pull A-Pro's permission to distribute PANE 95 with the clone boxes they sold, but with his company under investigation by the Federal Trade Commission for muscling computer vendors, he realized he was blocked. So in mid-November, he called together his top lieutenants, and they hatched a plan of action to deal with Welch that wouldn't tip off the Feds.

## The Last Mile

But the glossy ads, the planned IPO, the Inno Award tucked under his arm, and the flood of good press weren't enough to stop the two FBI agents who had cornered Welch in his office's underground garage.

"Mr. Welch, you're under arrest," repeated one of the agents to the pale and confused man, who had just gotten an unexpected birthday present.

"What—what have I done?" he stammered.

"Software piracy," the gray-suited agent responded, and read Welch his Miranda rights. They took him away, and Welch spent the next 24 hours in a holding cell, until his lawyer could spring him after posting bail for $50,000.

In court documents filed subsequently, Welch maintained that he had had no idea when Johnny Hu told him "not to worry about Aggro" that it was because Hu's nephews had been instructed to import thousands of counterfeit copies of PANE 95 and bundle it with every PC that A-Pro shipped. Welch's lawyer pleaded every known defense, but the judge was hard, and believed that a CEO's "duty to know" overshadowed any other factor, including not being able to understand Chinese and being totally involved with a "pervasive computing device."

## The Crossing

On the day before the verdict against Johnny Hu, Welch, and the Hu nephews was to be ordered, Welch suffered the worst nightmare of his life. He dreamt he was in prep school back in Colorado, surrounded by evil, thuggish teenagers, who beat him up, tied him down, and made him beg and cry for his life. He woke up at 4 a.m., his heart racing, certain that he was going to prison. He got his passport, his wallet, his car keys, and his WebMan, and jumped into in his BMW.

He drove south all day, then headed west across Arizona and New Mexico. He arrived near the Mexican border by early morning of the next day. He knew the border patrols would be watching for him—he was now a fugitive from justice—so Welch drove deeper into the desert, until he found the dusty track of road he recognized from his attempted Mesa Prep escape years before. He slept in his car until nightfall and then made his way south again on foot. He crossed the border near Nogales and walked on. He heard the gay, drunken sounds of a brothel in the night, but kept moving.

Welch walked far into the desert and saw visions. Buzzards flew wirelessly around a great invisible portal in the sky, Pfeiffer-like lizards snapped at dragonflies, and children danced in the shimmering distance, waving and laughing at the bedraggled gringo moving south. Dusty and hungry, he stopped at an adobe hut along the way and was offered food and drink. The home lacked a computer—in fact, it lacked a telephone line, and its power came from a wind generator in a nearby beanfield.

As he sat there eating his beans, Welch meditated on the primitive surroundings and wondered whether he hadn't finally discovered the promised land he'd been looking for all his life—a world of limitless revenue potential where the only predators patrolling the shrubby hills were real ones: wildcats, rattlesnakes, and scorpions. Even Royster G. Pfeiffer was an unknown quantity here—just an arrogant gringo with no hypnotic claim on the people's mindshare. It was a New World—fresh, unspoiled, and free to take a man to whatever heights he'd dare let his mind aspire to.

"Mundo Computers," Welch suddenly said out loud. "The Lone Horse on the Value Trail!"

And with that, the astonished Mexican family looked at this strange man with the wild, haunted eyes, brandishing his glowing palmtop device, and decided that his brain had been baked too long by the sun.

## *Epilogue*

HyperDynasty's IPO registration was withdrawn within a week of Welch's indictment, which made front-page news throughout the trade press. A-Pro computers was dissolved a few weeks later, leaving Hedge-Downs with a $360,000 bad debt on advertising it would never receive payment for. Johnny Hu and his nephews were each sentenced to five years in prison, but their sentences were commuted after a "friend" in Washington intervened on their behalf.

WebMan never came to market, and 5,000 unsold units were dumped into an open grave outside of San Jose. The FCC, to its everlasting credit, had denied them certification, and forbade their sale in the United States. Its engineers had demonstrated beyond a shadow of a doubt that WebMan's noisy, unshielded processor could easily cause airliners to land at the wrong airport if the device was operated within 100 meters of the plane's cockpit.

Mundo Computers launched in mid-1998, using funds that Welch had pulled out of his Swiss account. Most of the components included within its popular Value Line came directly from unpatrolled loading docks and unsecured containers that came through Nogales on freight trains. Many still believe that Mundo's computers are shoddily built and poorly supported, and often run questionably acquired software, but all agree that the company's bargain-basement prices can't be beat throughout the Western Hemisphere.

Welch, who remains a fugitive, now lives on a remote ranch and usually stays out of the public eye to avoid being extradited. But his grinning face still occasionally appears in Mundo Computers' glossy advertisements. Wearing a large sombrero and sporting a gold tooth, Welch's latest incarnation is as "El Bandito de Value."

SUBLEVEL -1.0

# Mole People

**Living Large in the Net's Hoovervilles**

# Bug Report: Virus Scan Has Detected Mole People on Your Hard Drive

This book has so far been about people who work the Web for a living, and Steve and I therefore restricted the bulk of our reporting efforts to illustrating the work lives of these "Internet professionals." But a large and significant group of people subsist apart from the caste of Web workers, and it would be a disservice to the reader not to include a section devoted to them.

Mole People, unlike Web workers, do what they do online for reasons which are primarily personal, political, or avocational. Unlike passive online consumers, the millions of industrious Moles now inhabiting the Net produce content—a lot of it—so much, in fact, that a massive online hosting infrastructure has been created to let them easily erect, modify, and promote their virtual soapboxes. Unlike Web workers, the siren call of professional achievement and e-greed aren't the primary motivations driving the Mole's industrious content-building efforts—it's the fundamental human need to say their piece in a place they can call their own.

Unpaid, underappreciated, and often completely unknown outside a small circle of friends, Mole People are responsible for creating the anarchic, crazy-quilt, cultic content pattern of the Web. Unconstrained by any stuffy norms of propriety, good taste, or Correct Web Design, their Web efforts are often egregiously amateurish, ugly, and eminently forgettable. Sometimes, however, their Mole-eye perspective and down-and-dirty attitude toward this medium create advanced, innovative Web content that's light-years ahead of the tepid, look-alike efforts launched, often at great expense, by "professional" Internet companies.

You can judge for yourself in the profile and story that follow.

## −1.1 Who/What Are They?

When Steve and I began our journey to uncover the real human beings behind the Internet, we were laboring under the common misperception that Molehood is a caste composed solely of hackers, sex freaks, revolutionaries, and other assorted weirdos who have taken to the electrosphere to preach their cause, be it religious, political, sexual, or technological (for example, "Amiga people ONLY!").

But as we plunged deeper into the Net's Heart of Darkness, what we found was by turns even more disturbing and consoling. Rather than being limited to a certain group of disenfranchised individuals engaged in suspicious and, in some cases criminal, activities, almost anyone with an AOL account, we realized, could fall into this caste. Mole People could be doctors, lawyers, bus drivers, butchers, stockbrokers, what-have-you—provided that they possessed a single quality which separates them from the rest of the Wired Nation.

"And what is that?" you ask.

It's the desire to escape, to leave behind the demands of the "real world" in order to pursue a specific interest, activity, or sense of community that's missing from their "normal" lives. It could be as innocent as someone who spends hours each night on the knitting forum or as sinister as someone who uses the Net to trade bomb-making recipes.

While the media would have us believe that anyone who has a personal home page and is online for more than five minutes a day is two clicks away from the funny farm, the truth is far more pedestrian. Granted, there are some rabid, crazed Moles scurrying around out there. But most are quite friendly and, dare we say, lovable. Hell, Steve and I, it turns out, are Moles. And if you're reading a book like this, chances are you're one too.

Following is a list of common traits we have found that make up the "typical" Mole. It should be noted that, while the self-appointed members of the e-moral majority seek to censor and destroy all Moles, Steve and I think they should be allowed to roam free, even if their opinions are at times extreme and repugnant. It's their constitutional right to express themselves in any way they see fit, as long as they don't encroach on anyone else's rights. Besides, getting rid of them would rob the Web of its last trace of wildness and would cure the symptom, rather than the underlying illness. The Internet is made of people, not wires and servers and microprocessors.

Put this in your e-commerce pipe and smoke it!

## −1.2 General Characteristics

*Where they can be found:* Mole people gather on obscure chat channels, restricted-access newsgroups, special-interest bulletin boards, electronic porn emporia, abandoned Web sites–basically, anywhere far away from the mainstream crowd.

*Average age:* Varies. Mole People, given the breadth of their population, can run the gamut from middle-aged members of militia groups to adolescent hackers.

*Interests:* Also varies. Mole People, by definition, are an eclectic bunch, prone to states of near ecstasy when discussing the most obscure subjects–feline vegetarianism, Vietnam-era cereal boxes, Klingon grammar, and, of course, every shade of conspiracy theory and superstition (for example, both Lincoln and Kennedy were assassinated by proalien Masons who wanted to get their puppets–Ulysses S. Grant and Richard Nixon, respectively–into office).

*Famous/infamous Moles:* Serial hacker Kevin Mitnick; the members of the "Heaven's Gate" cult; Melissa virus creator David Smith; hyperlinked, yellow-journalist terrorist turned media wonk, Matt Drudge.

*What pisses Mole People off:* People who invade their "space" to ridicule their interests. ("The iMac? It's a wonderful machine–for target practice.")

*Favorite offline activities:* Uh, would you mind repeating the question?

*Favorite color:* Black. (Did we even have to say it?)

*Percentage of the NetSlave population:* 30 percent (with a bullet). Given the Internet fever which has swept the globe, Mole People represent the most rapidly growing group of NetSlaves.

*Average number of hours spent online weekly:* 962.3 (not counting e-mail answered while on the toilet).

*Chance of upward/downward mobility:* Irrelevant. They don't care about getting anywhere because they have already arrived. What concerns Mole People, however, is being ready for the Big One–be it the Linux Revolution, the penny stock that becomes the next Microsoft, or the end-of-the-world showdown between Elvis and Michael J. Fox (the Anti-Elvis).

## −1.3 The Story of Outis

*When Outis, at the tender age of 11, became the youngest Apple IIe technician in the history of Massachusetts, he had no idea that he had taken the first big step into Molehood—a rite of passage that would have been completely painless, if it weren't for those darn Nazis.*

"Are you going to work?"

"Yeah, Ma, I'm going. I just have to finish something first."

Outis squatted on the kitchen floor, rummaging through the pile of belongings the hospice had sent over after his father died. There were two cardboard boxes filled with papers, a clock radio, a stack of back issues of *Reader's Digest,* and one larger box filled with some washed-out-looking clothing—sad linen shirts and baggy khaki trousers from another era.

Near the bottom of one of the boxes was a yellowed registration card that his father had filled out but never mailed in—a warranty notification for a TRS-80 personal computer his old man had bought him as a sixth birthday gift back in the early '80s. Outis had no idea why his father had never mailed it in to Tandy, but he remembered the machine well—it ran big, 8-inch floppy disks, CP/M, BASIC, and a crude version of DOS. For a brief moment, Outis regretted disposing of it years ago at the annual yard sale his mother held to raise money. The clunky old machine might have been the only useful thing his father had ever given him, but it went cheap—65 bucks, with a boxful of software and a complete set of bound documentation.

Outis rocked gently back and forth, thinking wistfully about the machine's small beige screen, and was on the verge of tears, when suddenly he heard feet pounding down the stairs. A second later, his mother came flying into the room.

"I told you to get ready for work!" she screamed. "Don't make me repeat myself!"

"I'll be going in a few minutes," Outis said, staring at the floor.

Outis's mother was a short, redheaded woman of about 45, given to violent mood swings and incredible feats of strength. Although he was almost twice her height, Outis lived in constant fear of her. When he was growing up, she suffered from a serious drinking problem that manifested itself in a mania for throwing things at near supersonic velocities around the house. Outis had a curving scar over his right eyebrow from a saucer his mother had thrown at him, and he half-suspected that some undetected piece of domestic shrapnel might well have been the proximate cause of his father's long illness, which ultimately laid him into an earlier-than-expected grave.

Outis's mother had stopped drinking about five years ago, but despite her newfound sobriety and claims to having "found Jesus," she was still a keg of dynamite waiting to go off. Outis hated her for all she had done to him, but he was no fool. He treated her with the utmost respect to her face, while keeping his real feelings bubbling just below the surface.

"Crazy religious bitch," Outis mumbled to himself as he pushed the boxes to the side and sprang up from the spot where he'd been sitting. He took a quick shower before heading out to his late-afternoon shift at Motor Chef, the local burger joint that was part of a large international chain of look-alike restaurants that stretched from California to the small, depressed city of Pittsfield, Massachusetts, where he and his mother now lived.

## *13'd Out*

Outis worked the afternoon shift out of habit. It was tailored to let high school kids get home early enough to do their homework, but the fact was that Outis no longer had to worry about such things. He had already dropped out—or to be more exact, he had exceeded the maximum number of absences and, rather than repeat his entire senior year, he had simply decided to stop going.

It wasn't his obsession with PCs and late-night BBSs that had sunk him. He'd been sidelined with a painful condition called "torsion" that he'd gotten while running like a madman from one end of the mall to the other passing out fliers to promote Motor Chef's latest hamburger, the "Hearty Handful." Torsion, for those unversed in such medical matters, is an extremely painful condition in which one of the testicles becomes dislocated and hangs down on a blood string. In any case, Outis got himself "torsioned" in a big way, and when he heard the doctor's prognosis, he felt like he was on the verge of becoming "double-torsioned."

"A week or so of bed-rest should return things to normal."

"I can't be laid up that long," Outis nervously told the doctor. "I'll lose my job—I'll get thrown out of school!"

"I'll give you a note," the doctor replied.

It sounded like a good plan, except that Mrs. Scully, Outis's English teacher, had already pegged him as a malingerer and wasn't about to let him off the hook, even with a doctor's note. She had never heard of "torsion" and wasn't about to personally inspect Outis's groin to verify his malady. To her, Outis's excuse was merely the latest in a long string of faked absences that he'd been conning her with since the first day of the fall semester. Deciding that she had had quite enough of this nonsense, Mrs. Scully concluded that a lesson in responsibility was in order for the morbid-spirited, argumentative youngster, and she punished him with the dreaded "13."

While others might have gone back for more punishment just to get that piece of paper, Outis would sooner have stuck his head in a flaming oven than waste another second of his life on higher education.

His mother's reaction to his dismissal from school was remarkably calm. "You've been sleeping in a lot lately," she observed one night at the dinner table.

"I suppose so," Outis answered.

"You're out of there, aren't you?"

"Uh huh," he said sheepishly.

He more than half expected a fork to go sailing toward his head. But his mother cleared the table and never mentioned it again. Apparently, she didn't care what he did anymore, as long as he stayed out of her way and didn't discuss religion.

Outis was more than happy to accommodate her in this regard.

## *I Walk Alone*

Outis decided to take the long way to work. Rummaging through the boxes had put him in a reflective mood and he walked past his old elementary school, remembering what was probably the happiest time of his life. His best and only friend in grade school was Mr. Bannerman, the principal. Mr. Bannerman was a large man with a brown beard and a perpetually wrinkled tweed jacket. Although his colleagues dismissed him as an eccentric, his fair and congenial manner endeared him to the students. In his spare time, Bannerman was also a computer hobbyist, spending countless hours on his machine at home and making sure that the computer lab was stocked with the most up-to-date technology.

The downside of Mr. Bannerman's technological progressiveness was that his budget was chronically in the red. Because he believed that kids shouldn't have to fight over a few scarce computers, he'd bought a lot of them, and they kept breaking down. The district administrator had chewed him out for going overbudget, and wasn't about to pay a dime for a techie to repair the crippled machines that piled up in the computer lab. So it was in a somewhat dazed and desperate condition that Bannerman came across Outis squatting alone in the corner of the schoolyard, drawing abstract symbols on the asphalt with a discarded piece of chalk. Bannerman knew that Outis knew a thing or two about computers, so he made him what must have sounded like an outlandish proposal.

"Young man, how would you like to become the youngest Apple IIe technician in Massachusetts?"

"Apple II's suck," Outis remarked gloomily, without looking up.

"You haven't seen the new GS," Bannerman countered. "I just got one—it's up in the lab. Sound, color graphics—the works."

"Can I see it?" Outis asked, finally looking up.

"That's the spirit! Meet me in my office today at dismissal."

It was slow going at first, considering that Outis was only 11 years old. But he caught on quickly, and it wasn't long before he stayed after school every day to work on the machines. Mr. Bannerman was very grateful for the help and showed infinite patience toward his eager pupil.

"Gentle, gentle," Bannerman would advise, as the kid pried the monitor casing from a IIe whose display parameters had badly drifted. "These monitors are very temperamental. Don't electrocute yourself."

It was a strange team, but it succeeded. The IIe's were soon repaired and kept running long after they should have succumbed to kid-induced abuse. Poring over the IIe's innards, Outis often found chewing gum, crazily bent paper clips, and torn-up baseball cards clogging the machines' 5½-inch floppy drives, or keys jammed by the repeated poundings of small fists.

Outis worked with Mr. Bannerman from sixth grade all the way until the end of eighth grade. In this time, he gained both a valuable knowledge of computers and, more important, someone who cared about him—a surrogate father, if you will. That Mr. Bannerman, a childless bachelor, had an equal love and respect for Outis was evident to anyone who saw them together or heard about what he had given the young man as a graduation present.

"What's that?" asked Outis, pointing to the large gift box sitting on the floor in the middle of the lab.

"It's my way of saying thank you—now, open it!"

Outis couldn't believe his eyes: a refurbished IIe, complete with 80-column graphics, RAM expansion card, thermal printer, and 300-bps external modem.

"So, what do you think?"

Outis couldn't say anything—he was trying to turn away, to hide the tears of joy that were filling his eyes.

## Project Roadkill

Outis took his new toy home and spent the entire summer holed up in his tiny attic bedroom playing with it. Since he already knew the machine inside out, he decided to take the modem for a spin. He wanted to find out for himself what all the fuss over BBSs was about—the way *BoardWorld* and the other computer magazines talked them up, they were the geek equivalent of dying and going to heaven.

But there was one thing standing between him and this electronic paradise: his mother. She watched the phone bill like a hawk and would burst into a rage if the bill exceeded $40. On one occasion, she got so angry that she pulled the cord out of the wall and didn't have it fixed for a month—all in retaliation for the bill's being 50 cents over the limit.

Outis had no desire to suffer such wrath and carefully confined his online explorations to the handful of local BBSs based in Pittsfield. Unfortunately, these boards were just as boring as the town itself—nothing but a bunch of dull text files about ham radio, monster trucks, Agent Orange, and those Dukakis liberals destroying this country. Outis wasn't impressed in the least. He didn't have to go online to hear such ramblings; they were no further away than Pittsfield's only newspaper.

One afternoon at the beginning of his freshman year, Outis stopped by the lab to say hi to Mr. Bannerman, only to have a flier stuck under his nose. "This is for you, boy. Right up your alley."

Mr. Bannerman was right as usual. The flier was about something called "the Roadkill Project" and the title alone piqued Outis's morbid attention. Reading further he found out that it was a quasi-official program whose purpose was to get kids in Massachusetts rural schools involved in computers by having them jot down notes of any fatal automobile collisions with hedgehogs, squirrels, porcupines, and other unfortunate wildlife. They'd then log this information into a central database, analyze the results, and plot them on a big map in the computer lab. Run by a retired school administrator and friend of Mr. Bannerman's known only as "Dr. Splat," information in the roadkill database might some day be used to inform the Highway Department about where to post warning signs, and it might even be used in feasibility studies for "turtle tunnels" and "bear bridges."

Outis didn't particularly love forest creatures—not even bats—but he seized the opportunity to become his class's "roadkill coordinator" with gusto, and helped put recruitment fliers up on every available bulletin board in the school. Overcoming his antisocial nature, he convinced a handful of students to participate. At the end of every week, Outis would tabulate the animal fatality results and transmit them to Dr. Splat. Even though the project died out after six months or so—Dr. Splat, unfortunately, had to drop the board for unknown personal reasons—Outis advanced his computer knowledge. Even better, at the end of sophomore year, Outis got a gift of a lightning-fast 2,400-bps modem from Mr. Bannerman as a reward. That night, Outis retired his 300-bps modem and archived the database of dead animals on a stack of floppies, on the off chance that "Roadkill II" might someday become necessary.

## *Infinity Halo*

The modem turned out to be the last present that he'd ever receive from Mr. Bannerman. At the beginning of junior year, Outis stopped by the lab to see how he was doing, only to find out that Mr. Bannerman no longer worked there—he had taken a principal's job at a prestigious school in California.

"Did he leave a forwarding address?"

"No," responded the bored-looking secretary.

"Do you at least know the name of the school?"

"No, I'm not privy to that sort of information."

Outis stormed out of the office. With Roadkill dead, and Mr. Bannerman vanished without a trace, he drifted into a deep depression. He'd walk along the rusty railroad tracks on the outskirts of Pittsfield and wait for a train to come by. When it did, he'd watch the wheels of the train passing—thousands of spinning guillotines slicing through a dead, hopeless existence. Outis knew that suicide was a loser's game—a cheap way out. But he still thought about it—something about it felt comfortable, almost noble.

He fought off the urges by plunging even deeper into the online world and spent hours each night with the role-playing fantasy games his local BBSs offered. He played Abyss of the Red Dragon, Alien Assassins, and The Dreadful Claw, but after a while, the sameness of the RPGs depressed him—their phony challenges and character-building exercises were just a cartoonish simulation of evil that didn't begin to scratch the surface of what was really wrong with the world.

Toward the middle of junior year, when he had all but given up on the local scene and was starting to think about the train wheels again, a new bulletin board appeared in the 413 area code called Infinity

Halo. To Outis's delight, Infinity Halo was a lot darker and a lot deeper than anything he had ever seen online. Unlike Pittsfield's typical "monster truck" BBS, Infinity Halo contained a swelling archive of shareware, a comprehensive library of porn, and, most important, a complete archive of "zines": underground, self-published magazines from shadowy organizations like Cult of the Dead Cow, the Computer Disinformation Network, and the Computer Underground Archive.

It was a lot for a 17-year-old to assimilate—a swarm of Nazi tracts, bomb-making instructions, environmental terrorist alerts, phone phreaking primers, and more, all concocted by invisible people who could barely compose a single cogent sentence, much less construct a coherent theory of history. But it was infinitely more refreshing to be living in this shadowy world of warped misanthropes than having to face the facts of being a nobody in a nothing town like Pittsfield, where very little ever happened. Outis loved the idea that a subliterature existed, and that losers like himself were able to read and create something that was real, albeit despised and ignored by the real world.

Being plugged into Infinity Halo also firmly impressed upon Outis the fact that, while he was most certainly a loser, he was hardly an illiterate one—his sixth grade essays on Hawthorne put most of this tripe to shame. And from that time on, Outis began carrying a small, black-leather notebook with him, so that he could jot down every dark thought that occurred to him by day or in the dead of night.

## Rendezvous @ the Chef

Outis entered Motor Chef through the service entrance and exchanged his black street garb for the cheerful white-and-red striped uniform and cardboard hat that each employee wore. Although just being near his place of employment was usually enough to put him in the foulest of moods, today he was smiling, much to the shock of his fellow food service representatives.

"Hey, what's with you?" asked Steve, the 22-year-old manager. "Did you finally have sex or something?"

"Not exactly."

Outis's dark mood from going through his father's boxes had all but vanished and been replaced by a feeling of joyful expectation. Tonight, at the end of his shift, he was finally going to meet 4Dioxin, the sysop of the Infinity Halo bulletin board, who'd become his online hero and role model. While the purpose of the meeting wasn't made clear from the short e-mail that 4Dioxin had sent, Outis hoped that the pair might explore collaboration—two misfits, after all, were exponentially more powerful than one.

As he worked the Frylator, Outis was brimming with ideas about what he and 4Dioxin might do—perhaps a list of the "Top 10 Reasons for Not Eating at Motor Chef" or, even better, a tract explaining "What Really Goes into a Hamburger." But his reverie was soon broken by an angry voice calling him from beyond the counter.

"This is a regular Chef!" screamed an older man with sky-blue pants. "I ordered a Junior!"

"Oh, sorry, sir. I'll get you the correct order," Outis cheerfully answered, imagining worms wiggling through the man's hollowed-out eye sockets.

A young man about the same age as Outis with green spiky hair that stood on end like electrified Easter-basket grass arrived five minutes before closing and took a seat in a corner booth. Outis watched him from the corner of his eye as he finished mopping the kitchen floor. The visitor laid a large manila folder on the table in front of him and stared out the window into the darkness. The older diners gave him dirty looks between chomps on their burgers, but he didn't seem to notice or care.

Outis washed his hands and quickly changed back into his black street clothes. He went over to nervously introduce himself, fearing for a second that he might have the wrong guy.

"4Dioxin?"

The bespiked young man nodded his head, whereupon Outis introduced himself with his online alias, which he had taken from an e-tract claiming that "Outis" would be the name of the eighth Anti-Christ—his given name, Dylan, didn't seem to have the malevolence required for an effective Mole persona. In any case, 4Dioxin wasn't much for chitchat, so once the initial pleasantries were exchanged, he got down to business by sliding the manila folder toward Outis.

"You should look at this."

The folder contained printouts of a bunch of designs 4Dioxin had recently released in something called an "ANSI pack." Among bulletin board operators in the early '90s, ASCII and ANSI graphics were the easiest way to give BBSs a distinctive look and feel, and packs were freely available. They functioned to dress up the main page of a BBS to give it a distinctive (and usually Gothic) attitude, and the ANSI scene was a tight, highly obscure circle dominated by a few genuine "eLITe" teenage artists and a whole crowd of imitators, who modified the work of the masters and called them their own.

4Dioxin saw the excitement in Outis's face and opined, "It's going somewhere—the whole BBS scene is going somewhere."

"I want to do a real zine," Outis began. "And I want to call it 'Evil Thoughts.'" And with that, Outis handed 4Dioxin his notebook, which by that time contained about 100 pages of grisly stories, free-verse poems, abstract designs, and a hundred or so epigrams and aphorisms dealing with decay and desperation. 4Dioxin's eyes focused on one in particular, simply titled "Pittsfield":

> Bodies burning in the street,
> Birds burning in the sky,
> Hound of Hell on the loose—
> Home Sweet Home.

"This is truly dark," he said. "Type it in and I'll put it up on Infinity Halo."

## Evil Thoughts 1.0

Within a month, Outis had put up the first 20 pages of what he'd later call "his collected works" on Infinity Halo, along with the first two installments of Evil Thoughts. In this short time, he'd become reasonably proficient with ANSI graphics, producing about 50 text-only designs that were vaguely Poe-like, in terms of having lots of pictures of crows, manacled legs, and lightning bolts.

A handful of users downloaded Outis's texts, but his ANSI packs were far more popular—dark, angular, and jutting. Outis's ability to turn text into an abstract graphical form was impressive to the crowd of teenage miscreants who frequented the Infinity Halo, and 4Dioxin stroked his ego with unexpected praise.

Still, Outis felt that with all the hours he whiled away perfecting his cryptic and powerful ANSI designs, a little more recognition might be due, and he told 4Dioxin the same one night at Motor Chef.

"What we really need is a Cyber-America account," Outis offered.

"You can't get one without a credit card," 4Dioxin rejoined, alluding to the fact that neither of them was yet old enough to vote.

"Not if we can scam a password," Outis answered, and proceeded, over the next week, to coax a password from Steve, the Motor Chef manager whose nickname was "the spitter," because of his penchant to "spice up" the burgers whenever a customer pissed him off.

It wasn't hard to get Steve to give up the password—in place of their usual exchange of "Your Mother" jokes, Outis simply began a guessing game with him. When Steve finally grew quiet, Outis knew he'd come very close to finding the answer. Steve's password, AB32, was the initials and birthday of his girlfriend. With that, Outis began skimming Steve's account whenever he knew he was asleep or out working under his car.

It didn't take long for Outis and 4Dioxin to begin getting themselves into trouble. After spending several weeks familiarizing themselves with Cyber-America's extensive labyrinth of chat rooms, they wrote a program that would gather up the names of unsuspecting members in each room and dump them into a giant mailing list, which soon grew to 3,000 names. To make a big splash with C-A's sex-hungry audience, they engineered what they called "porn packs," zipped files which contained a mix of porn graphics gathered from BBSs, along with a few text files. Their first pack, called "Godzilla Meets the She-Males," contained 17 pictures of hermaphrodites, plus 17 pictures of the famous lizard. They followed up with "Long-Dong Thunderstud and the Three Bears," a similarly mixed collection that juxtaposed digitized snapshots of long-penised males with bear photos gathered from a local wildlife BBS.

The response to these unsolicited mailings was mixed. Some Cyber-America members recoiled, screaming, "GET ME OFF THIS GODDAMN LIST." But others stayed on, impressed with the twisted satirical content of the pair's packs.

The next step was to seriously ramp up production on Evil Thoughts, whose first three issues, while less popular than the porn packs, provided a closer approximation of Outis's brooding worldview. To make a deeper mark on Cyber-America, Outis decided to do something controversial: Evil Thoughts would single-handedly take on the Pure White Aryan Network, one of many neo-Nazi groups that circulated electronic hate pamphlets through the burgeoning online underground.

## *Toe to Toe with the Nazis*

Outis's simple approach to ridiculing this particular band of online Nazis was to print portions of their manifesto in Evil Thoughts, along with a point-by-point rebuttal that would deconstruct their claims and reveal the pathological nature of their movement. After a short preface, in which Outis pointed out that the Pure White Aryan Network was "the sickest bunch of ignoramuses that I've seen so far," Outis excerpted sections of the Nazi manifesto verbatim, in purple, while his comments were printed in gray. The exchange wasn't exactly on the same level as Plato's discourse with the Sophists, but it made its point.

> The Pure White Aryan Network has as its objective the racial, ethnic, and moral cleansing of North America. PAWM would prefer to assume power by legal means, but we regard the present governments of the United States and Canada as illegal, corrupt and immoral. Thus we consider it our God-given right to resort to extraordinary means to seize power as well.

To which Outis responded:

> Who gives you the right to decide the racial composition of America? On what basis have you decided that the government of the United States is illegal? Furthermore, why is it called PAWM when it is the "Pure White Aryan Network"?

Feeling proud and more than a bit patriotic, Outis sent off the fourth issue of Evil Thoughts to his Cyber-America e-mail list late one Friday night, and spent the weekend feeling good about America. By Monday afternoon, however, it had all hit the fan: Outis and 4Dioxin had been banned from C-A for life.

It was weeks before Outis could piece together the reasons why Cyber-America had banished them for attacking the Nazis. Apparently, some Aryan with a C-A account had gotten a copy of Evil Thoughts #4, and had simply excised all of Outis's comments, re-assembled PAWM's text into an intact manifesto, forged a phony e-mail return address, and mass-mailed it to thousands of unsuspecting members. The response from C-A's guardians of morality was immediate, draconian, and irreversible, and Outis's efforts to have the sentence overturned by repeatedly calling C-A's Member Support representatives were in vain.

"The hell with it all," Outis said, and sank into a depression that kept him away from the keyboard for three months. The worst part of this was that Cyber-America kept sending him free diskettes, with a "50 hours free" come-on that mocked Outis and made him wonder whether the Nazis weren't already running things.

## A Place on the Net

Had it not been for 4Dioxin, Outis might even have succumbed to his favorite self-termination strategy: immolating himself in the front yard, using a gasoline-soaked stack of Cyber-America disks as fuel.

"Come on, man, snap out of it," 4Dioxin would say. "Don't let them win, man—there's a new ISP in town called MountainNet that can give you full Net access, and, get this, they'll take cash!"

Within weeks, the first incarnation of the Evil Thoughts Web site appeared, but like most Web sites launched as obscure literary projects, it got no more than a trickle of traffic. So Outis and 4Dioxin geared up their promotional efforts by going around to other Web sites that published dark, existential e-zines and e-mailing their Webmasters to "come check us out." This kind of one-to-one promotion was a lot more time consuming than spamming Cyber-America, but it usually led to at least a few additional hits each day. At this rate, evilthoughts.com would be getting its 10,000th weekly viewer by the year 2050.

"We need a gimmick, or something," Outis complained.

"How about we sacrifice a cow online," 4Dioxin suggested.

"No, a sheep—we'll kill a sheep online," Outis answered back.

"How about we just run an AVI of a sheep that's already dead?"

"That's close enough," Outis said.

Thus the concept of the "dead sheep movie" was born. In actuality, the movie that launched on Evil Thoughts was of a sleeping sheep, but the movie was so jerky and pixelated that the sheep's breathing was undetectable by all but the most astute viewers. To promote the launch of this new experiment in interactive animal morbidity, Outis repeated the process of e-mailing e-zine Webmasters with the invitation to "come check out the dead sheep," and, sure enough, a small traffic spike caused Evil Thoughts' weekly Web counters to spin past the 1,000 mark for the first time. A few e-zine publishers, however, sent angry e-mail back to MountainNet, complaining about Outis's spam, and he got an angry phone call from Cobb, the president and only employee, the next day.

"I don't know what the hell you're doing, but I want you to stop it!" Cobb screamed. "And what's this business about dead sheep? I used to be a detective in New York City and I moved up here to get away from lawyers and this kind of weird garbage. You're not trying to get me shut down, are you?"

"It's asleep," Outis answered calmly.

"OK, sleeping sheep. But that's the limit, no porn, no funny stuff, you get me?"

"It's just a marketing thing. I'm sorry about the spam—we'll be more careful about it."

"This is great!" 4Dioxin said, beaming over Evil Thoughts' latest hit reports, as the two of them ate a hamburger in Motor Chef late one night after Outis was through with his shift. "But we need a follow-up."

And so it was in late May of 1997 that Evil Thoughts became the permanent home of Roadkill II, the Net's definitive database of dead animals in the Northeast. Its core had been harvested from the floppy disks that Outis had culled from Dr. Splat's legendary BBS, but with user submissions, its database was vastly expanded to include up to 350,000 entries that were updated weekly. Roadkill II was the application that would make Outis and 4Dioxin as famous as they would ever become online. Although it would never make a penny, nor would it propel Outis beyond the rank of senior food service representative at Motor Chef, it gave him a sense of self-worth that prevents him from ever again entertaining thoughts of suicide.

## Epilogue

After another year of kitchen slavery, Outis would finally find a job that made better use of his computer skills: systems administrator at MountainNet, a position that earns him about $20,000 a year, plus unlimited T1 access and free hosting for evilthoughts.com. Outis never did repeat his senior year and has no plans to attend college. Evilthoughts.com continues to serve Outis as a dark and foreboding gateway to his mercurial inner state, but Roadkill II and the "dead sheep movie" have been taken down because Outis believes that they're played out. Although he still lives with his mother, he rarely sees her anymore because he spends most of his day at the ISP, updating his site, upgrading the server, and answering customer e-mail. Like most Mole People, Outis is happiest when he's typing at his keyboard—at home in a world he can call his own.

# Afterword

**Not Ready for Beta**

This is where Steve and I are supposed to shrink-wrap this whole damned book into a few brilliant and pithy statements. At the risk of disappointing you, we are forced to paraphrase Joe Pesci's character in *JFK:* "It's a mystery wrapped in a riddle inside an enigma!"

OK, maybe it's not that bad–but don't expect the Gold Code. With the history of this industry still being written, the best we can offer you is a hastily compiled Alpha Release with enough bugs in it to disgust even the most underhanded code jockey. Of course, since we are talking about the Internet here–where lousy, half-baked software is constantly being passed off as the "real" thing–odds are we're right on target.

So, what's our grand pre-alpha statement about The Nature of Net-Slavery? Just this: technology has changed, but human nature hasn't. Whether it's the Gold Rush of 1849 or the Web Rush of 1999, people are people. More often than not, they're miserable, nasty, selfish creatures, driven by vanity and greed, doing whatever they can to get ahead, even if it means stepping on the person next to them, crushing the weak, and destroying themselves in the process.

Although it's convenient to pin the onus for NetSlavery on the clueless, white-collared shoulders of New Media Management, NetSlaves are partially responsible for the hells they've put themselves in. Many NetSlaves don't examine the fundamentals of companies before accepting jobs. They fail to ask important questions such as: Is the technology really what it's cracked up to be? What's the buzz on the street about these people? Do they have a high turnover rate? Is the venture capital about to run out? Is the CEO the Web equivalent of captain Ahab–willing to sacrifice the entire crew in his mad quest for the E-Whale?

Investors have lost their shirts by ignoring such details. NetSlaves, however, lost much more–their résumés end up looking like Swiss cheese and their quality of life approaches Absolute Zero. If you've worked in this business, you know what you're in for: the complete absence of a social life, a lousy diet, lack of exercise, chain smoking, repetitive stress disorders, and last but not least, hemorrhoids. If Steve and I are permitted one prediction in this half-baked "conclusion," it's that if the Workers of the Web don't cool it, if they continue to buy into the myth of the 22-year-old codeboy genius subsisting on pizza and soda and going 36 hours at a clip, there's going to be a lot of sick people out there in a few years and, worse, they won't even have health benefits!

The good news is that if NetSlaves do make "value investments" in their careers, if they sign on with relatively stable companies that have a baseline respect for their employees, if they have realistic expectations about what their ROI will be, they can do very well for themselves. They will learn the tools, earn good salaries in an ever growing field, and still be in the Net game long after everyone else has burned out trying to become the next Bill Gates. And unlike a traditional caste system, the New Media Caste System allows for a great deal of mobility. The kid who was crawling under your desk to fix your printer port in 1996 can end up as a high-priced consultant if he/she plays the game right and doesn't let "Internet time" speed the path to an early grave.

For Steve and me, it's already too late—we're Old Men in our thirties and forties who've been to the war and have returned the chattering madmen you've listened to in these pages and between the swirling hyperlinks of the NetSlaves Web site (www.netslaves.com). Our hope is that we've snared a few of you before you've left Basic Training. It's a vain hope, perhaps, but it keeps us going.

We would be lying to you if we said we didn't want to have this book serve as a quasi-historical, quasi-anthropological "study" of a particular moment and the people and cultural values that constitute that moment. We hope we've delivered—if we haven't, this book will probably end up in the dustbin, at a garage sale, or reincarnated as the widget that holds your bedroom window open. Or, to use a metaphor from the very industry we've written about, it may become an inexplicable "artifact" with as much relevance as a 5½-inch floppy disk you've dug out of the bottom of your closet.

We would also be lying to you if we said we wrote this book with purely noble intentions. No way! Steve and I are two angry, cranky bastards out for blood. On behalf of ourselves, our unfortunate friends in the tech biz, the people we interviewed, the people who've written to us from as far away as New Zealand, hell, for all NetSlaves everywhere—we want these words to function as a bit of "chin music" (to use the Spillane terminology) for the Robber Barons and Robber Barons-in-training who've done us wrong. You haven't heard the last of us, suckers!

This is war.